Praise for
What Would Ben Graham Do Now?

"With more than half the world's GDP growth coming from developing countries and regions like China, India, Brazil, and Africa by 2020, a clear approach to participating in this new global landscape is imperative. Jeffrey Towson delivers one such view. He takes a powerful old paradigm—that of fundamental value from Ben Graham—and applies it to the financial and cultural nuances of the developing world. Towson's real world experience and application of Graham's theory is a thoughtful read for any business leader."

> —**Dominic Barton**, Global Managing Director, McKinsey & Company

"Throughout my career, I've found it difficult to identify international professionals with a grasp of the intricacies of investing in the Middle East. Jeffrey successfully draws on his vast experience accumulated through working closely with HRH Prince Alwaleed bin Talal to develop an optimal investment approach, marrying the well-understood principles of international investing with the idiosyncratic aspects of emerging markets, including the requisite differentiated risk perception, eye for value, and intricate understanding of local business culture. This book is an excellent reference for any international investor looking to spot value and avoid pitfalls in emerging markets."

> —**Tony Hchaime**, Head of Middle East and North Africa,
> The D. E. Shaw Group

"Identifying and profiting from market inefficiencies has always been at the core of value investing. Yet most investors are still trying to uncover these in overworked, developed markets. Towson's book is a wake-up call to the powerful fact that in the 21st century the real opportunities lie elsewhere: in the inefficiencies that are thrown up when developing and developed markets collide. Not only does he show investors where to look to profit from today's globalization, he provides a practical guide as to how to go about investing on the basis of this new paradigm. Rich in ideas and examples [of] how this new approach has spectacularly delivered, this book will revolutionize your investment strategy."

> —**Peter Williamson**, Professor of International Management,
> University of Cambridge, Judge Business School

"This is more than just an offering on value investing. Without realizing it, or at least without intending to do so, the author has set before policy makers a startling analysis of the world in which America competes. If it doesn't challenge your concepts of the global competitive environment, you aren't paying attention."

> —**Congressman Mick Mulvaney**, United House of Representatives

"Jeff has a view of global investing that incorporates both the developed and developing economies that is virtually unmatched … the dislocations occurring daily have the potential to create many opportunities … his insights and investing framework will help investors better understand this changing world."

> —**Jerry Leamon**, Global Managing Partner, Services and Mergers & Acquisitions,
> Deloitte Touche Tohmatsu

"In drawing on his unique experiences in the three critical sectors affecting the geopolitics of the new century, Towson has managed the rare feat of marrying a rigorous economic prognosis with acute cultural awareness."

—**David Watt**, International Director, Head of Business Development and
Client Services, Asia Pacific, DTZ

"Dr. Towson, a brilliant young insider who worked for Prince Waleed, takes the reader on an exciting investing journey that goes beyond Graham's 'value investing' to 'value point,' the latter adding the critical political dynamics factor necessary for global investing."

—**Donald J. Palmisano**, MD, JD, Former President of AMA,
and author of *On Leadership*

"Towson's book addresses one of the greatest challenges for today's investor—the world might be globalizing, but that doesn't make it easier to understand. Towson wisely shows how the differences between developed and developing countries are not barriers to investment, but instead value opportunities, whether by bringing Western management expertise to a deal, or leveraging political relationships. Neither East nor West has the right model. But finding the value in each is the way forward. Towson points the way."

—**Ben Simpfendorfer**, author of *The New Silk Road: How a Rising Arab World
Is Turning Away from the West and Rediscovering China*
and Former Chief China Economist of RBS Global Banking & Markets

"In a decade of opening distressed asset markets in Asia, I've never met anyone quite like Jeffrey Towson, which explains why so many international investors lost money."

—**Jack Rodman**, President, Global Distressed Solutions, LLC

"If you subscribe to the theory that equity-investing exclusively in Western markets in coming years will provide lackluster returns, read Jeff Towson's thought-provoking analysis of how to create a modern framework for global investment. A value investor to the core, Jeff has modified the historic model with new concepts such as 'value point' and 'capabilities migration' which make value investing more effective in complex regions offering high growth potential, such as the BRIC countries and the Middle East."

—**Eric Gleacher**, Chairman and CEO, Broadpoint Gleacher

"…an insightful roadmap to surgical cross-border investment in volatile emerging markets, based on a decade of successfully finding mispriced value across the globe."

—**Robin Panovka**, Partner, Wachtell Lipton Rosen & Katz; Adjunct Professor,
Columbia School of Business; Founding Director, International Institute for the
Study of Cross-Border Investment and M&A

"Forget the account of well-informed markets that we all learned in college—except as an ideal. Jeff Towson gives us a firsthand account of the way markets and businesses work in the emerging economies, where most of global growth is occurring. And the story is one in which state actors, affiliates, and entrepreneurs teaming up with them dominate business growth. Whether you approve or not, or believe this is a long term success formula or not, matters less at the moment than that U.S. investors and business men and women understand this new world. Towson is a first-class guide to understanding."

—**William T. Allen**, Nusbaum Professor of Law & Business, NYU Stern School of Business and NYU School of Law; Director, NYU Pollack Center for Law & Business

"Investors seeking returns in emerging markets must adapt tried and tested techniques to a daunting array of country-specific circumstances. Jeffrey Towson is uniquely qualified to help value-hunters sharpen the tools they already possess to capture unprecedented opportunities in a new, hyperglobalized era."

—**Tom Mitchell**, Deputy News Editor, *The Financial Times*

"Jeff Towson combines a fascinating narrative of his experience in emerging market investing with specifics for us all to engage on a professional level over the decades to come in securing value for our investors."

—**Steven Rockefeller**, Chairman and CEO, Rose Rock Partners, LLC

"Insightful strategies to value investing in today's global markets."

—**Ragnar Meitern**, Managing Director, Regional Head of Telecoms, Media and Technology, Standard Chartered Bank

"Jeff's book is a fantastic framework for going global—and investing into the unstructured universe of emerging markets opportunities."

—**Bertrand Valet**, Head of MENA SWFs and Financial Sponsors Coverage, Bank of America Merrill Lynch

"Jeffrey Towson lives at the intersection of multiple worlds. He is able to put forth a timely and thought-provoking framework for cross-border investing. His raw intellect, interdisciplinary approach, and life experiences combine to demystify and provide a paradigm for investing in emerging markets."

—**Cary A. Kochman**, cross-border M&A expert

"A fresh take on the timeless Graham and Dodd by an author with exceptional global business credentials."

—**Erik Bethel**, Founding Partner and CEO, SinoLatin Capital

"Jeff Towson presents the first practical guide for global value investors. His unique experience and perspective makes this a must-read for the professional investor or for anyone interested in better understanding how the rules of modern finance apply in a global world. I recommend it highly!"

—**Jonathan Woetzel**, Director, McKinsey & Company

What Would
Ben Graham Do Now?

What Would
Ben Graham Do Now?

A New Value Investing Playbook
for a Global Age

Jeffrey Towson

Vice President, Publisher: Tim Moore
Associate Publisher and Director of Marketing: Amy Neidlinger
Executive Editor: Jeanne Glasser
Editorial Assistant: Pamela Boland
Development Editor: Russ Hall
Operations Manager: Gina Kanouse
Senior Marketing Manager: Julie Phifer
Publicity Manager: Laura Czaja
Assistant Marketing Manager: Megan Colvin
Cover Designer: Chuti Prasertsith
Managing Editor: Kristy Hart
Project Editor: Anne Goebel
Copy Editor: Gayle Johnson
Proofreader: Gill Editorial Services
Indexer: Erika Millen
Senior Compositor: Gloria Schurick
Manufacturing Buyer: Dan Uhrig

Second Printing July 2011

ISBN-10: 0-13-217323-9
ISBN-13: 978-0-13-217323-0

Pearson Education LTD.
Pearson Education Australia PTY, Limited
Pearson Education Singapore, Pte. Ltd.
Pearson Education Asia, Ltd.
Pearson Education Canada, Ltd.
Pearson Educatión de Mexico, S.A. de C.V.
Pearson Education—Japan
Pearson Education Malaysia, Pte. Ltd.

Library of Congress Cataloging-in-Publication Data:

Towson, Jeffrey Alan, 1970-
  What would Ben Graham do now? : a new value investing playbook for a global age / Jeffrey Towson. — 1st ed.
    p. cm.
  ISBN 978-0-13-217323-0 (hardback : alk. paper)
  1. Investment analysis. 2. Securities. I. Title.
  HG4529.T696 2011
  332.6—dc22
                          2011000081

For my parents, Wayne and Linda Towson

Contents

Acknowledgments

I have without question pushed the limits of friendship and goodwill from a great number of people in writing this book. My thanks to everyone who was kind enough to give a bit of time and advice. A special thanks to Herb Schaffner of Schaffner Media Partners, who, with seemingly endless patience and positive encouragement, helped an often floundering first-time author find his way.

In no specific order, thanks to Martin Michael, master of all things graphical. Thanks to Dave Conti for his invaluable help on the proposal. Thanks to Barry Adler and Kelley Holland for help editing the manuscript. Thanks to my now fellow authors Jonathan Woetzel and Ben Simpfendorfer for their early advice. Thanks to Tom Mitchell for proofing the proposal over drinks in Hong Kong. Thanks to Leo Chu and Eric Garcia, who generously took my random calls between producing ever more entertaining episodes of Afro Samurai. Thanks to my new neighbors, Peilin and Eric Almeraz, for proposal feedback (and home-buying advice). Thanks to Dr. Kris Crawford, who seems to have unlimited bandwidth for helping friends. Thanks to Prince Khaled Alwaleed for being a patient guy when I got swamped. Thanks to Shirley Yeung for letting me borrow an office to hide out and write. Thanks to Patrick Maher, Doug Goodman, Meredith Spatz, Paul Lockmiller, Avi Kulkarni, Scott Gallin, Reshma Paranjpe, Jon Zifferblatt, and many others for all the support and encouragement along the way.

A special thanks to the many students from Columbia Business School, London Business School, Cambridge Judge, and Peking Guanghua who provided valuable feedback at various stages. Lots of editing was done based on how many people were dozing during what sections of class. Thanks to Wendy Liu, Marcus Matuszek, Garth Reucassel, and many others for their feedback and encouragement. For research, thanks to Cao Zining, who knows everything about Chinese automotive, and to Bin Yang and Larry Xie.

Of course, thanks to Jeanne Glasser, Julie Phifer, Anne Goebel, and everyone at Pearson/FT Press. Finally, special thanks to Eric, Jolene, Jack, Amelia, Alan, Maria, David, Michael, Gwen, Larry, Jamie, and Katie—well, just because.

About the Author

Jeffrey Towson is a specialist in global and cross-border investing. He has developed more than $15 billion in investments across multiple geographies (United States, China, the Middle East) and industries (real estate, hotels, banks/financial services, insurance, healthcare, retail, technology, petrochemicals, energy/infrastructure). He is currently Managing Partner of the Towson Group and is based in New York, Dubai, and Shanghai.

Previously, Mr. Towson served as Head of Direct Investments for Middle East North Africa and Asia Pacific for Prince Waleed, who could be considered the world's first private global investor. Nicknamed the "Arabian Warren Buffett" by *Time* magazine, Waleed's distinctions include being the world's fourth-richest person (2004, *Forbes*); the largest foreign investor in the U.S.; the biggest shareholder of the world's largest bank (Citigroup, 2007); and the world's second-largest media owner, after Rupert Murdoch.

Mr. Towson is a frequent speaker and writer (visit www. jeffreytowson.com). He is a fellow at Cambridge University's Judge Business School in the UK and is cohead of the Current Topics in Chinese Strategy and Investment course at Peking University Guanghua School of Management in Beijing. He holds an MBA from the Columbia Business School, an MD from the Stanford University School of Medicine, a BA in physics from Pomona College, and a Fulbright from the Karolinska Institute in Stockholm, Sweden.

Preface

I have a pet theory about Ben Graham—the father of value investing—and the lasting impact of his books on generation after generation of investors. Certainly, the logic of his thinking is both compelling and convincing, but I think it's the emotional impact that has made his ideas particularly widespread. Emotional impact is not something one usually expects in a business book.

Reading *The Intelligent Investor* for the first time gave me a somewhat euphoric feeling—a feeling of insight, of "I can understand this." Almost immediately, I found the confusing and anxious world of stocks and investing becoming understandable. For many of us, this initial feeling of insight was followed quickly by a secondary feeling of greed, of "I can get rich doing this." For most, this second feeling passes, and life returns to its normal daily habits. For some, it lasts a lifetime (greetings, Mr. Buffett).

But I think the emotional impact is unmistakable—and its deepest roots are in the appeal of a logical method to those of us with overly rational minds. We have been completely won over by its staunchly logical approach to business and investing.

With Graham's value approach as their weapon, generations of investors have laid siege to confusing and seemingly chaotic markets. And slowly and grudgingly, previously inscrutable markets and systems have become both understandable and actionable. Graham's approach has proved to not only be exceedingly profitable but also fascinating. The opportunity to understand the business world as it really exists, outside of our limited perceptions, is as satisfying as the returns. Graham's thinking offers what physicist and Nobel Laureate Richard Feynman called "the pleasure of finding things out." Unsurprisingly, value investing tends to attract both the ambitious and Feynman-type "curious characters."

This book started with a similar emotional reaction. Almost a gut feeling—that at the start of the first global century, confusion and anxiety seem to be growing. I am increasingly struck by the sense of gloom and doom Westerners in particular have about globalization and a changing world. The U.S. is in decline? Globalization will move my job overseas? The global financial system is precariously unstable and will inevitably collapse? The future is one of belt tightening and lowered ambitions? China's rise fundamentally threatens the West? (How many ways can the word *dragon* be used in a book title?)

Since returning to the U.S. after a decade in the emerging markets, and particularly following conversations with and readings of macroeconomists, I have been startled by the pervasive sense of anxiety and pessimism. And this mostly Western anxiety is such a stark contrast to the feeling of ambition and excitement I encounter almost everywhere else. If nothing else, this book is intended as a good solid whack at what I believe is an overly fearful and completely false worldview with an almost Hobbesian sense of human limitation. And my baseball bat of choice is a worldview and investment strategy based on Graham's thinking—rational, value-focused, ambitious, curious, and optimistic.

One of the nice things about being a value investor is that we are occupationally optimistic. We are almost always betting on prices going up. We are also one of the few groups that get excited by recessions (but we generally try to keep quiet about this). And rather than being frustrated by changing times, we both learn and profit from them. Graham's value concept gives the rational mind an anchor in times of changing markets, companies, and actors. And somehow, surprisingly, occupational optimism leads to real optimism. Somehow, out of this stubbornly rational approach, comes an optimism about business and life—and a deep belief in principles-based capitalism.

For value-obsessed investors, the arrival of a new and chaotic global investment landscape is anything but anxious or depressing. It is truly fascinating. And I suggest that if you are willing to walk out onto this new global terrain, you will re-encounter, as I have, those same original *Intelligent Investor* feelings. A blast of insight and confidence, of "I can understand this" and "I can get rich doing this." These are truly thrilling and unique times. Good hunting.

Chapter Descriptions

Chapter 1 introduces some of the opportunities and challenges value investors face in a rapidly changing world. How to deal with fundamentally different economic systems and their increasing impact on developed markets? How to apply Ben Graham's thinking to such situations? I begin to introduce a framework for investing, making deals, and building wealth in a global age.

Chapters 2 and 3 introduce value point as an extension of and complement to traditional value investment strategies. I reapply Graham's method to various investment environments and from this generate a series of frameworks and methodologies for global value-based investing.

Chapters 4 and 5 introduce political access as a tool in value-added deal-making. This is about recognizing and taking advantage of the fundamental role of government in many markets, industries, and companies. This view stands in contrast to the traditional value investing view that most often sees government involvement as something that decreases the attractiveness of specific companies or creates additional long-tail risks.

Chapters 6 and 7 discuss the strengths and limitations of reputation and capital in various environments. As new markets emerge and cross-border deals increase in number and size, differences in politico-economic systems, cultures, regulatory structures, and behavioral patterns become more important. Within this, reputation can have a particularly strong effect and can be used to turn these large cross-border inefficiencies—inherent to a colliding world—into returns.

Chapters 8 and 9 extend investing and deal-making to include the use of various businesss capabilities. Capabilities such as brands, technologies, operating systems, and management are continually migrating into developing economies from more advanced economies. Leveraging such capabilities into deal-making can be particularly effective in many situations and can create significant advantages for the investor.

Chapter 10 pulls everything together and shows how all the introduced tools (political access, reputable capital, capabilities, and management) can be combined into investments in a powerful way. I detail how this approach has been used by private equity firms, multinationals, entrepreneurs, and global tycoons.

Chapter 11 presents various tactics for finding and structuring investments. This includes going from focusing on screening investments to more actively networking. It includes expanding traditional concerns about competitive advantage to concerns about defensibility. And it focuses on simplifying deal-making in complicated locations to the primary goal of capturing companies of the highest possible quality at the lowest possible price.

Chapter 12 details a global investment playbook for the next several years. I show where I believe the most attractive opportunities are and the strategies to capture them.

Finally, Chapter 13 looks ahead to the next twenty years. We are only at the beginning of global investing. Investors and deal-makers from around the world are beginning to meet, but the strategies are still evolving. This chapter looks at the various investors and market players and assesses their various approaches going forward.

1

Introduction

This book was written to help you profit from the arrival of a new global investment landscape—a "new destination" created from the bending, shifting, and reshaping of economic power centers around the world.

Instead of Wall Street and European money centers dominating the investment world, multiple systems are now coming to prominence. China, India, Brazil, Russia, and the Middle East are all coming to the fore, both rivaling the traditional investment hubs in their ability to create economic wealth and challenging their way of doing business. Autocratic governments, regulatory uncertainty, limited legal structures, exotic consumer habits, and odd kinds of company ownership (including government and quasi-government ownership) are all characteristics of the new investment world. In many ways, it is a post-Wall Street economy.

For investors, it's an exciting time. Markets and companies are emerging everywhere, offering more and more opportunities. This is in turn attracting, and perhaps creating, a new breed of global investor who crosses borders and sees the entire world as his hunting ground. I was fortunate to spend much of the last decade working for the most prominent of this new breed of global investor, Prince Waleed. Often regarded as the world's #2 investor after Warren Buffett, Waleed is arguably the world's first private global investor. With projects and holdings in more than 130 countries, he is one of a rare few who can definitively claim the title of global tycoon. This book reflects many of the lessons I learned working on his investment team.

The Struggle to Go Global

Going global as an investor is conspicuously problematic—particularly for the value crowd. When we dig into the public markets in places like China and India, we find that corporate behavior is far different from what we have learned to expect in the United States and Europe. The companies just don't appear to be very stable, making calculations of a useful intrinsic value difficult. In fact, the economies themselves appear to be changing rapidly (that is, developing). Additionally, information, even in published financial reports, appears questionable. Unless you're investing short-term, it's a struggle to invest in changing companies in changing environments with limited and/or incorrect information.

Looking at private companies, of which there appear to be a truly large and increasing number, there are problems as well. First, it's hard to find information. And then you discover that you can't get access to the deal anyway. These private companies often are owned by entrepreneurs, families, conglomerates, and state-backed vehicles, and they don't sell easily. And if they do, it's only a minority percentage, never a majority. Plus, significant cross-cultural and cross-border problems exist—language gaps; cultural gaps; differing political, economic, and legal systems. If value-based investing in the U.S. is mostly about finding and accurately measuring unrecognized value, value investing globally seems to be mostly about getting information and access to deals.

Finally, if you do manage to get a deal done, you find yourself a minority owner of an emerging-market company, frequently known as the "sucker at the table." You quickly discover that your contract and Board seat mean little. Corporate governance and minority shareholder rights are nonexistent. A foreigner and his money are very easily parted. Don't be surprised if you are diluted or forced out after you have paid in.

The classic long-term value investing approach assumes many things: ready access to deals, the rule of law, shareholder rights, accurate and available information, a separation of commercial and government activities, and a significant degree of stability in both the company and the market. Few of these assumptions hold as you start to go global. So Western investors either stay in the West or go global but limit themselves to short-term, highly liquid, or speculative and technical strategies.

In doing so, they miss the point and ignore the most important lesson of value investing: An investor can build the most wealth not by speculating or going short-term, but by capturing real economic value in companies. This means staying focused on economic value. It means thinking long-term. And that is the crux of the problem. How do you focus on economic value over the long term, particularly for private companies and illiquid assets, in environments that are inherently unstable and uncertain? The struggle to go global is really the struggle to apply a long-term and value-based investment approach in unstable and uncertain landscapes.

What Would Ben Graham Do?

How would the "father of value" have viewed the global investment landscape of the 21st century?

What would Ben Graham—the father of value investing, author of the classic text *The Intelligent Investor*, and coauthor with David Dodd of *Security Analysis*—have thought of the 21st century? Could he have imagined the rapid rise of China, India, Brazil, and Russia? What would he have thought of an investment world that included autocratic governments, limited (or absent) legal and regulatory structures, and odd kinds of company ownership (public, private, government, quasi-government)? What would Graham have thought about investing in a state capitalist system like Russia?

At the start of the 21st century, it is startling to see how far the world has moved from the investment landscape in which Graham invested and taught. The increasing collision of developed and developing markets has created a very new and different terrain.

On one side, half of the human population is rapidly rising, creating new markets for both business and investment. We see thousands of companies emerging in non-Western markets, offering investment opportunities and changing the competitive dynamic for Western companies. These markets, socioeconomic systems, and companies are clearly different from their developed counterparts. Yes, China and India have billions of new customers for products and services, but the average gross domestic product (GDP) per capita is around $2,000. Yes, China has the world's largest mobile company, but it is state-controlled. Yes, there are thousands of new small family businesses to invest in, but there is no consistent rule of law to protect the investor.

On the other side, developed markets and companies are changing in response. Traditional value investing targets such as Coca-Cola and Sees Candies now have both customers and competitors in Asia and Eastern Europe. Is Coke's competitive advantage sustainable in Russia?

Could Graham have imagined the collision of these worlds? Brazilian capital is starting to enter the U.S. at the same time that all foreign capital is trying to exit Dubai. Filipino labor is entering the Middle East while American companies are opening call centers in Manila. American-owned casinos are opening in Macau to serve a flood of Chinese gamblers (often using black-market consumer loans) while reporting to the Nevada gaming authorities but being indirectly controlled by Beijing. Such investment situations would have been unimaginable just 20 years ago. Could Graham have imagined that the world's richest person would make his fortune in Mexico? Or that one day Warren Buffett, his greatest student, would buy PetroChina, a state-owned oil giant under the direction of the Chinese politburo?

More important, how would he have thought about "value" in a global age?

It has been 76 years since Graham published *Security Analysis*, laying the foundation for an investment methodology and mindset based on fundamental value. But Graham and most of his disciples' approach cannot be separated from the economic and historical circumstances under which it was developed and used. Even the best of thinkers are captives to their experiences and environments. What would value investing have become if Graham had invented it not in America in the 1930s but in China in 2010? What if his investing experience was not in moderately regulated free markets but in state capitalist systems with gray regulations, shifting laws, and active government involvement? Would he have spoken of Mr. Market or Mr. Government? Are we sure Mr. Market still returns to intrinsic value in Russia?

What would value investing have become if Graham had invented it in Singapore or Dubai? In these environments, skilled investors operate agnostically between these small city-state economies, the nearby autocratic systems of China and Russia, the chaotic developing markets of India and Latin America, and the developed markets of the U.S. and Europe. Would U.S. equities still have constituted most of his portfolio?

How much of what we refer to as value investing has been shaped by the American experience and not by the value principles themselves? And what is the best value-based methodology going forward into the first global century? Are we really targeting the best value opportunities in a rapidly changing environment? Or are we simply holding on to what we know as the ground moves beneath our feet?

About That Nagging Feeling That You're Missing Out

Much of the tension between economists/policy-makers/globalization theorists and global value investors can be understood this way. They see a globalizing macroeconomy with interconnected but fragile financial systems, while we see a rising sea of new companies that are wildly mispriced.

We are witnessing the breakneck chaotic development of half the planet's markets and their collision with the Western economies. At the company and asset level it is pure chaos, which is great for value investors. If China is building the equivalent of one to two Chicagos per year, how can this not create huge market inefficiencies? The pure scale and complexity of the activity, combined with erratic investor behavior, guarantee mispricings.

But many value investors, the experts at identifying such mispriced value, are conspicuously quiet. How can a Marriott spin-off be an exciting market inefficiency and the chaotic development of half the planet not be? I suspect more and more Western-based investors, staying strictly in their home markets, have a quiet nagging feeling that they are missing out.

I suspect that if Graham were looking at this chaotic sea of rising companies, he would see a world of opportunity. My guess is that he would mostly ignore the rampant theories of globalization and stay tethered to the concept of value. He would examine the fundamentals of companies around the world and build an investment methodology from the bottom up. Instead of going big and thinking macroeconomics, I think he would have gone small and thought of fundamentals.

Graham might also have seen it as a great intellectual challenge— a chance to understand a truly new and singular event in human history—the emergence of a global world. And instead of limiting oneself to the opportunities current strategies could capture, why not try to retarget the largest inefficiencies this event offers? This book, and much of my last decade, is my best attempt at this type of approach to the newly arrived global landscape—a *de novo* reapplication of fundamental value, learned on the ground and in the trenches around the world.

The investment strategies presented are the result of *de novo* reapplication of value and specifically target what I believe is the core "going global" problem: how to invest long-term in inherently unstable and uncertain environments. I call the resulting strategies *value point*. It is a logical extension of well-known value techniques and, hopefully, easily recognizable to most readers. It also explains most of the successes I have witnessed of Western firms going global—as well as the startling rise of developing market tycoons such as Carlos Slim and Prince Waleed. It is an action plan for profiting in a colliding world.

The Search for the Opportunity to Add Value

Going global is about capturing quality companies at a low price through a really big advantage

The animating idea at the core of Graham's (and Buffett's) methods is the search for value—a quest for unrecognized value caused by seemingly endless market inefficiencies. On a daily basis, the classic value investor estimates the economic value of companies, mostly by screening stocks, reading annual reports, and calculating intrinsic value. Accessing the deals, acquiring the assets, and managing the assets are key steps but not the major focus (you buy the shares and put them in your portfolio). A prototypical value investment would be Warren Buffett's purchase of Coca-Cola. He recognized the mispriced value, purchased the shares on the public market, and put them in his portfolio.

Value point is the search for the opportunity to add value. Finding unrecognized value is actually not the primary challenge in most global markets today. These are rapidly developing markets with limited and often inaccurate information—and they are overwhelmingly inefficient. The value point investor's problems are accessing inaccessible investments, eliminating the larger uncertainties, and strengthening the weak and often impractical claims to the enterprise.

A prototypical value point investment is Prince Waleed's launch of two Four Seasons hotels in Egypt. He partnered with the Four Seasons and made private bids for both prime land and existing hotels in Cairo and Sharm El-Sheikh. The offer added so much value beyond just capital that the local owners and government officials were willing to sell a minority share at a good price. His added value (the Four Seasons brand and management contract) made an inaccessible deal accessible. Furthermore, his long-term control of the hotel management contract enabled him to comfortably become a minority shareholder of an illiquid private asset in a country with limited rule of law. Per Graham, it was a value-based surgical investment. The risk was minimized by a large margin of safety, and the returns were effectively secured at the time of the investment.

In both examples, we see that the investors identified a quality company, acquired it at a cheap price, and secured a margin of safety. The key to value point is knowing what constitutes a quality company in a developing economy or cross-border situation and how to solve the "going global" problems mentioned. I have found that a surgical addition of value at the time of investment is the most effective approach. It both increases access and expands the margin of safety to compensate for the increased uncertainty and instability of these environments.

Intelligent Global Investing

Five simple recommendations for investing in a colliding world

Much of the presented strategies can be reduced to the following five recommendations/observations for moving to a more global posture for value investing and deal-making.

Point #1: The World Has Changed—and Our Worldview Must Change with It

Dislocations such as economic crises—and wars—often reveal changes that have been quietly accumulating. The 2009 financial crisis revealed that a global economy defined for the past two centuries by dominant Western markets and systems has become just one part of a much larger and more complicated global economy.

From 1950 to approximately 1995, the investment world can be described as "Western-centric" or "unipolar," as shown in Figure 1.1. The world's developed economies all had advanced legal and regulatory systems and were relatively comfortable places to do both domestic and cross-border deals and investments. Investors between London, New York, and Tokyo were fairly good at doing deals together.

Beginning in the early to mid-1990s, interactions with the developing economies began to grow exponentially, as shown in Figure 1.2. American factories were moved to China, Saudi investors were buying office buildings in London, and call centers were moved to India. Western investors began tentatively "reaching out" from their home markets to these very different systems. But investments and deals were conspicuously limited, mainly because of a lack of comfort. Large risks were perceived and avoided. Activities were circumscribed to what was similar to Western investment strategies and operating methods. In practice it resembled classic value investing, but with a larger, and often impractical, margin of safety demanded.

There is the impression that for the past 15 years, we have been awkwardly stretching out from this unipolar core, trying to apply familiar techniques to fundamentally different economic systems. But as the world evolves further and further from what we knew, we are stretching and contorting ourselves more and more.

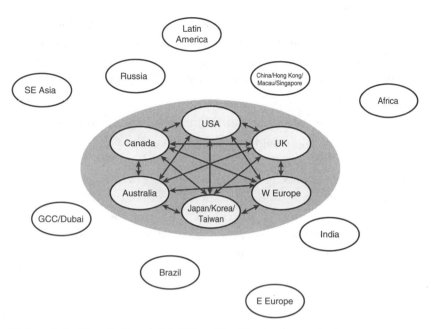

Figure 1.1   The 1950s to the 1990s: The Western-centric investment worldview

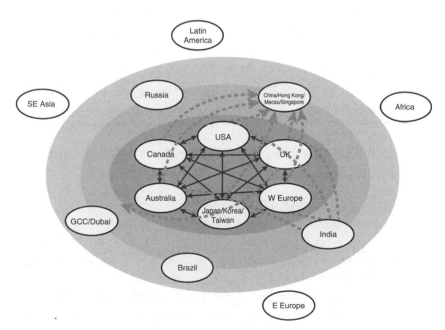

Figure 1.2   The 1990s to the 2000s: A Western-centric accommodation to a changing world

To create wealth in a multipolar economy, we need a mindset free of the Copernican model of Western developed economies as the centers of gravity with developing nations circling us. The biases of this Western-centric strategy are profoundly limiting to investing across national borders.

The international capitalism of the U.S. and Europe has now been joined by the state capitalism of places such as Russia and China and the "godfather capitalism" of places such as the United Arab Emirates (UAE) and Singapore. The world now has more systems, and many of them are fundamentally different. Competitive dynamics, the role of government, the role of the press, the rule of law, cultural traditions, governance practices, and many other important investment factors are very different depending where you are. Capabilities, particularly management ability, also vary dramatically depending on the location. The world is multipolar.

It is also colliding and surprisingly local. We are witnessing a great migration of capabilities from developed economies to developing. The migration of professional management is the most important, but many others exist, such as technology, brands, products, and business models. The increasing collision of differing ecnomic systems is an important part of the value worldview. And this collision is increasingly being fueled by local competitive pressures. As will be discussed at length, the multipolar world is not only colliding but increasingly local.

Point #2: The Key Is to Reapply Graham's Thinking to New Environments

Ben Graham's value principles are the key to direct investing within this multipolar, colliding, and local worldview. However, the starting point is not in his conclusions—Mr. Market, intrinsic value, and margin of safety—but in his method. We look at the value approach before many of the developed economy assumptions were incorporated into the methodology. "Graham's Method" turns out to be far more valuable than any particular strategy. My own approach for translating fundamental value to different landscapes is to combine security analysis with uncertainty analysis and hands-on deal-making. So I have followed Graham's Method but reached a different methodology. In this book, I focus less on measuring a margin of safety and more on strengthening the claim to the enterprise. I talk less about Mr. Market and more about Mr. Government. To be honest, I am somewhat pleased with this, as I have never really liked the term Mr. Market. It sounds odd in Chinese (shi chang xian sheng) and ridiculous in Spanish (Señor Mercado).

Graham's Method could be considered the scientific method for investing. His assertion that a company has an independent value is very similar to scientists' assertion that the world has independent natural laws to which it adheres. And although it is somewhat common to argue that finance is alchemy without any sort of independent or stable natural laws, this underestimates the insights to be gained by testing measurements against an independent and stable thesis. It also overestimates the actual consistency of most natural laws. Newtonian physics and quantum mechanics work only in specific situations and fail in others. Seeing where a thesis holds and where it fails can be equally valuable. Much of this book is about studying the margins where traditional value investing breaks down.

For the purposes of this book, I have taken some liberties and inferred Graham's Method to be the following three steps:

1. **Eliminate the uncertainties** in both your direct measurements (past versus future revenue, tangible versus intangible assets) and your calculated values (cash flows, intrinsic value). Calculating an answer is fairly easy. Calculating the uncertainty around an answer is the real challenge.

2. **Quantify the risk.** Remove the human element, and set a standard quantitative measurement for the risk of loss from the investment. Note that I am claiming something different from the usual statement that value investing is about minimizing risk. The real insight in Graham's Method is to quantify risk and then to invest only in situations where it happens to be acceptable.

3. **Invest surgically,** and make your returns at the time of investment.

Using Graham's Method on public stocks in the U.S., you naturally derive the well-known value investing methodology (buy when

Mr. Market is 30% below a stable intrinsic value, and hold). However, when using Graham's Method on developed, developing, and cross-border environments (the global landscape), you derive a broader methodology that combines both value investing and value point concepts. Mr. Market is joined by Mr. Government. Sustainable competitive advantage is joined by the concept of defensible investments. And the search for value is complemented by the search for the opportunity to add value. Traditional value investing in developed economies can be seen as a simplified subset of a longer equation.

This makes intuitive sense. As we move from U.S.-style developed markets to a larger global investment landscape with multiple types of investment environments, we lose many of our simplifying assumptions. We should expect our methodology to expand and our tool kit to get larger.

Point #3: Seen Through the Prism of Value, the World Is Full of Inefficiencies and Opportunities

Value investing and value point methodologies show a global landscape full of attractive opportunities. And it appears much larger, more varied, and more inefficient than the investment landscape previous generations had to work with. But its biggest inefficiencies and its most attractive opportunities turn out not to be the ones frequently considered when going global. Western-listed companies with exposure to India are not terribly compelling, and Hong Kong pre-IPOs are nice but not thrilling. However, family-owned private companies in China and India are a deep pool of mispriced value. And crane-leasing companies in the UAE and infrastructure deals in Saudi Arabia offer huge upside. At the moment, agribusiness deals between Chinese state-owned enterprises and Mexican companies get my attention. As will be detailed, a chaotic, developing, and colliding world is full of market inefficiencies and value opportunities, but they are not necessarily in places where investors are comfortable. But what you see depends on the prism through which you look.

Point #4: It's Still About Price and Quality

Value point is a more complicated and hands-on version of value investing but seeks the same end result: a quality company purchased at a low price, relative to value. The higher the company's quality and the lower the price, generally the higher the returns.

In fact, value point is, for all effective purposes, a series of techniques to significantly expand the number of companies that can be targeted and to boost the margin of safety. Logically, that is the only way to eliminate the additional uncertainties and instabilities of many global landscapes. As we move to more developing-type environments, we need to significantly increase the margin of safety, both at the time of the investment and long-term.

Point #5: A Value Personality Is the Same Everywhere

With the right worldview and a consistently applied value methodology, we seem to naturally evolve in our mindset and posture to the "intelligent investor" that Graham described so well. We are value-focused. We don't speculate. We are microfundamentalists. We are on the ground and in the trenches, spending our days studying the details of specific companies. We are skeptics, constantly retesting our assumptions and always doing all our own research. We invest only when we are assured of making money, and we never lose money. And when we do find an investment that meets our criteria, we go in big. We don't diversify. We concentrate (and obsess).

Most importantly, we are optimists. Whether this is by personality or a natural result of a rational approach to business and life, we see a world of attractive investment opportunities. That makes us optimistic about business and investing. None of this changes when going global. A value framework and personality are the same everywhere.

The Prince Waleed Years

Second only to Graham's influence, this book is the result of working for the world's first private global investor

I began writing this book in 2009 in Riyadh, Saudi Arabia. It had been almost ten years since I had left New York City financial services to work for Prince Waleed internationally. It was a fairly radical move at the time. Few people left New York to go off to the emerging markets back then, let alone to the Middle East, let alone to Saudi Arabia. But Waleed was the world's fourth-wealthiest person (*Time* magazine had nicknamed him the "Arabian Warren Buffett") and arguably one of the few master investors. Having met him on a consulting engagement, I had been struck by what I called the "Waleed mystery": How had a pure investor with only two or three staff members built $30,000 into a $22 billion fortune? Furthermore, how did he walk so effortlessly between developed and developing markets when so many others struggled? He could buy Fortune 500 companies in the U.S. on Monday, hotels in Africa on Tuesday, and banks in China on Wednesday. So I took a chance and became one of his few staffers. In the first year of the first global century, I had joined the world's first global investor.

Of all the major investors (George Soros, Buffett, and so on), Waleed is unique in that he is the only one to have come from a developing economy. He made his first fortune in the Middle East, yet he also became the largest foreign investor in the U.S., the largest shareholder of the world's largest bank (Citigroup, 2007), and the world's second-largest media owner, after Rupert Murdoch. Even Warren Buffett has wryly called himself the "Waleed of America." He is the only master investor who has been equally successful in developing and developed environments.

His Western investments are fairly well known: 5% of Citi, more than 200 hotels (Movenpick, Fairmont, The Plaza, George V, the Savoy, the Four Seasons hotels), EuroDisney, Canary Wharf, News Corp., Saks Fifth Avenue, TimeWarner, Apple, eBay, priceline.com, and many others. Less-well-known investments include Bank of China, a Manhattan-sized real estate development (27 square miles of land), a private Airbus 380, multiple Africa projects and private equity funds, a one-mile-high skyscraper, hospitals, insurance companies, schools, petrochemical facilities, banks, architecture firms, market research companies, and many others. His deal history is an interesting combination of public stocks and private investments in both developed and developing economies.

Sitting at my desk in Riyadh in 2009 and thinking about this book, I began rereading Graham's *Security Analysis* and Mohamed El-Erian's *When Markets Collide*. And I began asking many of the questions posed at the start of this chapter. What would Graham have thought of the colliding world El-Erian so accurately described? Why didn't Graham's methodology work very well in other economic systems? And why is it that so many Western-based investors seem to be sitting on the global sidelines while investors like Waleed are making money hand over foot? In my experience, I have found that Graham's concepts are the theoretical anchor for global investing but Waleed's deal history is the Rosetta Stone.

I concluded I had gotten unbelievably, and unintentionally, lucky. I had somehow become part of the first generation of investors trained on a global playing field. Not only did I have a front-row seat at a singular time of global transformation, but I had also ended up in the inner circle of likely the most successful global investor thus far. Now, almost ten years later, I was in a position of being equally comfortable buying hospitals in India, buying stocks in Chicago, and building mortgage companies in Africa.

I think my entire generation has gotten lucky. We are the first wave of investors to see the entire world as our opportunity—being equally excited and comfortable in Shanghai, New York, Dubai, and Mumbai. It is a thrilling time if you are ambitious. And, like many value-focused people, I have a fascination (compulsion?) with understanding things as they are. And now there is much more of the world to learn about. Beijing banks. India–U.S. cross-border mergers and acquisitions (M&A). African natural resources. It's all fascinating—and profitable.

I am ridiculously optimistic about the new century and its opportunities. Absent some sort of new animal analogy, I could not be more bullish (a bull elephant?). For the intellectually curious, it is fascinating. And for the ambitious, money can be made almost everywhere. The first global century is as you would expect any grand new frontier to be—thrilling and chaotic, daunting and confusing, energizing and fascinating.

2

Rethinking Value in a Global Age

The world's tallest building is now in Dubai, its largest phone company is in China, and its richest person is in Mexico. The twenty-first century—the first global century—has arrived much faster than anticipated and in a fairly stunning fashion. And it has caught many smart investors flat-footed. Confident, experienced investors and deal-makers have found themselves on rapidly changing and increasingly unfamiliar terrain. Did Macau really surpass Las Vegas in revenues in just five years? Is Volkswagen really selling more cars in the BRIC countries (Brazil, Russia, India, and China) than in the United States? Have a million Chinese really moved to Africa to develop natural resources? The new global investment landscape is thrilling but, for many, increasingly uncomfortable.

Within this general chaos are real challenges for the traditional value methodology. In the previous chapter, I described the typical problems and concerns of Western-based value investors looking at global investments. Most of these "going global" problems can be classified as one of five types:

- Limited access to investments
- Increased uncertainty in the current intrinsic value
- Increased long-term uncertainty, including worries about instability
- The availability of only weak or impractical claims against the target enterprise
- Foreigner disadvantages

I also asserted that none of these problems is getting smaller. They are in fact inherent characteristics of many rising economic systems—and, therefore, of a colliding global world, which Mohamed El-Erian called "the new destination."

Ben Graham's core concept of intrinsic value is the anchor for understanding and investing in this new destination. It offers the one stable point in a sea of changing actors and dynamics. In the last century, Graham's value concept and methodology made a confusing Western investment world understandable. It is also the key to understanding the next century.

Having come to the end of almost ten years of investing between the developed and developing markets, I have found myself repeatedly returning to Graham's writings. It is impressive to see how easily his concepts can be reapplied to very different politico-economic environments. At the same time, I am an avid student of the global investment deals of the last 10 to 15 years, and I was fortunate enough to have worked for one of the leading practitioners. The presented investment strategies were built theoretically from Graham on one side and reverse-engineered from practitioners on the other. The point in the middle where these two approaches meet and, thankfully, agree is the investment strategy presented in this book, *value point*.

Essentially, value point asks three questions about potential investments and generates four answers:

1. Is it a good, potentially great, or great company?
2. Is it cheap? (Is there a market inefficiency?)
3. Is the margin of safety capturable and sustainable?

If the answer to all three is yes, the investment has all the characteristics we hope to see with a value approach. We consider the company attractive. We can purchase at a good price and secure a healthy margin of safety. The resulting four answers are as follows:

1. A margin of safety is captured.
2. The investment downside is minimized.
3. The potential upside is maintained.
4. The investment is made surgically, and returns are effectively captured at the time of investment.

Overall, the investor captures significant value at the time of investment and can benefit from the growth of the company's economic value over time. You win big over time by not losing.

These questions on the surface are almost identical to those posed by traditional value investors in developed economies when considering a public or private company, except for Question 3, which is usually just assumed. But as you move to different environments, additional factors are introduced, so the details of how you answer these questions become more complicated, as shown in Figure 2.1.

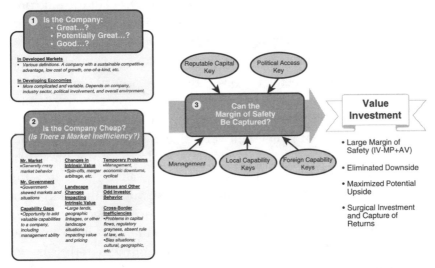

Figure 2.1   Value point: the search for the opportunity to add value

The main difference is an expansion of the traditional *search for value* philosophy to a *search for the opportunity to add value*. Buying a $10 million company for $5 million is good. Buying it for $5 million and increasing its value to $12 million at the same time is better. Instead of just pushing down the price relative to the intrinsic value, the margin of safety can also be expanded upward by surgically adding value at the time of investment. This has several other important effects, which will be discussed. But the goal is to capture and stabilize the current and future margin of safety with structured deal-making. In short, we are combining value investing with active deal-making.

In many ways, this is a classic value approach for coping with increased uncertainty or instability in an investment or environment. You compensate for uncertainty by expanding the margin of safety.

However, this is also a departure from and a rejection of the classic global value approach. In that approach, you compensate for additional perceived risks (currency fluctuations, governance problems, limited reporting, increased instability) by limiting your investments to those that are identified as having an exceptional margin of safety. The problem with demanding an exceptional margin of safety is that it is impractical. Too few investments reach this level of extreme precaution, and it is in many ways a denial of the fundamental characteristics of many increasingly important economic systems.

And as will be shown, a "search for the opportunity to add value" approach effectively solves the five primary going-global problems listed at the beginning of this chapter. You increase access. You eliminate uncertainty in both the current and future intrinsic values. You strengthen your claims to the enterprise, and you overcome the foreigner disadvantages. However, it is important to stress that the primary objective of adding value is to reduce the longer-term downside uncertainty (and "stabilize" the margin of safety). The big payoff is to be able to hold to a longer-term value approach in unstable and uncertain environments, which enables you to capture the growth in economic value of the enterprise.

This, hopefully, makes somewhat intuitive sense. As you leave the developed democracies, you start to lose stability, information accuracy, governance relationships, minority shareholder rights, and many other things. But you also start to gain an ability to significantly impact the value of companies that, like their economies, are rapidly developing. Both of these factors push you into a closer and more hands-on deal-making posture with the investment. If successful, you can take a rising sea of new companies with exceptionally large market inefficiencies and transform them into capturable value opportunities.

This chapter presents two important prerequisites for this approach. The first is a value-based worldview—a way to see global markets through the lens of a value investor and deal-maker. The second is a recasting of Graham's value concepts within this worldview. This lays the groundwork for the next chapter, which details the investment strategy.

A Value-Based Worldview

The Microfundamentalists Strike Back

A value worldview bears little resemblance to most of the globalization talk

"Globalization" as a subject (particularly for books) has long been the realm of economists, macro-traders, policy wonks, and portfolio managers. Their language is that of interest rates, government policy, capital flows, gross domestic product (GDP), and employment rates.

We value-focused microfundamentalists find little utility in this approach. Our language is that of management, customers, competitive advantage, intrinsic value, margin of safety, economic goodwill, and return on invested capital (ROIC). In a large and growing investment world, our favorite approach is to go very small. We do real estate investments in China, develop hospitals in India, and structure cross-border mergers and acquisitions (M&A) deals between the U.S. and the Middle East. And the only "globalization" theories we espouse are a sort of hazy aggregate of all this bottom-up fundamental analysis. My own experience has been that after a decade on the ground on three continents and in more than 15 industries, a fuzzy but consistent macro picture does emerge from lots of time spent at the micro level.

What we value-focused investors do see is a world that is full of new companies that are wildly mispriced. It is a place in which rising economies and colliding systems are creating huge gaps between price and value. For us, the global investment world looks like one big value opportunity.

The key question is how to capture it. The strategy presented is based on combining fundamental security analysis with uncertainty analysis and deal-making. The first has long been the domain and primary language of value investors. The second is the key to transporting fundamental analysis out of relatively stable developed economies and into more uncertain and unstable terrains. The third lets you remove the long-term uncertainty. The melding of uncertainty analysis and deal-making lets you do long-term fundamental investing in uncertain places.

Unsurprisingly, the value worldview conflicts with most of the current globalization talk. The world is flat. Its financial system is precarious. Foreign policy power and regional stability follow from wealth and trade relationships. If it's not a direct conflict, it's a situation of talking past each other. I can't see how the world is flat in any meaningful way, and I generally don't care what the trade policies or World Trade Organization (WTO) commitments are. I also find economic or multivariable macro analysis not particularly usable at the company and asset level. Globalization theorists and macroeconomists tend to be top-down analysts. We are bottom-up analysts. Or bottom and "we don't really care about up" analysts. But value investors and economists disagreeing is nothing new. Twentieth-century value investors had the Efficient Market Theory promoters to butt heads with. Global value investors have the globalization theorists to contend with.

In this vein, I thought it appropriate to make a clear declaration of fundamentalist principles at the start. I am presenting a worldview and investment strategy based on fundamental value that is staunchly micro. And I will probably not resist the urge to fire some gratuitous broadsides at the globalization crowd as I pass by.

The Unsexy Reality of Globalization

The global investment world is overwhelmingly local

I proffer the very exciting worldview that globalization is nothing new. It's fascinating, intellectually challenging, and very profitable. But it doesn't appear to be anything really new in terms of investing. The number of sizeable markets and economies is certainly increasing. The markets and economies of the U.S., Europe, and Japan have already been joined by established emerging markets such as China, India, Brazil, Russia, and the Gulf Cooperation Council (GCC). For investors, this means a lot more companies and assets to buy. And certainly some of these economic systems are fundamentally different from the developed Western economies. China and Russia, in particular, are completely different animals. But investment is still mostly about profits, and profits are still mostly about competition in local markets.

I assert that the global investment world is *multipolar, colliding,* and overwhelmingly *local.*

Let me immediately backtrack this big assertion with a big quali-
fier. I am terrible at economics, which implies that I am an order of
magnitude worse at global economics. I am a mathematician and
physicist by training, and I can pretty confidently model the radiation
scatter from an electron-positron collider (a nano-fundamentalist). I
can also tell you the laser penetration rates needed to remove tattoos
from LA gang members and the biophysics of Swedish fighter pilots
in high-speed turns. (Because Sweden has been officially neutral for
almost 200 years, flying around Sweden as a fighter pilot is about the
most fun you can have in a career.)

But I have no real idea what the GDP of Argentina will be in a
few years. I have no idea why foreign exchange rates move the way
they do. I am strictly micro and would go nano if I could. So the presented worldview (multipolar, colliding, and local) is mostly descrip-
tive and limited to factors relevant to direct investing. It has about the
same analytical rigor as cloud naming. ("That cloud looks like a castle,
that one a bunny.")

The World Is Multipolar

The investment world has seen an increase in both the number of
sizeable markets and the types of economic systems. If the last century was Western and unipolar, this century is global and multipolar. I
have given various examples, but it's really just cloud naming and
hopefully is self-evident. China and Russia are alternative economic
models with little in common with the U.S. or UK. And despite being
called developing economies, most are not developing toward the
developed economies. They are something new and different. State-
managed (and mismanaged) economies in Asia, Africa, and the Middle East come in various shades, just as Western capitalism varies
between historically free-market America and more tightly regulated
France and Germany. Brazil and India are also different entities,
offering an almost nineteenth-century version of large population,
low income, international capitalism. And the majority of the other
countries that are often grouped illogically but conveniently into the
"emerging markets" bucket show significant variation as well.

But overall, many more types of investment landscapes exist today, and avoiding them is getting harder and harder for Western investors. The world is multipolar.

The World Is Colliding

Mohamed El-Erian's book *When Markets Collide* describes the collision of these fundamentally different types of systems—the increasing interactions of a multipolar world. That book was written mostly at the macroeconomic and policy level, whereas I am viewing the same topic at the company and asset level. If *When Markets Collide* is at 30,000 feet, this book is in the trenches. But the conclusion is the same. The collision is dramatic and increasingly intense— although it is debatable at what level the collision is more interesting to watch. I get to see it in the unusual interactions between companies, investors, and partners from around the world. But people at the macro level get to watch the interconnected financial system and all its precarious chaos.

A quick scan of the *Wall Street Journal* or *Financial Times* on any given day shows the collision at the company level. United Arab Emirates (UAE) investors buy UK soccer teams. Indian industrial companies buy European steel makers. Chinese state-owned enterprises try (mostly unsuccessfully) to acquire U.S. assets. Besides producing frequent headlines, the increasing collision of companies, markets, and investors is creating interesting investment dynamics. The multipolar world is colliding.

Again, I am simply stating these first two observations without much support. ("That cloud looks like an elephant.")

The World Is Local

The key difference in how microfundamentalists (particularly fundamentalist microfundamentalists) view global investing is the primacy of competition and competitive advantage. Profits and investment returns are overwhelmingly a function of competition, and this drives most market participants' activity and behavior. Most of the activity that can be seen on the ground in Mumbai, Shanghai, and Dubai is about competitive dynamics. So I am far more interested in how local real estate companies in India compete with foreign entrants than with what the trade policies are. The fight for customers on the ground in local markets is the sharp end of the investing spear.

This mostly local competitive fight is creating a strong push toward an increasing localization of services, products, and capabilities. To win customers in a local market, you likely need to tailor your products and services to their tastes. If your competitor has achieved local economies of scale in, say, distribution in Bangalore, you need to build the same or risk being pushed out.

If the past decade was mostly about the emergence of a colliding, multipolar world, the next decade will be about the arrival of a multi-local world. Service industries such as banking, healthcare, insurance, and hospitality will all be local. Private clinics in Brazil are not terribly worried about competition from Germany. Even large multinational companies can be viewed as mostly multilocal in practice. Standardized products, such as Coca-Cola, are marketed, bottled, and distributed mostly domestically. Certainly, many industries (cars, manufacturing) have global value chains with different functions in different regions, but markets, customers, and competition tend to be mostly local, and that is the primary concern for direct-value investors.

This raises a conundrum that sits at the center of much of the presented investment strategy. Business and competition are increasingly local. But investing and capital are increasingly global. How do increasingly globally active investors engage with increasingly local businesses?

An important aspect of the competitive dynamics of most developing economies is also worth noting—the impact of foreign capabilities. The coffee shop in Abu Dhabi that first franchised with Starbucks suddenly acquired a significant advantage over its local competitors. The acquisition of Starbucks' capabilities (brand, operating systems, supply chain, management) quickly manifested itself in the local market share, earnings, growth prospects, intangible and tangible assets, and many other quantitative and qualitative parameters that value-concerned investors look at. The migration of capabilities across borders is a significant aspect of competition and therefore investment returns.

In fact, driving through Abu Dhabi, it is fairly hard to find any business that is not a combination of local operations and foreign capabilities. Competing in the developing economies has a lot to do with assembling best-of-breed combinations of global capabilities (brands, supplies, technology) and deploying them locally. U.S.-based companies usually assume that all their needed capabilities (and customers and capital) can be found domestically. In contrast, Middle Eastern companies, a fairly shallow market in terms of customers, skills, and technology, start virtually every project by looking for new foreign capabilities to bring into the market.

Most often this migration of capabilities between markets is a natural part of the never-ending race for operational efficiencies. Absent a competitive advantage, local companies are continually adding and refining capabilities, assets, and performance to stay competitive and make a moderate profit. Migrating capabilities typically appear first on the balance sheets of local companies (brands, factories) and then are translated over time to the income statement, depending on management ability. It is important to note the degree to which global value investing is about the interaction between competition, capabilities, management, asset value, and earnings power value.

That markets are becoming more local and that capabilities can be advantages should not be surprising. Developing markets are by definition developing. Moneylenders are being replaced by banks. Hutongs are being replaced by modern apartment buildings. Bicycles are being replaced by scooters and scooters by cars. As will be discussed, the migration of developed-market capabilities into rising economies is a big part of the direct investing worldview.

The World Is Uncertain and Unstable—But This Is Somewhat a Matter of Perspective

A final note on an issue that cuts across much of the "going global" discussion. The developed economies feel—and, for the most part, are—relatively stable. The public and private markets are large, have grown fairly predictably for 50 years, have relatively clear regulations, and are subject to only rare political risks. They are also deep and offer frequent mispricing opportunities. When going global, Western-based investors are confronted with much shallower markets that are constantly changing. They are less stable and pre-dictable—and feel even more so. Regulations can change suddenly and dramatically (five years is a very long time in India in terms of new regulations). This decreased "stability" (both real and perceived) will play out repeatedly in strategy discussions, particularly because many value investors tend to think longer-term when stability really matters. However, it should also be noted that investors in the Middle East, Russia, India, and China don't feel things are unstable. They long ago acquired their sea legs and consider this all very normal.

An increasingly uncertain and unstable world (both real and per-ceived) raises a core challenge to the value methodology. Value investing has most often been described as a long-term approach, buying and holding relatively stable companies in a stable environ-ment. The focus on sustainable competitive advantage is mainly about targeting companies that have the most stable (protected) prof-its. Yet, the worldview I have presented is overwhelmingly unstable, or at least uncertain. The markets are developing. The companies are young and growing in real economic value. The competition is con-stantly shifting. Capabilities are migrating. The regulatory grayness, lack of rule of law, active involvement of the government, and other factors all create additional uncertainties, especially in the long term.

This uncertainty question has always been central to a value approach. In *Security Analysis*, uncertainty as a topic runs through every chapter. And certainly the 1930s time period in which Ben Graham and David Dodd wrote it was much less stable and more volatile than most of the 70 years that have followed. Graham and Dodd discuss this uncertainty and instability question within the 1930s shift in the American economy from asset-heavy industries such as resources, manufacturing, and transportation to more asset-light service industries.

Uncertainty discussions take up most of this chapter, but I wanted to make a couple of key points early on:

- Because global investing is rife with a mixture of perceived and real uncertainties and instabilities, separating out the perceived uncertainties is both the first step and an opportunity.
- Dealing with the increase in real uncertainties and instabilities is the central challenge, particularly with a long-term approach.

Warren Buffett has said that he puts companies into one of three buckets: "good," "bad," or "too hard." But "too hard" can be a mix of real complexity, the limitations of your strategy, and investor perception. This investment strategy is mostly focused on putting back into play many of the companies that are frequently placed in the "too hard" category.

On a purely gratuitous side note, this perceived lack of stability also makes the global investing landscape largely free of what some would call questionable Western investment thought. There is not much talk about efficient markets or random walks in India. Nobody assumes Gaussian distributions in China.

The Inefficient Century

The global landscape is brimming with companies that are wildly mispriced

In 2002–2003, Warren Buffett purchased $488 million worth of Petro-China. Within five years he sold this stake for $4 billion, an eight-fold increase. In 2008, he purchased 9.89% of Shenzhen-based battery maker BYD for $230 million. Less than 24 months later, that investment had increased six-fold to $1.45 billion. When was the last time value investors made these types of returns? Not only are the returns in the six to eight times range, but this is also for some of China's largest companies. The number of mispriced companies increases dramatically as one moves to medium and smaller-sized companies.

The takeaway is that we are witnessing massive gaps between price and value in many of the world's new markets. The first global century may turn out to be the most inefficient.

Going global is still mostly about getting a cheap price. A $10 million company trading at $5 million is a 100% return, but if it's trading near $1 million, the returns jump to 900% to 1,000%. Value investors' number-one objective is to find such market inefficiencies—gaps between intrinsic value and market price—and the bigger they are, the better.

Cheap prices can result from a range of factors such as a real change in value, a change in company size, investor neglect and other biases, an economic downturn, management problems, or just crazy Mr. Market. But as you leave the developed economies and move to a larger, multipolar, colliding, and less stable playing field, all these inefficiencies get larger.

This is great news for investors. A host of new markets contain not only a sea of new companies but also much greater inefficiencies.

Three particularly global phenomena can also significantly impact price. They are not market inefficiencies as typically defined but can have the same effect. They are *large trends*, *cross-border inefficiencies*, and *capability gaps*.

Large Trends Swing Price Away from Value

In *The Age of Turbulence*, Alan Greenspan argued that rapid dislocations in markets and economic systems seem to be increasing in frequency. Financial crises regularly emerge in developing (and now developed) economies and ripple rapidly through the interconnected financial systems. Earthquakes in Ecuador can spike the price of copper, resulting in an increase in Chinese manufacturing costs and causing a rise in prices at Walmart. Far from diversifying risks and stabilizing the system, the connections between the world's financial systems seem to almost amplify the daily swings and periodic booms and busts.

But these crashing waves on the surface of the global economy can sometimes obscure deeper currents underneath. Within the past ten years, 1 million Chinese have moved into Africa and started over 500 Chinese companies (Mandarin has become the number-two language in many places). This is a result of Chinese manufacturing's growing demand for natural resources. In a few short years, Indian call centers and IT companies became a standard service for many Fortune 500 companies. This has fueled the rise of large Indian companies such as Infosys and has resulted in the migration of hundreds of thousands of people within India. The opening of Macau's casino market in 2002 led to a massive influx of Western, Asian, and Chinese businesses into a small territory. And in the GCC, the rising price of oil in the late 2000s led to a development and real estate boom across the region that gave rise to the world's tallest building.

Such larger and deeper trends appear to be increasing. And they are creating value opportunities.

I am not talking about normal growth. By large trends, I mean large and sudden changes in real economic value (or both companies and environments) that result in a lag between true value and market price. The subsequent growth can also increase returns, but the gap between current value and price is the starting point for the investment. Such trends are often the result of a new connection between two previously separate economies, such as Africa and China in natural resources. Buying office space in Macau in 2005 could have been done with a good margin of safety. The same thing was true of crane leasing in Dubai in 2007.

The key to distinguishing between turbulence on the surface and the deeper economic currents underneath is usually the size of the trend (either positive or negative) versus the size of the local economy. Capturing these large trends is one of the fastest paths to wealth in developing economies and explains many of the large investors emerging from these regions.

Colliding Cultures Are Creating New Biases

Behavioral finance issues seem inherent to colliding economic systems. Joint ventures between Mexican and Russian companies, for example, are rife with psychology. There are lots of biases. There are cultural and language gaps. There is an unfamiliarity with distant geographies and fundamentally different politicoeconomic systems. All this impacts price.

In the U.S., you can similarly see such cross-border inefficiencies when investment committees (of private equity firms, for example) are asked to approve, say, an investment in Bangalore. As experienced as the senior partners are, most have never invested outside the U.S. or Europe and are hesitant to approve large, particularly illiquid investments internationally. This lack of comfort and often strong bias (if the investment is in Africa, for example) show up in the discussion. Compare this to the price a local Indian private equity firm would pay for the same company. Whether it's private equity partners in the U.S. or business development executives in Moscow involved, cross-border deals are often as much about behavioral finance as business or investment strategy.

For investors, these cross-border inefficiencies are value opportunities. Mexico–China natural resources deals are underserved today, as are Middle East–India infrastructure deals. Large Chinese and GCC investment dollars are struggling to move into Western opportunities, while Western investment dollars are struggling to move into the developing economies. There are opportunities at both the company and capital level.

Gaps in Capabilities Are a Type of Inefficiency

The discussed movement of capabilities into developing economies creates another type of inefficiency. If bringing the Starbucks franchise to a coffee shop business in Abu Dhabi will significantly increase the economic value of that enterprise, I can capture part of that change in value. If it will increase the value from $10 million to $12 million, there is no way I can be told that my buy-in price is $12 million. It's partly about negotiation, but it's also a situation with a real gap between price and value. Another way to think about such a capability gap is that it is event-driven investing, but you are creating the event.

The following chapters expand on this by looking at how capabilities are moving between the world's economic hubs. This is overwhelmingly done by global investors and deal-makers. Someone had to bring Starbucks into Abu Dhabi. Someone struck a deal that put a 7-Eleven on what seems like every street corner in Hong Kong and Singapore. Capability gaps at both the industry and company level are capturable value opportunities.

Rederiving Graham's Method

Value Investing's Upper-Atmosphere Problem

Traditional value methodologies are failing to capture the really big opportunities

The power of value as a concept is that it isolates an independent and measurable variable from the general chaos of the market and its participants. The gaps between this variable and the market price (and between reality and perception) are value investors' primary targets. The presented worldview, with its colliding markets, companies, actors, and biases, is overflowing with these types of gaps. Going global, we are not looking for investments with a 15% internal rate of return (IRR); we are looking for 50%, 75%, 100%, 200%, and so on.

So why, in a period of massive market inefficiencies, are the value experts so hesitant? If the world is littered with dollars selling for 50 cents, why aren't they rushing about in a frenzy, grabbing them?

I suggest that this mostly Western hesitancy is the result of three factors. The first is an unclear worldview, as just discussed. The terrain is unfamiliar, and seeing the opportunities is half the battle. The second factor is the mentioned paradox of how to invest globally when most businesses are local. The third is that value investing's most common methodology has limited applicability outside of developed economies. At the edges of developed economies, the standard value approach begins to break down. This is what I call value investing's "upper-atmosphere problem."

Per my favorite Richard Feynman trick, I continually translate business and investing problems into physics problems, work through them, and then translate the result back. Feynman was famous for doing this when meeting with professionals in other fields such as biology or anthropology. He would translate their field's problems into physics, figure them out, and then startle the biologists or anthropologists by giving them the answers. Of course, he wouldn't tell them how he was doing it, so they thought he was mystically smart.

With this approach, value investing's limited applicability outside developed economies looks a lot like an upper-atmosphere problem. The Earth's upper atmosphere is where many of the physical laws start to fall apart. It's where a lot of our assumptions about life and our sense of the world start to break down (a gap between perception and reality). The world is not actually three-dimensional, as it seems to be when you're walking around on the ground. The shortest distance between two points is not a straight line. And as accurate as Newtonian mechanics is on the ground (objects falling, pendulums swinging), it starts to give the wrong answer when you reach the upper atmosphere and light and time begin to bend. Even international flights can show small changes in time. Value point is a lot about investing in situations where traditional value investing starts to break down.

But it's in situations where the established concepts begin to break down that we can learn something new and something old. We find new laws and rules, and we rediscover some of the hidden assumptions we have been relying on. Going to the extremes or to where the models break down is when things get interesting.

Value investing was invented to explain stocks in the American economy. It was a theory put forth to solve a practical problem, and it involves many unstated assumptions. George Soros caught one of them when he noticed that intrinsic value and market price are not always independent. In financial products, particularly with credit, they can form reflexive relationships with positive and negative feedback loops.

Working across the Middle Eastern and Asian markets, and observing their increasing interactions with the U.S. and Europe, I began to notice that lots of the value assumptions were breaking down (see Figure 2.2). Neither the companies nor environments were very stable. Continually involved government actors actively influenced both market value and intrinsic value. Governance and legal structures were often too underdeveloped to invest in a hands-off reader-of-annual-reports sort of way. As you go step by step through the standard value investing methodology, you discover problems and questions at virtually every point.

Unsurprisingly, prudent investors following this approach have avoided most developing markets. Or they have adopted the posture that global investing is U.S. investing with lots of additional problems. This is a common red flag that your framework is breaking down. The applicability becomes narrower and narrower, and the qualifiers become more and more numerous.

In the sixth edition of *Security Analysis*, Thomas Russo wrote an introduction for the chapter on global value investing. His introduction, titled "Globetrotting with Graham and Dodd," lists additional precautions to be aware of when going global. Avoid illiquid assets. Beware of high trading costs and currency risks. Note that disclosure is less transparent. That management practices are problematic. That capital movement is restricted. And that there are language, cultural, and political stability problems. The net conclusion is that extra protection is required when going global. The margin of safety must be much larger.

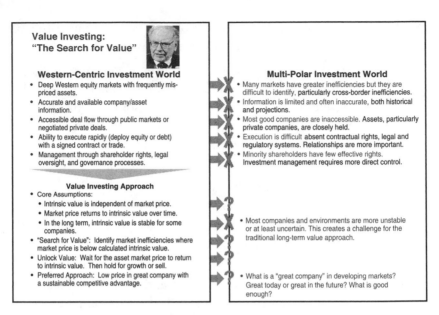

Figure 2.2   Value investing's upper-atmosphere problem

Value investing's upper-atmosphere problem manifests itself as a posture of extreme precaution. This is impractical for most investors, particularly those who lack Mr. Russo's ability and specialization. And beyond this, it results in investors avoiding the areas that have the largest market inefficiencies and offer some of the greatest opportunities for wealth creation.

I am arguing for an abandonment of this contorted stretching out from comfortable methodologies—and for a *de novo* targeting of the largest opportunities. In my experience, the largest value opportunities in a colliding world are in exactly the areas that this extreme prudence avoids: in *the long-term growth in per-share economic value of mostly private companies*. I am trying to go private and illiquid. I am trying to go long-term. And I am trying to go deep into the hunting grounds that everyone else avoids.

First, Eliminate Uncertainty

Graham's most important lesson is his treatment of uncertainty

Many of the key principles of Graham's Method are ironically unstated in his books. He talks about Mr. Market, intrinsic value, margin of safety, and circle of competence, but these are conclusions and a usable methodology. He states the end equation without showing the actual derivation. This is a shame, because I think some of his most impressive insights are in how he got there.

Given that the method is somewhat unstated, I am taking some large liberties and inferring it. Please cut me a lot of slack in this exercise if you can.

I think Graham had three steps in his derivation of value investing, as shown in Figure 2.3.

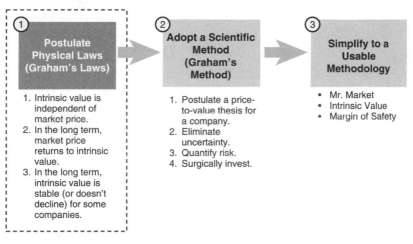

Figure 2.3   Derivation of value investing

In the first part, Graham postulated a series of "physical laws" for certain types of companies, which I will refer to as Graham's Laws. Similar to Newton's Law of Gravity, Graham's Laws serve as a theory to explain how the world works *outside and independent of any observers*. And similar to the physical laws of the sciences, his laws, by virtue of being independent, can be tested with measurable data.

Graham's Laws

1. Certain types of companies have an intrinsic value that is independent of the market.
2. The market price returns to this intrinsic value in the long term.
3. Intrinsic value is relatively stable in some types of companies.

This is a very simplistic summary and is just for discussion purposes. The point is that these physical laws for the investment world turn out to be true for a fairly large number of companies. There are many additional qualifiers related to the company's size, the degree to which the company is followed by the investment community, the actions of management, and so on, but I believe this is a fair summary of one of Graham's most common approaches. It can be represented graphically over time as shown in Figure 2.4.

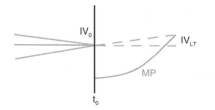

1. Intrinsic Value (IV) is independent of Market Price (MP).
2. In the long term, Market Price (MP) returns to Intrinsic Value (IV_{LT}).
3. In the long term, Intrinsic Value (IV_{LT}) is stable (or doesn't decrease) for some companies.

Figure 2.4   Graham's Laws

In the second part, Graham adopted an investing method that I call Graham's Method (see Figure 2.5). It is analogous to the scientific method and sets out a systematic process for investing. If it works, you make money—and if it fails, you gain valuable feedback on the accuracy of Graham's Laws. It is as much about organizing your thinking and putting in a process for systematic measurement and evaluation as it is about stating any inherent truth about the investing world.

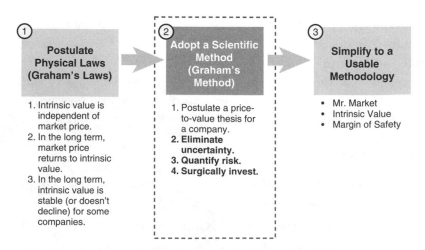

Figure 2.5   Graham's Method

Here are the key steps in Graham's Method, which are complete speculation on my part:

1. Postulate a price-to-value thesis for a specific company.
2. Eliminate uncertainty.
3. Quantify the risk.
4. Invest surgically.

Graham's Method starts with *postulating a relationship between the price and value* of a specific company. If the company's value is $10 million but the market price is $5 million, it is likely the type of company that fits Graham's Laws. This is how many investors generally see value investing. It is intrinsic value and Mr. Market. But I think the next three steps are the really clever insights.

Step 2 is the *elimination of uncertainty*. Any theory about how the world works (such as Graham's or Newton's Laws) requires prediction and direct measurement. For Graham, this means measuring companies' intrinsic value relative to price. But because intrinsic value cannot be measured directly, other factors are measured, and intrinsic value is then calculated. And doing this while eliminating uncertainty is most of the challenge.

This is one of those areas where coming from a physics background is a bit of an advantage. Physicists are used to spending 10% of the time calculating the answer and 90% calculating the uncertainty in the answer (which is always much harder). It's not really how fast the rocket flies but under what conditions it blows up that concerns you. It's also why so many of us detest Excel, which seems designed to do calculations without any consideration of uncertainties. There is an additional advantage if you did your training before computers took over, and you were forced to derive things empirically and without resorting to quantitative solutions.

Uncertainty runs through virtually every section of *Security Analysis*, but it lacks a coherent framework or clear language. Rather, it is discussed as a long list of fairly ambiguous terms such as "range of approximate value," "indistinctness," "adequate," "thorough analysis," "safety of principal," and "satisfactory return." There is almost a tangible struggle by Graham and Dodd over how to discuss uncertainty. This can especially be seen in the discussion about the inherent disconnect between intrinsic value and true value (which physicists would describe as definitional uncertainty). Based on what appear to be mostly uncertainty concerns, Graham is clearly at odds with the increasing reliance of the investor community on only future income to determine value, instead of using past and current balance sheets and income statements. Even the margin of safety concept itself is, at its core, a tool for dealing with uncertainty, although it is vaguely described as "a dependable conclusion for the relationship between price and value." Uncertainty analysis runs through the center of Graham's work, but in a somewhat vague way.

It is worth quickly noting the standard types of uncertainties. This exercise is tedious, but understanding the differences becomes important when we move to developing economies, where the uncertainties start exploding in every direction.

- **Definitional uncertainty.** The concept does not have an exact meaning, like height or weight. A president's favorability rating has definitional uncertainty because it is not exactly clear what favorable means. Intangible assets similarly have significant definitional uncertainty. And intrinsic value has big definitional uncertainties.

- **Measurement process error.** Random errors always occur in the measurement process. If you measure your weight on a scale multiple times, you will get multiple results. Similarly, measuring the resale or liquidation value of a fixed asset introduces significant measurement process error.

- **Variance in events.** Counting the number of babies born each day in a hospital will get you different daily results. Although the definition is certain and the measurement process is accurate, the measured event is continually changing. Similarly, assessing a company's cash balance can have significant variance depending on the company and on what days you check.

- **Reading scale uncertainty.** A digital clock can tell you the time only to the minute. So a reading of "6:55 p.m." is actually a reading of "6:55.00 p.m. to 6:55.59 p.m."

- **Systematic error.** Repeated measurements and frequent calibrations are needed to make sure that there are no systematic errors. Scientists routinely check to make certain that their scales are balanced. Financiers, not so much.

To go from direct measurements with various uncertainties, such as cash balance, assets, and revenue, to a calculated value such as intrinsic value, you need an appropriate definition of intrinsic value. And, unfortunately, you have to propagate the errors. A direct measurement with a 10% uncertainty multiplied by another direct measurement with 20% uncertainty gives you a calculated answer with 30% uncertainty. This is why most financial projections are nonsense. Not only are you guessing at future revenue and costs (the uncertainties increase dramatically going forward), but when you start adding and multiplying them, the uncertainties propagate so fast that the projection is meaningless. However, this has not stopped an entire generation of PowerPoint-wielding MBAs from creating linear projections for earnings five years into the future.

A few comments on definitional uncertainties versus calculated uncertainties for intrinsic value, and then I promise I will make my point and move off this somewhat tedious subject.

Significant attention is paid to what definition to use for intrinsic value. Graham famously used Net Nets. Many use the present value of the expected cash distributions over the lifetime of an enterprise. Some just look at last year's earnings. Or at net asset value (liquidation or reproducible), earnings power value, free cash flow, and so on. I raise this question: Is it more important to have an accurate definition of the intrinsic value or an accurately calculated value?

In Figure 2.6, I have mocked up three calculated intrinsic values—net asset value (NAV) on the left, earnings power value (EPV) in the center, and free cash flow (FCF) on the right—and put them against a theoretical "true value." Assume that the true value is the company's real economic value (which is, by definition, unknowable as it usually depends on future events, but is assumed here) and that all three estimates of intrinsic value capture it within their confidence intervals.

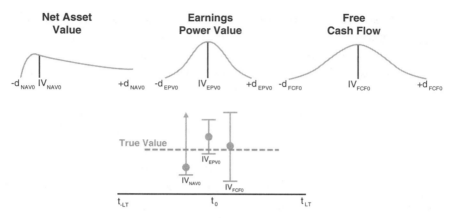

Figure 2.6   Intrinsic value uncertainties

Note that for EPV, in the center, the uncertainty is not too bad, but the calculated value is significantly above the true value (we've likely overestimated the margin of safety). Compare this to FCF, on the right, where the calculated value is closest to the true value but the uncertainties are the largest. Then look at NAV, on the left, in which the calculated value is the farthest from the true value and the uncertainty is very large and asymmetrical. Which is the best intrinsic value?

Note that the net asset value (IV_{nav0}) has a very different shape from the other intrinsic value calculations. It has a small calculated uncertainty (you know the value of the liquid assets) but a large asymmetrical definitional uncertainty. (Nobody really thinks the true value of Coca-Cola is the value of its assets at liquidation.) But all the uncertainty *is on one side*. The negative uncertainty is very small because we know the company's intrinsic value is not less than its net liquidation value. Graham's Net Nets are a terribly inaccurate calculation for what the intrinsic value is. But they are a very accurate calculation of *what it is not*.

This is an old physics trick. Calculating what something is with great accuracy is very difficult. Calculating what something is not, with great accuracy, is much easier. I can calculate with great accuracy that the value of Coca-Cola is not less than $1 billion.

Underneath the catchy terms Mr. Market and intrinsic value, Graham's Net Nets were a clever way to eliminate all the uncertainty in the direct company measurements and on one side of the calculated intrinsic value. And it was on the side that mattered, because we ultimately don't care about intrinsic value. We care about intrinsic value minus market price. It is an exact calculation of the company's minimum margin of safety.

The takeaway is that the critical second step in Graham's Method is *eliminating the uncertainty*. But this does not necessarily mean eliminating the uncertainty in the intrinsic value, or in every direct measurement, or in both the upside and downside uncertainties. It's about eliminating the downside uncertainty in the margin of safety, *both at the time of purchase and in the longer term*. Graham refers to this indirectly in multiple ways throughout *Security Analysis*. In particular, he emphasizes that an investor's duties include both buying the asset and owning it. I would change the language to say that eliminating the downside uncertainty at the time of the investment and over the long term are the real duties. As we move to developing and more uncertain environments, value investing becomes figuring out clever, wily ways, like Net Nets, to eliminate downside uncertainty at the time of purchase and in the long term.

But as I will show, when going global, we also have many additional ways to do this that Western investors lack. We can add capabilities and impact a company's replacement value quickly. We can structure deals to eliminate long-term uncertainty. We can impact management and change the relationship between asset value and earnings power value. We can structure political partnerships that limit entrants by competitors. Buying below liquidation value is even frequently possible (note real estate in Dubai in 2010). And absent high tax rates in many cases, we can sometimes do short-term balance sheet strategies, similar to those in Graham's time.

Quantify Risk and Invest Surgically

Graham's Method is not about eliminating risk, but about quantifying it

In the third step of Graham's Method (we're in the home stretch now), he *quantified the risk*. Risk is the investors' catchall concept for both a wide spectrum of human emotions (perceptions, biases, fears) and actual potential financial losses (margin of safety, value at risk, volatility). But by quantifying the risk, Graham removed the former and kept the latter. He accomplished the same thing physicists did using quantum mechanics and what pilots did using VPR instruments. He removed the brain from the process when it could not be trusted (or could no longer understand what was going on). When Richard Feynman could no longer conceptualize what he was seeing at the quantum level, he just did the linear algebra and accepted the results. When pilots are flying in snowy weather and they lose their sense of the horizon and of level flight, they ignore their eyes and look at their instruments.

Quantifying risk (the margin of safety) takes the investor's brain out of this step of the investment process. I don't care how much I like the company or how I'm feeling today. I invest only when there is a calculated >30% difference between the intrinsic value and the market price.

This approach also enables consistency over long periods of time, which is critical for accumulating wealth. It is one thing to be rational and level-headed most of the time. It's quite another to be that way all the time. This takes a quantitative system. Quantifying also has the benefit of standardizing risk, so one can cleanly compare investments across industries and years. This lets you slowly focus on the most profitable investment types over time. You get both richer and smarter as time passes.

Finally, Graham *invested surgically*. If the uncertainty is eliminated and the risk has been clearly quantified (hopefully low), you go in surgically by buying shares in one targeted move and making the returns at the time of the investment. There is no dependence on event-driven changes in the future. Or working with management over time to improve performance. Post-investment, the only requirement is to check that the intrinsic value is stable (or increasing), per Graham's Third Law.

If these can be considered Graham's Laws and Graham's Method, we should also note two Buffett "Great Company" Corollaries (yes, I'm making all this up). Within this approach (see Figure 2.7), the biggest weakness is the third law, which requires that the intrinsic value be stable (or increasing) over the long term. The risk of the investment is the risk of intrinsic value decreasing over time (the long-term downside uncertainty).

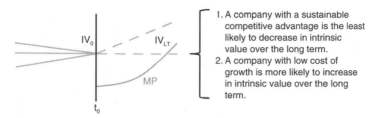

1. A company with a sustainable competitive advantage is the least likely to decrease in intrinsic value over the long term.
2. A company with low cost of growth is more likely to increase in intrinsic value over the long term.

Figure 2.7   Buffett "great company" corollaries

This is discussed in the section "Rethinking from Good to Great" in Chapter 10, but it is worth mentioning how "great companies" look in terms of uncertainty analysis. Great companies are those that have an economic value (per share) that is the least likely to decrease over time—the first corollary. Companies with a sustainable competitive advantage (among many other things) meet this criterion. Companies with protected profits have lower long-term downside uncertainties.

The second Buffett "Great Company" Corollary is that companies with a low cost of growth in addition to a sustainable competitive advantage are even better over the long term. They are less likely to decrease and the most likely to increase in economic value.

We finally reach the last step of my fabricated rederivation of Graham's approach, Simplify to a Usable Methodology (see Figure 2.8). The familiar Mr. Market, intrinsic value, and margin of safety concepts fall out.

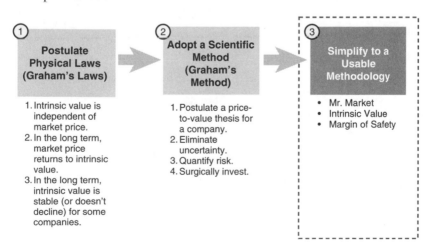

Figure 2.8   Simplify to a usable methodology

This chapter, admittedly dry for those who don't live their lives according to various frameworks (most everyone I suspect), presented both a value woldview and a logical method for approaching it. Graham's Method in particular turns out to be the key to opening the door to value investing in fundamentally different environments. In the next chapter, we reapply Graham's Method to the colliding, multipolar world described and generate a broader investment strategy for it.

3

Value Point

I summarized value point as asking three questions and getting four answers, as shown in Figure 3.1. On the surface, this is very similar to traditional value investing (such as buying a good company cheap). However, significant extra detail is included within the treatment of the margin of safety (Question 3 in the figure) to deal with all the mentioned problems when "going global." The previous chapter's focus on the mechanics of Graham's Method and on building uncertainty analysis into the language of value investing was in order to address the added complexities of Question 3.

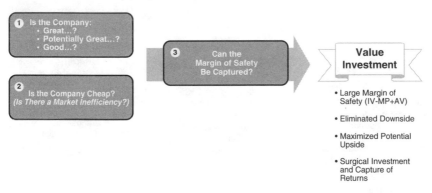

Figure 3.1   Value point

For all effective purposes, I am laying out a value approach for the opposite extreme of what is generally considered global value investing. Instead of stretching out somewhat to moderately more uncertain markets (such as short-term listed equities in Hong Kong), I am jumping to the furthest extreme (such as buying and holding minority shares in private Russian companies). If a long-term value strategy can work with these assets, it can work anywhere. If you can do emerging markets, you can do developed markets. If you can do China and Russia, you can do India and Brazil. If you can do negotiated private deals, you can do public purchases. If you can do small companies, you can do big companies. If you can do buy and hold, you can do buy to sell.

But the real key to overcoming the five "going global" challenges (limited access, increased current uncertainty, increased long-term uncertainty, weakened claims, and foreigner disadvantages) is Graham's Method.

Looking again at Graham's approach, but with a global worldview (see Figure 3.2), we can see that the first and second laws hold true for most companies in most environments around the world. Market price and intrinsic value are independent in most cases. And more importantly, market price returns to intrinsic value in the long term in most private assets and public equities. I am simply asserting this from experience. It has always seemed somewhat mysterious as to why this happens.

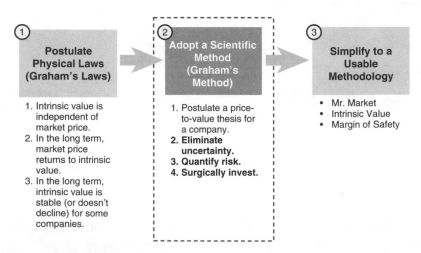

Figure 3.2   Derivation of value investing

However, you do see Soros-type reflexive relationships fairly frequently, particularly in real estate, infrastructure development, and other sectors where government credit is very active. I will argue later that this is inherent to many systems where government policies and credit are used to drive large-scale domestic development.

It is Graham's Third Law that becomes the biggest problem when we leave the developed world (see Figure 3.3). It greatly depends on intrinsic value staying relatively stable—or at least not decreasing. However, in developing and colliding markets, this just doesn't hold. Companies and markets are rising (and falling) rapidly. Governments are actively involved and frequently change the rules. Most of the assumptions about stability and the separation of government and private sectors are not there. These things are all considered exceptions in developed economies (and usually are avoided in practice). But in much of the multipolar world, they are now the norm.

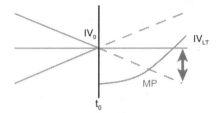

1. Intrinsic Value (IV) is still independent of Market Price (MP).
2. In the long term, Market Price still returns to Intrinsic Value (IV_{LT}).
3. In the long term, Intrinsic Value is NOT stable for most companies.

Figure 3.3   Graham's Laws in a colliding world

Because there are many cases when we cannot assume long-term stability, we need to actively eliminate the long-term downside uncertainty at the time of investment. The best way I know to do this is through a combination of a large margin of safety and a negotiated deal structure. This can include negotiating a lower price and adding value at the time of investment (see Figure 3.4), thereby increasing the margin of safety. But negotiated value-added deals can also impact the stability of the intrinsic value in the near and long term. So I expand Graham's Third Law in this way: *"In the long term, intrinsic value is stable for many companies, and it can be actively stabilized in many others."*

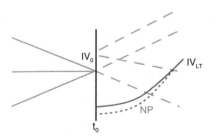

1. Intrinsic Value (IV) is independent of Market Price (MP).
2. In the long term, Market Price returns to Intrinsic Value (IV_{LT}).
3. In the long term, Intrinsic Value is stable for many companies and can be stabilized in many others.

Figure 3.4   Value point in a colliding world

Note that this is an expansion of traditional value investing into value-added deal-making. In the best-case scenario, adding value supercharges the margin of safety. But the most important impact is that it minimizes and often eliminates the downside long-term uncertainty, which effectively opens the door to value-based investing in many more situations. There is no set approach for doing this across all deals. The common element is that we are introducing additional variables and tools into the deal process by which we can construct deals that eliminate the current and long-term downside uncertainty.

Looking at Graham's Method, we can start going through its steps for various companies in various types of environments. The "mispriced value + added value" (MP + AV) approach basically greatly expands Graham's Net Nets trick. We cannot say what the future value will be, but in many carefully constructed deals we can very accurately say what it will not be. As soon as the current margin of safety is known and the long-term downside is eliminated, we can invest surgically and big. Graphically, the approach looks like Figure 3.5.

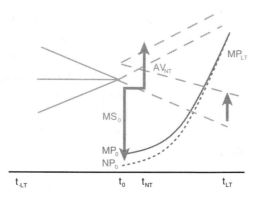

Figure 3.5   Mispriced value + added value

In both value investing and value point, the central problem is the downside uncertainty in the future intrinsic value. An accurate and healthy margin of safety does not help us if the intrinsic value can decrease over time. The main thrust of both value investing and value point is eliminating this possibility. But where value investing does this by choosing stable companies in stable environments, value point does this by constructing value-added deals.

And when going global, we discover we have tools that investors in developed economies do not. We are not limited to either being passive investors or adding value long term through active management. We can surgically add capabilities and other types of value at the time of investment. Capability migration, political partnerships, weak management environments, and many other uniquely global situations give us a lot of tools with which to do this. Most of the rest of this book is about deal structures that achieve this. But all deals follow Graham's Method:

1. Postulate a price-to-value thesis for a specific company.
2. Eliminate the uncertainty.
3. Quantify the risk.
4. Invest surgically.

In terms of *quantifying risk* and for those who think better with equations (yes, I am one of those who tried to adapt quantum mechanics to investing—it doesn't work but it's great fun), the standard value investing calculation is as follows:

$$(1 \,/\, \text{risk}_{VI}) \approx \text{margin of safety} = IV_{t=0} - \delta_{1\text{-}} - MP_{t=0}$$

where MP is market price and delta(1) is the downside uncertainty in the intrinsic value at time zero. Note that per the earlier discussion, I am including only the downside uncertainty of the intrinsic value. Investors often require that:

margin of safety > 30%

and we assume/hope that:

$$IV_{t=0} - \delta_{1\text{-}} < IV_{t=LT}$$

For value point, the calculation is similar:

$$(1 \,/\, \text{risk}_{VP}) \approx \text{margin of safety} = (IV_{t=0} - \delta_{1\text{-}}) + (AV_{t=NT} - \delta_{2\text{-}}) - NP_{t=0}$$

where NP is the negotiated price and AV is added value in the near term. And I am including the downside uncertainties for both the intrinsic value and the added value.

The key uncertainties are the minimum values of the intrinsic value and the added value (again, we are proving what it is not).

However, bracketing the final terms shows an important difference with value investing.

$$\text{margin of safety} = (IV_{t=0} - \delta_{1\text{-}}) + [(AV_{t=NT} - \delta_{2\text{-}}) - NP_{t=0}]$$

In value point, the investor's key skill is crafting an investment that maximizes the added value and pushes down the negotiated price (the bracketed term in the equation). Compare this to value investors who typically spend their time trying to calculate the intrinsic value with the greatest accuracy (the first term in the equation). Value point investors are both investors and deal-makers. We calculate the intrinsic value, and we structure deals that drop the negotiated price, maximize the added value, and eliminate the long-term downside uncertainty.

Putting it all together, we have a clear price-to-market thesis, we can eliminate the uncertainties, and we can quantify the risk. And the approach is very *surgical* (see Figure 3.6). We make our money at the time of the investment and avoid any long-term operating or management requirements. It is more hands-on than typical value investing but is still surgical investing.

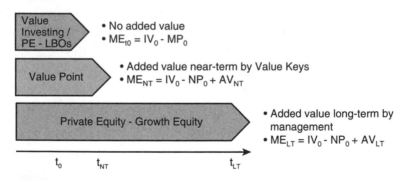

Figure 3.6   Value point versus value investing versus private equity

B2B: Back to the Balance Sheet

Value-added investing, particularly within unstable markets, depends heavily on balance sheet analysis

Graham wrote about the transition he witnessed during his career from a focus on the balance sheet to an increased focus on the income statement—particularly future earnings. This transition followed from both changes in the interests of the investment community and from changes in the American economy. During this period, the American economy transitioned from a heavy reliance on industries with extensive fixed assets (railroads, factories, natural resources) to more service-type industries. It also entered a period of much more stablity and with somewhat predictable growth.

"Going global" for many means rediscovering this earlier period of the U.S. economy, focusing on fixed-asset type businesses (manufacturing in China, natural resources in Africa), and returning to the balance sheet. And it's fairly obvious that if you are looking at environments with greater uncertainty and instability, relying heavily on earnings power values or discounted future cash flows becomes problematic. Additionally, "adding value" often means changing the assets and the asset value in the short term (and hopefully the earnings power value in the near term). So in terms of understanding an enterprise, the starting point is most often the changes in the balance sheet over time and the balance sheet's relationship to the income statement.

My intention is not to reiterate ideas that are well known and well presented elsewhere (and balance sheet analysis fits in that category). So I'll note just a few things in passing on the increased importance of balance sheet analysis when "going global."

Point #1: The Relationship Between Assets and Earnings Is a More Stable Starting Point

In traditional value approaches, this is a good check on reported earnings per share (and management performance) and enables you to discern the real relationship between resources and earnings. But in value-added deal-making, this relationship becomes the key to deal structures. Tangible assets, intangible assets, and replacement value (sometimes liquidation value, but rarely) are the primary initial targets in the analysis.

The instability in both the intrinsic value and the environment are the key problems. So forward projections of earnings aren't particularly useful. The balance sheet will give you a more stable assessment in the near term.

Point #2: The Relationship Between the Asset Value and Earnings Power Value Over Time Is Critical

When people talk about "developing economies," they are usually referring to geographies where assets are being deployed at a fairly rapid rate—a more accurate term would be "developing assets economies." Buildings, factories, and infrastructure are being thrown up, often at astonishing speeds. Intangible assets (such as brands, franchises, and licenses) are similarly being created and deployed. If markets are described as "emerging," economies are "developing assets." And when a mismatch occurs in the market emergence versus asset development rates, the results can be interesting. In 2007, Dubai was clogged with traffic as the market surged ahead of the infrastructure. In 2009, Dubai was a ghost town as the market pulled back and the assets remained.

Given the predominance of asset development, the current replacement value of an enterprise is one of the most measurable and meaningful values in most environments. The market and the competition may be changing rapidly, but we can know a particular company's position in the industry based on its existing intangible and tangible assets. And we know what it would cost for a competitor to build the same asset base, even in a rapidly changing situation. The balance sheet and the current replacement value of an enterprise are usually fairly solid starting points for changing environments.

Per standard security analysis, we can tell a lot about a company by the relationship between its asset value and its earning power value. Columbia Business School professor and "guru to Wall Street gurus" Bruce Greenwald describes three basic cases:

- **AV > EPV** normally implies ineffective management or some other problem that has the company producing lower earnings than such an asset base should. Typically this means that an investor needs to think about a catalyst or a management change.

  However, in developing economies this is a much more common and important case, because we can have an outsized impact on the effectiveness of management. As will be discussed, the migration of management ability around the world is an important trend and something a deal-maker can use in a deal. In many of these cases, by bringing foreign management to a management-weak situation, we can rapidly pull the EPV up to the AV. Changes in management can be a fairly powerful way to surgically add value in these AV > EPV cases.

- **AV = EPV** is the most common case, indicating that reasonable management is in place and is driving for continual operating and asset improvements without any significant protection from competition. It's pretty common and a pretty tough way to make a living.

  But as will be shown, this is actually a fairly attractive place to do value-added deals. If we can significantly increase the asset value of an enterprise at the time of investment (say, by bringing in capabilities or other assets to increase replacement value), the earnings power value should naturally follow over time, assuming no degradation in management ability.

- **AV < EPV** usually is evidence of a franchise or some other type of significant barrier to entry. In developed economies, this tends to be the most attractive target for value investors (everyone looks for a sustainable competitive advantage, but they are much rarer than people think). In developing environments, the other two cases can often be as attractive.

Looking at the relationship between earnings power value and replacement value *over time* is important. Having an impact on the replacement value is an important strategy, and how this affects earnings power value or discounted cash flow over time is critical. Looking at the current time, near term, and long term, there are actually nine cases to consider, six of which can be attractive opportunities. Note that these six cases graphically create an arrowhead or "point," as shown in Figure 3.7—hence the term value point.

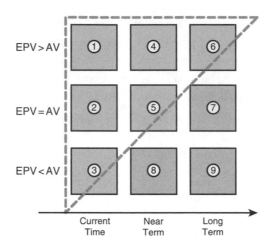

Figure 3.7   Six attractive EPV versus AV cases over time

Point #3: "Added Value" Often Shows Up on the Balance Sheet in the Near Term and on the Income Statement in the Long Term

If we improve a company's management in Case 3 of Figure 3.7 (EPV < AV at time 0), we can move it rapidly to Case 5 (EPV = AV in the near term). If we add significant value to a company's balance sheet in Case 1 or 2 (EPV > AV or EPV = AV at time 0), this should lead to an increase in the EPV (Case 4 or 5). If we add capabilities such as unique brands or technology to a company in Case 2 (EPV = AV at time 0), we can sometimes create a competitive advantage result in Case 4 or 5 (EPV > AV in the near or long term).

Types of added value vary by industry and company but generally can be placed into five categories:

- Tangible assets such as buildings and factories
- Intangible assets such as goodwill, trade names, and patents
- Earnings such as additional businesses with existing profits
- Management
- Value perceived by the seller or partner (reputation, political access)

Point #4: The Balance Sheet Sits at the Intersection of Competition, Management, Earnings, Assets, and Capabilities

This book began with a mild rant about how global investing is frequently viewed as Western investing with lots of additional problems. However, with the right worldview, you can see that global investing offers a host of advantages that developed markets do not have. Competition, assets, earnings, management, and capabilities all interact within changing environments (see Figure 3.8). This creates endless opportunities for value-added deal-making. And at the center is the most stable point in this interaction—the balance sheet.

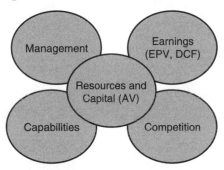

Figure 3.8   The intersection of competition, assets, management, earnings, and capabilities

Putting It All Together

Value point is a value strategy for a colliding, multipolar world

I stated that value point is about asking three questions and getting four answers:

1. Is it a good, potentially great, or great company?
2. Is it cheap? (Is there a market inefficiency?)
3. Is the margin of safety capturable and sustainable?

If the answer to all three is yes, we consider the company attractive, and we can purchase with a healthy margin of safety. The downside has been eliminated/minimized and the upside maximized. Time becomes our ally in the capture of the company's economic value.

Looking again at the summary chart, a lot of the details should now make more sense (see Figure 3.9).

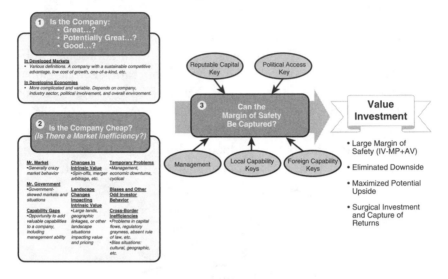

Figure 3.9   Value point: the search for opportunity to add value

Note on the left of the chart that the market inefficiencies we are targeting include both those we are familiar with in developed economies (change in value, investor bias, crazy Mr. Market) and new ones more characteristic of developing markets and cross-border situations. But the principle is the same: Get it cheap.

Note also Question 3 in the middle, which brings in all the deal-making and adding value aspects of the approach. We need to structure deals to truly capture the margin of safety, both now and in the long term. And that means adding value with various tools, which I call value keys. Also note that with this value-added approach, the number of companies and situations (the six presented EPV versus AV cases), we can target increases dramatically. Adding value in Question 3 increases the number of companies in Question 1.

On the right side, you see the end result of a smart value investment or deal. A good or great company has been purchased at a cheap price. The better the company and the cheaper the price, generally the better the investment.

Value investing's "search for value" is actually a subset of this broader approach, which makes sense (see Figure 3.10). As we

expand to more types of landscapes, we are also expanding our value
methodology and adding some tools to the tool kit. In practice, they
are often used in combination. We do both standard acquisitions and
value-added deal-making. We search for both value and the opportunity to add value. We target both the standard market inefficiencies
and a list of new ones. If you look at articles about Prince Waleed, you
will see he is often referred to as either the "Arabian Warren Buffett"
(implying traditional value investing) or the "Prince of Deals." Many
don't recognize that it is really one coherent value strategy.

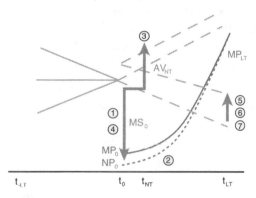

Figure 3.10   Negotiated deal-making's impact on the value approach

Hunting for deals and investments with the objective of adding
value has several other important effects. As shown in Figure 3.10, it
can do the following:

1. **Increase access to deals.** As mentioned, private companies
   tend to be particularly tightly held in developing markets. You
   almost always need to bring more to the table than just capital.
   A strong value-add can open the door to investments.

2. **Decrease the negotiated price.** Depending on the investment, a strong value-add such as a Starbucks brand, political
   connections, or a highly reputable investment name can enable
   you to decrease the negotiated price. This is particularly true of
   deals with multiple parts.

3. **Increase the intrinsic value of the asset or company.** As
   discussed, this can be very large in smaller companies, although
   I have also seen investors turn $400 million investments into
   $800 million at the time of purchase.

4. **Create an advantage when competing for deals.** If there are multiple bidders at the table, a value-add almost always beats no value-add.

5. **Create a long-term partnership with the company (strengthen your claim to the enterprise).** A strong value-add creates a true partnership between the company and the investor, and you are less dependent on contracts, board seats, or proper governance to protect your interests.

6. **Eliminate the future downside uncertainty (stabilize the margin of safety).** As discussed, deal structuring plus a margin of safety is the best approach to eliminating the long-term downside uncertainty. This is also achieved by creating a long-term partnership with the company.

7. **Eliminate some nonmarket risks (defensibility).** In many particularly difficult environments, nonmarket forces such as regulators and state-backed competitors can be significant threats. Defensibility will be discussed later, but value-add is a big part of this.

Adding value also enables value-focused investors to target many situations in the relationship between earnings and assets/resources, as shown in Figure 3.11.

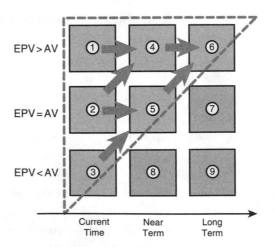

Figure 3.11   Multiple situations can be targeted

This approach solves most of the problems and limitations previously outlined: limited access to investments; uncertainty in current intrinsic value; long-term uncertainty, including worries about instability; the availability of only weak or impractical claims against the target enterprise; and foreigner disadvantages (see Figures 3.12 and 3.13). It solves value investing's upper atmosphere problem.

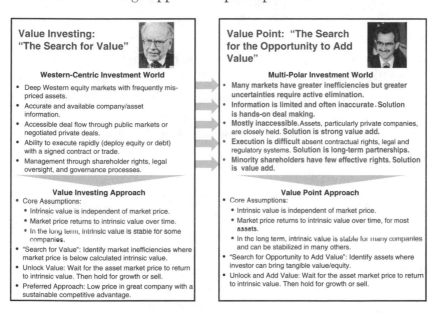

Figure 3.12   From Buffett to Waleed: From the search for value to the search for the opportunity to add value

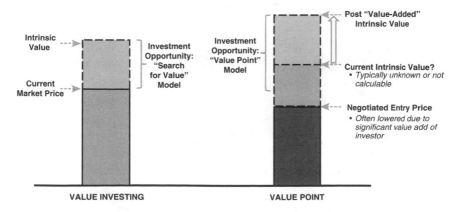

Figure 3.13   Value investing versus value point economics

Value Keys

Value keys are the building blocks of value point

Searching for value in practice is mostly about estimating an external and independent variable (intrinsic value). However, searching for the opportunity to add value in practice muddies this. You mix objective and perceived factors as well as independent and dependent ones. What is the company's value? How do you add value so that the downside uncertainty is removed and the margin of safety is stabilized? How do you add value so that the company or owner gives you access to the investment—and so that you create a strong, long-term partnership? The quantitative and qualitative factors that are involved can sometimes be independent of the observer and other times are dependent.

Therefore, we break "added value" into smaller component parts. I call them value keys because they both open the door to the investment and add value. The five main keys are political access, reputable capital, foreign capabilities, local capabilities, and management. Some of them are purely quantitative and independent of the observer, and others are more qualitative and perceptional. Adding value to an investment or deal becomes a matter of assembling the right combination of value keys, as shown in Figure 3.14.

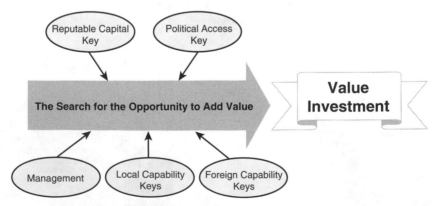

Figure 3.14 Value keys can both open the door and add value to investments

Subsequent chapters will detail the uses of various combinations of value keys in deals; the following is just a summary.

Political access is the value key that requires the largest break with a Western "unipolar" worldview. Active government involvement in both markets and companies is common in many parts of the world. Dealing with the government is the norm, not the exception. And it should not be perceived as a risk or problem, but as an opportunity.

Reputable capital is about the value of an investor's reputation in specific types of deals. Clearly in the West, reputation matters for investors. If you have to sell, Warren Buffett is everyone's buyer of choice. However, in a colliding world, reputation can have a much more powerful effect. Not only does it often gain you preferential access to investments, but it can also overcome inefficiencies in the capital markets, regulatory grayness, weak rule of law, and many of the other problems discussed. A partner with a strong reputation can be seen as the solution to all these problems. Deals between Africa and the Middle East are often done only if a reputable, trusted partner is involved.

The next two value keys are *capability keys*. Bringing a Four Seasons management contract to a hotel in Egypt adds value by adding capabilities—the brand, the operating system, the increased access to foreign customers, and so on.

We separate the capability keys into *foreign* and *local* types. The hotel's improved operating system is, by and large, a local capability. It is something you bring into Egypt and build there. The brand and access to foreign customers is a foreign key. If the deal is dissolved, the Four Seasons name and its reservations system (the foreign key) disappear. But likely the improved operating system (the local key) stays. One resides locally and the other at a distance. This difference between foreign and local capability keys becomes important in environments such as China and Russia.

The final value key is *management*, which could be considered a capability key. Private equity firms have long focused on adding value to an investment over time through their operational and management expertise, sometimes referred to as "solution capital." However, in developing economies, the impact of management can be much

greater and faster, particularly in parts of the world with very limited
professional management.

As a simple check, note that Figures 3.15 and 3.16 show that
value point reduces to both traditional value investing and common
private equity structures (absent the debt plays). Value investing
can be seen as the use of some reputable capital and some
management—particularly capital allocation, but very little. Private
equity of the leveraged buyout (LBO) type can be seen as the use of
some reputable capital and, some might say, political access. Private
equity of the management-intensive type, such as Cerberus, is the
use of reputable capital and long-term management.

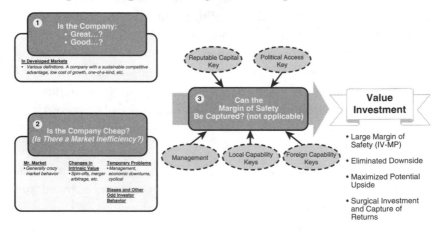

Figure 3.15   Value investing: the search for value

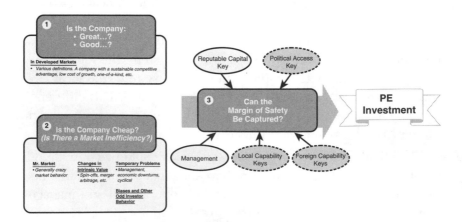

Figure 3.16   Private equity: buy-to-sell

The More Things Change...

Value point is an expansion of the value investing methodology

If traditional value investing is mostly about searching for opportunities in a fairly efficient market, value point is mostly about getting access to opportunities in overwhelmingly inefficient markets and then coming up with clever ways to eliminate the uncertainties. Our problems, as detailed, are mostly *access*, *uncertainty*, *control*, and *foreigner disadvantages*. Inefficiencies can be found virtually everywhere.

A broader value tool kit can capture a wider spectrum of inefficiencies and reach both unrecognized *and inaccessible* value. As you would expect, many of the familiar value investing terms and concepts are similarly expanded in this approach:

- The bipolar *Mr. Market* is joined by his giant cousin, *Mr. Government*. With the mixing of commercial and government activities in many markets, Mr. Market's chaotic pricing is also impacted by Mr. Government. And Mr. Government has the additional ability to impact intrinsic value.

- To the *margin of safety*, defined as the difference between the market price and intrinsic value, we add another term—*added value*. How "cheap" a company is can depend heavily on this other term.

- The focus on *competitive advantage* (hopefully sustainable) in value investing is joined by a focus on *defensibility*. A competitive advantage is your profit's protection from competitors, your moat around the castle. But in many environments, your profits face threats from more than just competitors. Partners, employees, customers, government regulators, and state-backed competitors can all be direct threats to your profits. Defensibility can be as important as competitive advantage.

- Instead of searching for value by *screening* lots of investments, you search for the opportunity to add value mostly by *networking*. This means spending more time traveling and meeting people and less time reading annual reports.

- Instead of positioning yourself in the market as the *buyer of choice* for investments, you focus on becoming the *partner of choice* or the *value-added partner of choice*. You are the person everyone approaches when entering a geography or expanding their capabilities in an industry. You bring more to the table than just capital.

...the More They Stay the Same

Value investing's core principles are good advice everywhere

I have found that when operating in more developing-type environments, a lot of the quieter principles of value investing become more pronounced. Chief among them is the value of reputation. I have briefly discussed reputation as a way to help deals happen. But over many years of doing this, I have found that reputation is, as Buffett has always said, your most valuable asset. And when you are operating in the global Wild West, this becomes even more true. Absent the rule of law, clear contracts, regulations, and such, reputation is everything.

I have hardwired this into the center of the presented strategy. Searching for the opportunity to add value means that you are always striving to become a more valuable and reputable partner. By the very definition of the investment thesis, we invest only when we bring value to the project and to our partners. Reputation and a strict adherence to principles-based capitalism is central to the strategy.

Some of the other value investing principles that I keep at the front of my brain as I hunt for investments around the world are:

- An investor's wealth is still created by capturing and growing economic value per share. Wealth follows from economic value, not speculation. Fortunately, a colliding world can be described as a time of historic growth in economic value.
- 80% of value investing still involves picking the right strategy and the right location to hunt for investments. The remaining 20% is waiting for the right pitch to swing at.

- Always choose your own area, do your own research, and find your own opportunities.
- Avoid crowds. Whether value investors are contrarian by personality or strategy is a matter of debate, but I do tend to quickly move to more remote areas as soon as crowds show up.
- Focus on good to great returns on a relatively small number of investments.

This last point is why it is so easy to be excited these days. You ultimately need to find only 20 to 30 really good investments in an investment world that just got a lot larger and a lot more inefficient. These are easy times for value investors.

4

Investing in Politicized Markets

Over the next 20 years, the international capitalism of the West will be increasingly joined by the state capitalism, "godfather" capitalism, and other politically infused forms of capitalism that are prevalent in many other countries. What the West calls crony capitalism, much of the world calls business. And as China, India, Brazil, and others become more potent forces in global finance, successful investors will learn to take advantage of the opportunities afforded by their forms of capitalism.

In these countries, companies cater to both customers and bureaucrats. Deals are combinations of commercial and government interests. Political power is often held by a privileged few, so economic opportunity is similarly concentrated. And the invisible hand of the market is paired with the heavy hand of government.

Societal implications aside, these systems can be very attractive for investors. A mixing of commercial and government activities can skew the markets, create large inefficiencies, and enable increased creativity in deal-making. I am certainly not asserting that these systems don't have large problems (economic and political freedom being top of the list), but that they are prevalent and do contain attractive value opportunities. If Mr. Market creates opportunities for investment by driving prices away from true value, his giant cousin, Mr. Government, can have an even bigger effect. Mr. Government can move prices but can also create large increases (and decreases) in the economic value of enterprises. If Mr. Market is bipolar in the short term but generally wise in the long term, Mr. Government is generally heavy-handed in the short term and slower to learn in the long term.

Government-skewed markets can also vary more widely than free markets—swinging between rapid growth (Dubai and Macau) and stagnation (much of Central Asia). This is a significant contrast to the Western markets, which, with the exception of occasional boom and bust cycles, have been fairly stable and dynamic over the past 50 years. Government-skewed markets and government-directed economic initiatives, usually structured to drive development or some other objective, also create competitive situations that can vary between monopoly (Qatar) and hypercompetitive (China). For value investors, the wider spectrum of market and competitive behavior creates lots of opportunities.

But if Mr. Government can create attractive opportunities for investors and deal-makers, he can also create risks. The rules can change on taxes, tariffs, and even private-property ownership. The government can take sides. And an investor who lacks political connections can make a tempting target for entrenched local powers. A rabbit on the savannah doesn't have to do anything wrong to be attacked. Being there is enough. The same could be said of foreign-owned companies in some government-infused markets.

Still, the investment and deal-making opportunities in government-skewed markets are in many ways larger than in the more efficient free markets of the West. Holding one of the few approved bank licenses in Saudi Arabia can be a guarantee of exceptionally high returns. Buying the shares of a Chinese petrochemical monopoly is a no-brainer at the right price.

Assumptions about the role of government represent one of the biggest differences between traditional investment approaches and a multipolar worldview. Traditional value investors view an active government as increasing uncertainty overall. And within industries, it varies between something that can decrease profitability through regulation (government-regulated entities often have less pricing power) or can increase it by limiting competition. Additionally, acute government actions such as regulatory changes are viewed as either events to be predicted in a short-term strategy or a source of long-tail risk.

In contrast, value point investors see politically inflected economies as opportunities for creative deal-making, and they aggressively target the market inefficiencies that government actors create. In many emerging markets, government is not just an actor in the market; it is the single largest player. We see government actors as partners for deals, and this can have very attractive results. An investor can secure land rights, redistrict property, obtain government contracts, receive bank licenses, borrow at low rates, and gain regulatory approvals (or, in the case of Carlyle Group's attempted purchase of Xugong in China, regulatory denials for competitors). The next section details some of the more effective strategies for capturing the inefficiencies of politically infused markets and adding value with a political access approach. The power of this approach in many economies cannot be overstated. It is not just a way to make outsized returns; it is frequently the best way.

The large returns possible in government-infused markets are responsible for many of the large companies and cash-rich investors we are now seeing on the global stage. These rising stars often first make headlines as bargain hunters for brand-name Western assets. It was an unknown young Saudi prince who shocked the United States with his investment in a distressed Citigroup in 1991. Carlos Slim's Mexican holdings propelled him past Bill Gates as the world's richest person and into New York to buy a large stake in the New York Times Company. From state-owned enterprises out of China to oligarchs out of Russia, we are increasingly seeing companies and newly cash-rich investors from government-infused markets entering Western markets.

That said, a politically focused strategy should never imply doing anything that is less than aboveboard. The intersection of commercial and government interests can be a fairly disreputable place, and one should tread carefully. In politically infused markets, we strictly adhere to the core value point philosophy that investors and dealmakers search for the opportunity to add value. We capture wealth by building economic value in projects and by helping our partners. By adding value, we chart a strictly honorable course in any situation.

In the previous chapters, I outlined a value framework that adapts Graham's Method to the increased uncertainty and instability that are inherent characteristics of many politico-economic systems. Politicized markets and active governments strike to the core of the "going global" problem. What would Graham have done in a market like China or Qatar?

Mapping the New Political-Economic World Order

A simplistic worldview to orient the microfundamentalists (and offend the macroeconomists)

To better understand different political environments, I have sorted national economies into four categories: godfather capitalism, state capitalism, advanced international capitalism, and developing international capitalism (see Figure 4.1). This is simple "cloud naming" that will surely offend economists and political thinkers of all types. But it is just for orienting direct investors and deal-makers. I am focusing on only those factors that matter for direct investing—the role of government, the degree of competition, the level of local management ability, and so on.

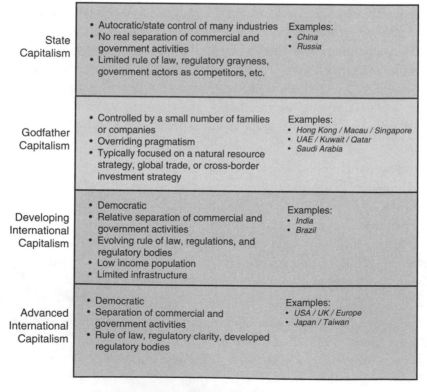

State Capitalism	• Autocratic/state control of many industries • No real separation of commercial and government activities • Limited rule of law, regulatory grayness, government actors as competitors, etc.	Examples: • *China* • *Russia*
Godfather Capitalism	• Controlled by a small number of families or companies • Overriding pragmatism • Typically focused on a natural resource strategy, global trade, or cross-border investment strategy	Examples: • *Hong Kong / Macau / Singapore* • *UAE / Kuwait / Qatar* • *Saudi Arabia*
Developing International Capitalism	• Democratic • Relative separation of commercial and government activities • Evolving rule of law, regulations, and regulatory bodies • Low income population • Limited infrastructure	Examples: • *India* • *Brazil*
Advanced International Capitalism	• Democratic • Separation of commercial and government activities • Rule of law, regulatory clarity, developed regulatory bodies	Examples: • *USA / UK / Europe* • *Japan / Taiwan*

Figure 4.1   A simplistic investment worldview

The next section describes the first two clusters in detail and explains some of the opportunities and challenges that each presents. The other two, developing and advanced international capitalism, are not as politicized and are not discussed at length.

Liar's Poker and Liar's Dice

The arrival of surprisingly high-performance state capitalism

Go to any bar or nightclub in any Chinese town, and you will likely encounter people playing Liar's Dice, with dice-filled cups slamming down on the tables and hand signals flashing back and forth. The game (which is great fun) often perplexes foreigners, because every player lies about what he has at every turn. The game is raucous and can be somewhat overwhelming for the uninitiated.

In a game with two people, each player slams down a cup with five dice hidden underneath. After checking your dice, you give a hand signal for what you think you and your opponent have collectively. If he flashes 7-2, it means he thinks that in his hand and yours are at least seven dice with 2s showing. You must then say this is a lie or raise the guess (such as eight dice with 2s, or seven dice with 3s). The game quickly becomes a sequence of falsehoods. Because I lied about this, his subsequent lie was likely about that, so my next lie should be....

Liar's Dice is similar to the Wall Street game Liar's Poker, described in Michael Lewis's book of the same name. Players bet on the combined numbers of the serial numbers of bills (but in Liar's Dice, you can't cheat by carrying special bills in your wallet for the occasion). And the Chinese game is faster and louder, the falsehoods are more complicated, and a lot more drinking goes on. All in all, it's an excellent analogy for the differences between doing business in state capitalist China versus international capitalist America.

For value investors and deal-makers, China is something new. It is autocratic, with no consistent rule of law, no separation of commercial and government activities, direct state control of many aspects of business, nebulous regulations with shifting implementation, and, most importantly, different rules for local and foreign businesses and investors. This is a system where who you are matters. It's also state capitalism of a scale and sophistication never before seen.

China's population is three to four times larger than any other globally competitive country. Chinese markets are almost always described by their very impressive aggregate sizes. But it is enlightening to divide that number by the 1.3 billion population. For investors, the key factor is that it's overwhelmingly a very low GDP per capita environment. The second key factor is that the growth story is actually more impressive than it first appears. Historically China has constituted about one-third of the global GDP. Even after 20 years of 10% GDP growth, China is at only 8% of global GDP. It's only directional analysis, but at the macro-level, lots of future growth is likely still possible. But if you look at the micro-level, at various local industries and markets (say, auto sales in Chongqing), the growth story is truly impressive. For value investors, China represents an interesting mix of high-growth, large-volume, low-income state capitalism.

However, in stark contrast to virtually all other large-population/ low-income economies, China has a robust physical and government infrastructure and a history of fairly effective bureaucracy dating back several thousand years. You can look back 1,000 years and read about the Treasurer of Beijing or Nanjing. This unique strength in physical infrastructure and government bureaucracy makes China a particularly attractive landscape for investors. It doesn't suffer from the chaos and dysfunction of many developing economies.

Most importantly, the Chinese economy can perform at a surprisingly high level. After 20 years of consistently high GDP growth, it is undeniably successful financially. China is now the world's second-largest economy. The government reports over $2.4 trillion in official reserves. Beijing's banking system is now larger than Australia's. And China's infrastructure, which direct investors care a lot about, is in many situations world-class (phones, Internet). In other situations it is leapfrogging developed economies (high-speed trains, continental integration of shipping).

For value investors, the primary issue is, as always, competition. And in China, the competitive dynamics are fascinating. The business and political environment is constantly shifting at the same time new capabilities and competitors are rapidly emerging. And all this occurs while talent shortages and information asymmetries abound. Chinese competitive dynamics are an entire subtopic of value investing in themselves.

In his book *Competitive Advantage of Nations*, Harvard professor and competitiveness guru Michael Porter argues that at the country level, competitive advantage is the ability to add tangible value to locally based businesses. This can be accomplished by deploying infrastructure that benefits companies or creating specialized clusters (Silicon Valley, Hollywood) in which a critical mass of customers, specialized labor, and specialized support companies can be concentrated. Both beneficial infrastructure and specialized clusters can give local businesses a competitive advantage domestically, regionally, and sometimes globally. China's rapidly improving continental infrastructure is a big part of the competitive dynamics I consider in direct investments. A big market for consumer products such as Coca-Cola is only valuable if you have the roads and logistics to move the products within it. In a developing economy, the ability to deploy infrastructure is a big invesment factor.

China's government has shown a truly impressive ability to create specialized clusters in areas like finance, technology, and manufacturing. The world's next Wall Street, Hollywood, and Silicon Valley are already being built, and at a truly staggering pace. Next time you visit Shenzhen, across the border from Hong Kong, keep in mind that this modern city of 9 million people, with its airport, subways, parks, and skyscrapers, did not exist 30 years ago. And Futian, Shenzhen's main commercial district, went from empty land to modern thoroughfares lined with skyscrapers and parks in about six years. China's high urbanization rates combined with an ability to rapidly deploy large-scale infrastructure may turn out to be its most powerful competitive advantage in the long term.

Consider Shanghai's deepwater port. It connects the Yangtze River to the Pacific, but it also effectively connects China's exporters to the world's markets. As recently as 2003, the shipping from Shanghai's deepwater port was approximately 4 million TEU—roughly equal to the throughput of the Long Beach and New York ports. By 2008, Shanghai's throughput had increased to 20 million TEU, five times that of any Western port.

During the same period, the products being transported through Shanghai went from shoes and bicycles to cars and laptops. The market share of Chinese manufacturers is both surging and moving up the global value chain. This is mostly a story of infrastructure providing a competitive strength to locally based companies.

Even for newer products like solar panels, Chinese companies such as Suntech Power Holdings are both gaining market share and pushing down global prices (decreasing by 50% in the last year alone). Suntech, based in Wuxi, is now set to overtake Q-Cells of Germany and become the world's second-largest solar panel supplier. From an investment viewpoint, the unique Chinese landscape with its high-performance state capitalism, ability to deploy infrastructure, and critical mass in manufacturing is now critical to understanding the competitive dynamics of many companies and industries.

When I review individual investments and industries in China and other state capitalist systems, such questions related to competitiveness come up repeatedly. How do companies win on the hypercompetitive Chinese landscape? How does a large low-income population change the competitive dynamic? In acquisitions, is it better to target a highly scalable company, or does that make a buyer too dependent on infrastructure? Doesn't a truly sustainable competitive advantage require political support? How does the dynamic differ between local and foreign companies? Does Coca-Cola still have a competitive advantage in places like China? (Yes.) Is it the same as in the U.S.? (Sort of.)

The key takeaway for investors and deal-makers is that high-performance state capitalism is a new landscape on which they will have to learn to operate. It is a large part of the present and future. And this means understanding the inherent political aspects of these markets and how they impact individual companies, industry structures, competitive dynamics, factors such as infrastructure, and investment strategy.

An Aside on the China-Versus-U.S. Question

I teach at business schools in China, the UK, and sometimes the U.S. My courses cover global and cross-border investing, the competitive dynamics of different economic systems, and private deal structuring. These discussions frequently segue into a more general conversation about U.S.-versus-China competitiveness. It's an important question, but as I'm strictly a micro person, I generally leave this question to wiser people.

But this topic comes up a lot, so I thought I would address it briefly by pointing out three events that caught my attention this past year.

The first was the collapse of General Motors. One can make an interesting (not totally accurate, but interesting) analogy between U.S. and China competitiveness and the competition between GM and Toyota. As recently as 1991, American GM was the world's largest automaker and had been for as long as anyone could remember. It was inconceivable that it was not number one. But it was taking on sizable debt in the form of pension and healthcare liabilities. Japanese Toyota at that time was still fourth in the world but had the highest operating margins in the industry. And it was investing its high cash flow in technology and processes. Its market share both globally and within the U.S. was slowly and consistently increasing. From that point, it took just ten years for Toyota to surpass GM as the leading car company and for the symbol of American automotive leadership to be shattered. And not long after that, a suddenly shrinking GM (all business cases had assumed continued growth) collapsed quickly under its large debt obligations. Too much of this story strikes me as similar to the current situation between leading but cash-poor and increasingly debt-ridden America and rising, market-share expanding, and cash-rich China. My general and completely simplistic takeaway is that in globally competitive industries, Debt + Competition from Asia = Defeat.

The second event that caught my attention was actually a nonevent. It was something that didn't happen. I watched the 2009–2010 U.S. political fighting (budgets, healthcare, financial reform) from afar in my home in Shanghai. What caught my attention was the absence of any competitive considerations in any of the discussions on spending and debt. It just never came up as a topic. This is a sharp difference from the Chinese government's fairly consistent focus on building infrastructure, acquiring resources, and saving money, all with the stated purpose of making the country and its industries more globally competitive.

The third event was the groundbreaking for the approximately 1,900-foot Shanghai Tower in the Liujiazui financial district. The fascinating aspect is that this skyscraper is almost identical in size and ambition to New York City's under-construction 1 World Trade Center (originally named Freedom Tower). Both are the same height, both have similar designs, and both carry deep symbolism. The Shanghai tower is set to be completed by 2013. 1 World Trade Center is finally under construction after a 7-year delay and is set to be completed by 2013–2017—maybe. That one country can build its symbolic tower in 4 years and the other in 12 to 16 is symbolic. And certainly the ability to deploy (and upgrade) infrastructure has a direct impact on the competitiveness of companies in certain industries (manufacturing, logistics, natural resources, etc.). I have no real, solid conclusions from these U.S.-versus-China anecdotes, but they did catch my attention.

Rise of the Arab and Asian Godfathers

Pragmatic elites dominate smaller, often slower-growth economies

A number of investment landscapes in Asia, Africa, and the Middle East can be described as "godfather capitalism"—capitalist systems dominated by a small group of people. Author Joe Studwell, in his book *The Asian Godfathers*, originally used this term to describe the economic systems of Hong Kong, Singapore, Malaysia, Thailand, Indonesia, and the Philippines, but you can see similar systems across the emerging markets today. Because we are not primarily concerned with the real macro nature of politico-economic systems, but instead with how to do direct investments within them, the defining characteristic of such smaller systems for us is companies and who you do deals with.

Continuing my simplistic and offensive-to-every-macroeconomist worldview, such godfather economies typically are smaller than the so-called BRIC economies of Brazil, Russia, India, and China. They are sometimes little more than city-states and are often located far from larger, more stable economies such as Europe and the U.S. A sense of isolation or of being more exposed is a significant part of the psychology of companies and investors in these economies. Although it is common to describe most of them by their size and their politico-economic system (autocratic, benevolent dictatorships, a few democracies), I tend to characterize them as "mostly pragmatic." The political leaders, business heads, and other decision-makers are overwhelmingly concerned with growth, protecting a critical resource, or surviving in a perceived exposed situation. They exhibit an overriding pragmatism when it comes to business and investing. This is sometimes a nice contrast to the more complex political forces of international and state capitalist systems. For investors and deal-makers, the godfather economies are particularly attractive and straightforward environments in which to operate.

These smaller, godfather-type economies have also shown fairly dramatic improvements in their domestic investment and management capabilities in recent years. It is getting easier and easier to operate as a foreign investor in places such as Qatar. The events in Dubai, Abu Dhabi, Macau, and other locations that have caught the world's attention—the meteoric rise of Macau's gaming market, the creation of the Middle Eastern mega real estate industry, and the rise of sovereign wealth funds—have a lot to do with the increasing combination of godfather capitalism and professional management. Meetings with the Abu Dhabi Investment Authority now likely entail talking with ex-Goldman Sachs and Morgan Stanley bankers. This is a fairly dramatic change from just five years ago. Indeed, many of these godfather economies operate more and more like sophisticated investment firms. For example, Kuwait recently received a report titled "Kuwait Vision 2035," detailing a clear development strategy for the country and prepared by an international, professional team including former British Prime Minister Tony Blair.

In general, godfather economies catch my attention as an investor when one of two things happens.

First, they tap into the global capital and trade flows. They capture a position in a global value chain and begin to benefit from an inflow of foreign capital and/or trade. Singapore achieved this in logistics in Asia; Dubai in logistics, tourism, and capital markets; and Macau in gaming and entertainment. In some cases, this can result in dramatic economic booms, especially if the capital or trade flows are large compared to the economy.

Second, they have a valuable resource, such as Saudi Arabia in oil or Qatar in natural gas. This tends to create both significant wealth and significant needs, resulting in opportunities for alert global investors. In the best cases, growing wealth and a growing need for foreign expertise are matched with effective management and execution. More often, the valuable resource tends to breed complacency. There is a reason why Dubai, the GCC city that ran out of oil, has been so effective in its execution, and why oil-rich Riyadh in 2011 looks pretty much like it did in 2001. These are all attractive investment situations, but not all are necessarily growth stories.

Deals in such environments can often be done with a single person or group. For example, just about any real estate deal in Qatar can be done through Qatari Diar, the real estate arm of the sovereign wealth fund. One deal can result in access to an entire industry, and all permits and regulations can sometimes be approved in one meeting.

In addition, the overwhelming pragmatism that often pervades the political establishment in these countries means that investments and deals can be discussed in terms of both strategic and financial benefits. In practice, these types of commercial-to-government deals are very similar to commercial-to-commercial deals. Singapore, Macau, Qatar, and others have clear strategic plans, making deals easy to discuss. An investor can propose a new high-speed ferry from Hong Kong to the Cotai Strip and cite its potential to increase traffic for the casino industry. The more a discussion includes strategy and business aspects, as opposed to purely price, the more room there is for creative deal-making.

Finally, godfather economies are rarely self-sufficient. American businesses can use American capabilities and American financing to create American companies that serve American consumers. Qatar does not have the technology to develop its natural gas, and its customers are overwhelmingly overseas. The country has strong needs for foreign capabilities, whether it be management, capital, brands, products, services, or technologies. Cross-border deals and foreign investment tend to happen naturally and quickly in such situations.

The key takeaway is that these economies can be attractive and comfortable environments for investing. And they are often open to dealing with foreign investors in a way that more rapidly developing economies are not.

The purpose of this exercise is to provide a few simple analogies for different landscapes and enough basic language that we can discuss specific value strategies in the following chapters.

The New Political-Economic Powers Are Deal-Makers, Too

Government and quasi-government players are out in force

In 2005 and 2006, when CNOOC and DP World attempted acquisitions of American companies, public reaction was swift—and strong. What surprised me, however, was that these two widely reported "almost deals" were the only two that got noticed. Few pundits or politicians seemed to pay much attention when Google effectively partnered with the Chinese government to enter the Chinese market, or when UK investors partnered, mostly to their peril, with Russian state-backed companies in energy deals. Cross-border deals that mix commercial and government players were occurring every couple of months.

Government and quasi-government entities are now active investors and participants in markets around the world. And this is a completely expected result of the rising wealth and prominence of many economic systems in which government has a much more direct, active role. Sovereign wealth funds, state-owned enterprises (SOEs), development banks, and government-supported companies are numerous and increasingly active. At the start of this book I mentioned the world's tallest tower was in Dubai, its largest mobile company is in China, and its wealthiest person is in Mexico. At least the first two are clearly quasi-government players.

Government and quasi-government players can operate with a strange mix of strategic, political, financial, and other interests. Sometimes the interests are clear, such as Chinese SOE resource acquisitions in Africa and Australia. Sometimes the interests appear mixed, such as Chinese loans against oil deliveries for Venezuela. And sometimes the interests just appear confused. Why did Dubai build the world's tallest building? (Why is the U.S. building high-speed rail?) Such activity can clearly benefit private-sector sellers, who can construct deals that appeal to these other interests even when they do not make perfect financial sense. In other cases, the impact of these government players on investments can be fairly mixed.

In 2008, Mubadala, one of Abu Dhabi's many sovereign wealth groups, partnered with GE to create a strategic partnership that was a clear win-win for both parties. The multibillion-dollar partnership included projects in clean energy, commercial finance, aviation, and corporate learning. The joint investments expanded GE into an attractive market and brought desired skills and technology into the country. A clear win-win on a strategic and ROI basis.

In contrast, Sabic's purchase of GE Plastics was a significant loss for the competing private Western bidders. Sabic is 70% owned by the Saudi government and operates with an effective domestic monopoly. Its $11.6 billion bid for GE Plastics was well above the $10 billion bids by TPG-Carlyle, Blackstone-Bain, and KRR-Koch. In an increasingly competitive world, it is hard to maintain a private-government separation when your competitors are not.

Deals between state-owned enterprises are another increasing phenomenon worth paying attention to. In 2007, Sinopec and Saudi Aramco signed an approximately $5 billion joint venture to triple the capacity of Sinopec's Fujian refinery (from 80,000 bpd to 240,000 bpd) and add a petrochemical complex. They also agreed to operate a chain of 750 fuel stations in China. What is particularly notable is that this deal, like many SOE-to-SOE deals, involved industry sectors that are mostly off-limits to private companies and foreign investment. And it had support at the highest levels of both governments.

Where the Visible Hand of Government Helps Investors

When politics skews markets, astute investors can find good companies and great bargains

Jim Chanos, founder of the hedge fund Kynikos Associates, recently claimed that China was "Dubai times 1,000—or worse." The pronouncement made headlines everywhere and earned him the title of leading "China contrarian." A review of the Chinese real estate market numbers certainly supports his claim of a very large bubble. But does it matter?

Claiming that China may have a bubble is like warning that a rocket ship may have turbulence. Yes, it's true but shouldn't you already know this? China is a rocket ship of a country that is equal in geographic size to the U.S. (with four times its population) that has grown from agrarian poverty to developed superpower status in less than 30 years. Of course it's a bubble. How could it not be? There are multiple bubbles in China at all times. China is state-directed development writ large.

Government action through state-directed and state-subsidized credit, commercial-state collusion, and dominant state-owned entities is continually altering the economics of China's markets—particularly real estate, construction, and infrastructure. In this sense, state capitalism is doing what it does best—fueling the creation of fixed assets. The result is not market growth per se (the obsession of the multinationals), nor is it always imminently collapsing market bubbles (the dream of the shorts); it is the rapid development of the country's assets and infrastructure.

Keep in mind, we saw a similar Chinese real estate "bubble" just ten years ago. In 1999, Shanghai and Beijing Grade-A commercial property had vacancy rates of 38% and 30%. And the state banks had nonperforming loan (NPL) ratios of 15% to 25%. A clear bubble, or turbulence, depending on your viewpoint. But just five years later, the state banks had reduced their nonperforming loans dramatically, and many had successfully gone public. China Construction Bank went public with an NPL of 4%. And at the same time, the vacancy rate for Grade-A office space in Shanghai dropped from 38% to 6%. Post "bubble," things quickly took off again and by 2006, 80% of the world's cranes were again in China.

Looking at China today, I expect we will shortly see the same pattern play out. Real estate prices will fall, possibly quickly. Troubled loans will increase. Banks and state-operated enterprises will recapitalize through the public markets or government support. And the country will continue on its 30-year deployment of new assets and infrastructure. This is government-fueled and -directed development, which goes hand-in-hand with booms, busts, and other forms of turbulence. And all this government-directed activity creates endless opportunities for value investors.

The pervasive role of government in state and godfather capitalist systems distorts their commercial markets, not periodically but continually. Government actors are continually acting simultaneously as regulators, competitors, customers, and providers of credit. The fairly subtle invisible hand of the free market is paired with the heavy visible hand of government. This means that places such as China and Russia offer exciting opportunities—provided that you can manage the uncertainties. That, in fact, is the central investment challenge.

I would characterize Dubai's spectacular rise and fall not as a bubble, but as a government-directed boom/bust cycle that got out of hand. There is a reason why Dubai built such eye-catching projects like the Burj Al Arab, why it created an international airline with daily flights to JFK, and why it put billboards of sunny Dubai beaches all over Moscow every winter. It was a government-directed "Build it and they will come" strategy—or, more accurately, a strategy of "Build it huge, hype it everywhere, and they will come—and then the economy will grow."

And it worked. An unknown city located in a problematic part of the world became a brand name with world-class capabilities in logistics, real estate, and finance. But the strategy got away from the government around 2006, and projects went from ambitious to ludicrous, credit went from prudent to risky, and the markets went from development-oriented to speculative. When the financial crisis erupted in 2008, foreign demand abruptly disappeared, and the real estate sector collapsed. This was helped along by the excess debt taken on in recent years, but it was more an income statement than a balance sheet problem.

I am admittedly terrible at economics and really everything at the macro level. My understanding of various markets and the simplistic descriptions presented in this chapter come almost entirely from looking at individual deals on the ground around the world. This sort of state-directed development occurs primarily because government actors, in places like Dubai, structure the rules so that everyone at the table can say yes to the deal. If the project doesn't have a proven or realistic market (which is the most common problem in emerging markets), or if the economics of the deal just don't work (usually due to large initial infrastructure costs), a government actor of some type generally fixes the rules so that the deal can proceed. It is the sheikh or the city official sitting at the end of the table that provides credit, provides a sovereign guarantee, or grants additional land that can be sold early on in the project. In practice, it is state actors altering the economics of deals so everyone can say yes that, in aggregate, causes such altered and turbulent markets. And the more tools the state actors have in their tool kit (development banks, state-backed companies, commercial banks), the more room there is for creativity in the deal structuring.

Therefore, in many ways booms and busts are inherent, or at least should always be expected, in developing countries and markets. I just assume that any rapidly developing country is in this state. It is inherent to many of the systems that are now part of the investment landscape.

The key question for investors is not whether China is a bubble but whether it can manage its perpetual booms and busts. A quick review of the past 20 years indicates that Chinese officials are actually quite adept at controlling state banks and credit. They are good at flying the rocket ship. And the local population is also well conditioned to this turbulent environment. They have very high savings rates, purchase property early in life, and develop extended personal networks for security. Per Nassim Taleb, it's not a black swan if you see it coming.

For investors and deal-makers, these situations are obviously value opportunities. Although the free market may not be as efficient as the efficient market hypothesis advocates hoped, it is relatively stable, and booms and busts are relatively uncommon (the financial sector not included). In government-skewed markets, mispricing is everywhere, and booms and busts are the norm. Recall that in the opening of this book, I argued that the real challenge in going global as a value investor is managing the uncertainties in inherently unstable environments.

The negative of this situation at the deal level is that activist governments lead to more regulatory scrutiny, which can easily slow or impede investment. I often think of Robert Fisk's book *Pity the Nation* in which he describes a period in Beirut's civil war when there were so many militias and occupying armies in the city that driving across town meant stopping at 10 to 15 checkpoints in a single trip. You go three blocks and then are stopped and need to show a pass or pay money to proceed. Heavily government-infused markets are similar. There are more points in the process where you need to get approval to go forward, and this can be a positive or negative in terms of competing for deals. If the checkpoints limit you, it's problematic. If they limit competitors, it's beneficial. It was Carlyle's competitor for the Xugong investment that slowed and eventually killed their deal. There is a common saying that doing business in China means successfully partnering with the government. Doing business in India successfully means being able to overcome the government. The multiple checkpoints can play out in various ways, usually depending on who you are.

As described, the heavy hand of government can have a significant impact at both the market and deal levels. But it is at the company level that the effect can be most powerful. The number of bank or mobile licenses can be limited. Industry-wide monopolies can be created. Access to land or development rights can be controlled. Regulatory requirements can drive up overhead or other fixed costs such that smaller firms find it harder to enter. In general, government action and involvement can create numerous types of limited-competition situations at the company level, enabling returns on invested capital to stay well above the cost of capital (and sometimes that cost can be driven down with state support). Politically infused markets can create value investors' favorite targets—companies with very sustainable competitive advantages.

Limited-competition situations can be cash cows for investors. Until very recently, there were only a handful of bank licenses in Saudi Arabia, a country with hundreds of billions in annual oil revenue. In China today, only three (actually, two) mobile phone companies are allowed in a market with more than 790 million mobile phone users. Owning any of these limited-competition companies can be a gold mine. It's notable that Warren Buffett's first major investment in China was in state-owned Petrochina, which operates with a government monopoly. The intersection of a strong advantage at the deal-level and limited competition at the company-level is the holy grail of investing in politicized markets.

On a side note, in the last year there has been a fascinating new collision between such state-created monopolies and free-market competitors. In 2010, Visa fired the "shot not heard around the world" when it took the step of blocking Chinese Unionpay in many international markets as it attempted to expand globally. Without receiving much media attention, Visa had fired the first shot in a new global front between state and international capitalism. Chinese Unionpay, since its founding in 2002, has done exceptionally well under a politically granted credit and debit card monopoly in mainland China. By 2009, it was processing over 1 trillion annual transactions. Visa, which processed $4.4 trillion in transactions internationally in 2009, has long struggled against this monopoly in its attempt to get a foothold in the mainland China market. But as Unionpay began to expand internationally, Visa was finally able to respond in similar fashion. They moved to have Unionpay blocked in many international markets. The fight between international and state capitalism, traditionally within developing economies, is increasingly moving to a global playing field. It will be interesting to see how far the benefits of a limited-competition situation in a home market can be leveraged internationally.

But if government-infused markets can create attractive limited competition situations on one hand, they can create brutal hypercompetition on the other. China's steel industry is an example. Extensive loans by state-owned banks have created a massive oversupply in iron smelters and other stages of steel production. The resulting hyper-competition in steel production has resulted in falling prices, with the investment returns well below the private market cost of capital. This type of hyper-competition is about the last place a value investor wants to be.

Investing in politicized markets is a core question for the traditional value strategy in a global world. In many cases, such as Buffett buying public PetroChina shares, these types of markets are just offering companies that have another type of competitive advantage. One could argue that a state monopoly is possibly the most sustainable of competitive advantages. But beneath this case, investors can confront a fairly wide variety of investment environments and competitive situations. Rapid booms and busts, slow booms and busts, limited competition, hypercompetition, and others are all inherent to government-infused markets. Generally speaking, this means greater market inefficiencies for value-focused investors to target, but it also means dealing with greater uncertainty and instability. As mentioned, my best answer for this conundrum is to combine traditional value methodologies (for example, PetroChina purchases) with value-added deal-making, which will be discussed in detail in the next chapter.

5

How Political Access Adds Value

Traveling around the world, I am continually astounded by how many businesspeople know Ben Graham. Not just executives in places like Hong Kong and Dubai, but business students and investing enthusiasts in places like Bangalore, Chengdu, and Jeddah. Giving talks in these regions, I have found that if I put up a slide of Ben Graham, 10% to 20% of the group can identify him by his picture alone. And I suspect it is now only a matter of time before some large real estate developer in the Middle East or China builds two small twin cities and names them Graham and Doddsville.

It's clear that Graham's value approach is compatible with the government-infused markets described in the preceding chapter. Not only do the investors and deal-makers in these regions understand highly political systems and how to deal with active government actors, but they also understand and follow Graham. It's really just a matter of adapting Graham's Method and the well-known techniques to these politicized environments. This chapter is about how to do this, with a focus on private assets. Value strategies for companies on emerging market exchanges such as Hong Kong and Dubai are well known and are not repeated here.

Princes, SOEs, and Government Sachs

Seven ways political access can help investors

The large and persistent role of government in a multipolar world effectively guarantees the ongoing creation of large market inefficiencies. Fortunately, using political access is a fairly effective way to capture these opportunities. It is difficult to overemphasize the power of this approach in state capitalist and godfather capitalist economies. This approach explains the rise of many—sometimes I think all—of the wealthy investors from many regions.

Note in Figure 5.1, that politically created inefficiencies show up in Question 2, and political access is marked as a value key for constructing deals and securing a margin of safety. Recall that value keys both open the door to investments and add value with the primary goal of eliminating the current and long-term downside uncertainty.

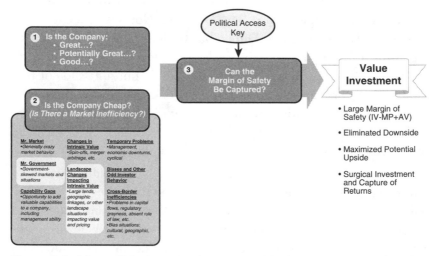

Figure 5.1   The political access key and politically created inefficiencies

Question 1 asks whether a company is good, potentially great, or great. Government rules and the choices of government actors can positively and negatively impact the attractiveness of both individual companies and industry structures. Politically limited competition can create particularly sustainable competitive advantages. State-owned enterprises themselves can be very attractive companies for investment. And Mr. Government can directly increase the intrinsic value of many types of companies. So political factors are significant for Question 1.

Question 2 asks whether the company is cheap. As discussed in the preceding chapter, government-skewed markets are far more inefficient and can swing price far away from value. Both Mr. Market and Mr. Government can create mispricing opportunities. And if you are purchasing a company or asset directly from a government agency or state-owned enterprise (SOE), negotiated prices can be quite attractive. At the industry level, government-directed development activities, such as were described for China and Dubai, can generate large trends in which significant lags between value and price almost always exist. I have highlighted government-created inefficiencies under Question 2 as both "Mr. Government" and "Landscape Changes."

Question 3 asks whether the margin of safety can be captured. But this middle section of the chart is also about deal advantages. Can you access the investment? Can you beat out competing bids? What is your advantage in bidding on companies in Dubai or Singapore? Is being a foreigner a disadvantage? Political access is a requirement in many of these situations and can be a very strong advantage in some. In the best-case scenario, you structure the deal such that you end up as the only bidder for a project or company.

Generally, if you are investing in politically infused markets then political access and government-skewed economics are significant determinants of company quality, price, and the margin of safety.

Although it is interesting to detail large investments involving high-level officials in Beijing, Doha, and Moscow, most political-type deals are actually at lower and smaller levels. Vancouver legal firms are doing mining deals with government officials in Kunming. Investment bankers in London are dealing with Saudi regulators for their corporate clients. And venture capitalists, private equity groups, and business development executives going global are rapidly building political expertise, if not capabilities, around the world.

In terms of the uncertainty language presented in Chapter 3, "Value Point," political access can have seven significant effects on a value-focused transaction, as shown in Figure 5.2:

1. **Increased access to deals.** This is clearly the primary opportunity. And not just deals, but special deals. Getting land in China. Acquiring licenses in limited-competition situations in Latin America. Obtaining construction contracts in Qatar or oil and gas allocations in Saudi Arabia. Winning access to natural resources or state-owned assets or, in the case of the Russian oligarchs, getting actual ownership. The ideal situation is when you have preferential access to a company with politically limited competition.

2. **Decreased entry price.** This is occasionally possible. Whether it is assets or contracts, governments are often un-skilled at setting prices, and this doesn't seem to worry them much.

3. **Increasing the intrinsic value of an asset or company.** Buying a company and putting in place a significant government contract or benefiting from the actions of a state-owned entity can create a large increase in economic value.

4. **Eliminating future downside uncertainty (stabilizing the margin of safety).** This is most commonly done through a significant government contract or investing in a company with politically limited competition.

5. **Creating an advantage when competing for deals.** Politically connected locals typically are in a strong position relative to foreign companies. This is the reason for many foreign-local joint ventures in politicized markets.

6. **Occasionally creating a long-term partnership with a company (strengthening a claim to the enterprise).** Political access tends to be a short-term value-add for foreigners. It's better for securing contracts or assets as opposed to creating long-term operating partnerships.

7. **Eliminating nonmarket risks (defensibility).** This is critical. The government is the primary nonmarket risk in many systems, and it's better to be on the inside than the outside. This speaks to the long-term downside uncertainty.

Figure 5.2 shows the net impact on the value framework.

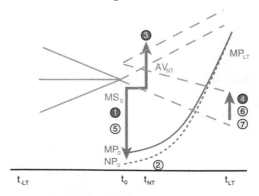

Figure 5.2   The uses of political access

These seven uses of political access are a different "value approach" than that taken by traditional value investors and private equity groups. Value investors have traditionally limited political connections to information gathering (particularly by event-driven short-term investors). Private equity firms have traditionally used political access both for information and for enhancing their management and operational efforts. It is a secondary consideration at best. Value point directly focuses on adding value with political access, which can be fairly powerful at the company and deal level in highly politicized markets. This approach is very common by local investors in these markets.

Political Access Success Stories

In 2010, Carlos Slim Helu became the world's richest person, inching past Bill Gates at $53.5 billion. That Slim's wealth increased by $19 billion in one year (averaging $2.2 million per hour) was particularly startling. He is also the first person from a developing economy to top the list, being propelled there by his Mexican telecommunications empire. Emerging-market giants like Carlos Slim are growing in number and offer important case studies in how to generate large wealth in economies with different politico-economic structures. You really cannot separate most of the emerging-market giants like Slim from such politicized economics.

Emerging-market giants most commonly are the result of exceedingly profitable industry positions in government-skewed economies. Typically, the individual or company captures a limited competition (very good) or monopoly position (phenomenal) at the regional or national level. And, given the rising wealth of many emerging markets, they become prominent and often highly liquid global investors fairly rapidly. The abnormally high domestic cash flows enable Western acquisitions so they are most often first noticed as bargain hunters for premier Western assets (see Figure 5.3). Whether it's Slim into the United States or Russian oligarchs into the UK, we see this pattern repeatedly. A select few (such as Prince Waleed) then combine their developed and developing market assets to do global deal-making.

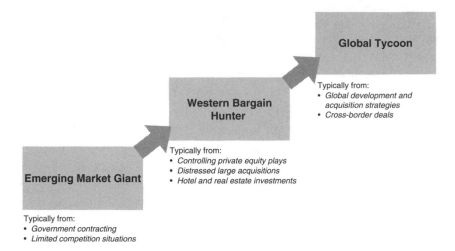

Figure 5.3   Government-skewed economics fuel the rise of many emerging-market giants

Emerging-market giants are one manifestation of the increasing wealth of government-skewed markets. There are many others such as state-owned enterprises, government-connected or -financed multinationals, and sovereign wealth funds. Understanding how political access is deployed in government-skewed economies is critical to understanding the wealth creation that is the engine of many rising companies and investors.

The Value of Political Access in State Capitalist Systems

In state capitalist China and Russia, political access is the number-one, -two, and -three strategy for investing and deal-making. I grew up with the idea that first you make your fortune in business, and then you serve in the government. In state capitalist systems, the approach is basically the reverse. People accumulate power through a government position, and then use that to make their fortune. This is not as Machiavellian as it sounds. It simply reflects the fact that state entities are the largest players in the economy, and that is where most of the economic opportunities are. Working in "politics" could mean working in a state-owned entity such as China Mobile or in a state-supported innovation hub such as Founder Group, a Beijing-based technology conglomerate. It can be building a private company with close ties to the government, such as Chinese search engine Baidu. But for those who invest in these environments, political access is part of most every successful company and therefore most deals.

A good example of one of China's emerging-market giants is Vincent Lo, the chairman of Shui On Group and arguably the most famous Shanghai real estate developer. Lo was an aggressive early mover in large-scale Chinese real estate. In the 1990s, he successfully acquired and master-planned a very large section of downtown Shanghai, something unheard of at the time. The resulting now-quite-famous Xintiandi development covers approximately 129 acres of land in the central Luwan district of Shanghai and contains a historic shikumen district, residential housing, and premier office space. It is still a singular achievement in terms of Chinese real estate development. One can watch tour buses arrive at Xintiandi every morning filled with Chinese tourists who want to take pictures in front of its sign. When large numbers of tourists want to take photos in front of your Coffee Bean, that is a fairly good sign that you have succeeded.

When Lo first proposed the large master-planned development in 1997 to Han Zheng, then an up-and-coming Luwan officer (and a future Shanghai mayor), acquiring land in China was entirely a political process. Land is not even actually acquired as it belongs to the state; it is technically leased for 20 to 40 years. And typically, government departments master-plan the areas and then sell smaller sections to developers on a lot-by-lot basis. This unfortunately has resulted in most Chinese cities having very high-quality buildings but, as of yet, few memorable large developments. Shanghai has no Trafalgar Square or Champs d'Elysees. Within this highly political process, acquiring such a large space in central Shanghai and then being able to master-plan it was a demonstration of outstanding political access. To my knowledge such a thing has not been repeated since.

Over time, the land-acquisition process in China has become less political. Open bids are now held for most tracts in the major cities, but the bidding process is still influenced, and successful bids are sometimes "arranged." Even today, such real estate deals, many of them politically connected, account for a large number of China's emerging-market giants.

However, my favorite example of the use of political access in Chinese real estate is a developer I met in Changsha, Hunan, whom I will call Mr. Zhang. It is a good lesson in how even a small amount of political access can be leveraged into a fortune in such a system.

Changsha is the capital of Hunan, but it is certainly not a wealthy city. It has none of the economic scale or growth of Shanghai. So those with strong political connections typically focus on building hotels for visiting businessmen or luxury residential apartments for the still small local upper class. In starting his business, Mr. Zhang had little capital but some political access. He was able to leverage his political connections to buy some land far outside the city that nobody really wanted. As necessity is the mother of invention, he hit upon the idea of building private cemeteries. The land outside of town that nobody wanted was relatively cheap, and cemeteries don't need central locations. There are also no real capital costs for building cemeteries, because there is really nothing to build. The only operating costs are for gardeners, which, as you can imagine, are pretty cheap in Hunan, and advertising space in downtown Changsha offering plots for people's parents. Plus you can sign contracts and receive payments for the plots on a reservation basis almost immediately. In a respect-your-elders society, private cemeteries turned out to be a low-capital expenditure, low cost of growth, high cash-flow business. Within five years, Mr. Zhang became one of the most successful private cemetery owners.

Such success stories are fairly common in most of the state capitalist systems. A deal is done between a private business person and a government official or department (usually in construction, real estate, or infrastructure) and that propels the investor upward, often at astonishing speeds.

Still, the most spectacular example of the use of political access is without question the loans-for-shares deals in Russia in the mid-1990s. Relatively unknown individuals became billionaire oligarchs almost overnight by acquiring previously state-owned assets. This story is covered in fascinating detail in Chrystia Freeland's book *Sale of the Century* and is not repeated here.

The Value of Political Access in Godfather Economies

In the godfather economies (Hong Kong, Qatar, Macau, the UAE, etc.), political access is a similarly powerful way to create wealth. The dynamics are also much easier to understand in these smaller and simple economies. A small number of individuals or families control much of the economy and local businesses in either strong or weak fashion, and they tend to be fairly easy to work with. Additionally, these economies are often not self-sufficient. They need foreign technology, products, brands, and business models, so the locals in power have a greater interest in working with foreign partners. A foreigner may have difficulty getting state approval for a deal in Moscow, but it is quite a natural thing in Singapore or Qatar.

Qatar is an interesting example because it is a rapidly growing economy and is controlled by a single group, the Al Thani family. Most of the country's major projects are developed by entities controlled by his family. Additionally, as a small country, Qatar also lacks virtually all the capabilities required for domestic development (technology, management, businesses). So, unsurprisingly, Qatari Diar has launched a series of joint ventures with foreign partners. Qatari and the Saudi BinLadin group have launched a new construction and industrial services company. Qatari Diar and Deutsche Bahn, a leading passenger and logistics company, launched a joint venture to develop the country's railways. Qatari Diar and Prince Waleed struck a hotel development and management deal in which Qatari Diar purchased 23% of Fairmont Raffles and then provided multiple hotel management contracts. And so on. Such deals are quite simply, and are mostly, and sometimes entirely, about political access.

You can see the same pattern across the godfather economies. A small group of individuals control significant parts of the economy and are quite comfortable with foreign partners. For example, in Dubai, most real estate is controlled by three state-owned companies—Emaar, Nakheel, and Jumeirah. And in Abu Dhabi, local real estate is developed by five primary real estate companies—coincidentally the same number of main members of the royal family.

From Mexico to China to the Middle East, companies and investors who leverage political access into returns are in ascension. Rising tycoons such as Slim in Mexico and Prince Waleed in Saudi Arabia; overnight billionaires such as the oligarchs in Russia; and family dynasty heads such as Li Kai Shing in Hong Kong and Stanley Ho in Macau are experts at understanding politically infused markets and at structuring political access into their deals. Understanding such political aspects at both the deal and company level is critical within a value approach in such systems.

Investment Strategies for Politicized Markets

The following sections detail two examples of particularly effective strategies for particularly government-skewed markets. These are both value-added strategies consistent with Graham's Method previously outlined. You eliminate uncertainty, quantify risk, and invest surgically (and big). Again, the primary challenge is to eliminate the long-term downside uncertainty—through both company selection (the traditional value approach) and negotiated value-added deal-making (value point approach).

Strategy #1: "Bird on a Rhino"

A multipolar world contains many types of what I call corporate, government, and financial "rhinos." These are the very large animals in the economy. They command large assets and large investment dollars and often they are focused on overriding strategic or government interests, as opposed to purely financial returns. They also tend to show herding effects, running in packs after various investment opportunities. Moving out of the West and into smaller and shallower economies, such rhinos can have a disproportionately large impact.

The state-owned enterprises of China, Russia, and the GCC countries are good examples of emerging-market rhinos. Their interests are a shifting mix of government and commercial priorities. And they regularly invest tens of billions of dollars with a long-term focus. Saudi Aramco, the Saudi government oil giant, routinely makes large strategic investments around the world in order to move downstream in the oil and gas industry. Chinese state-owned enterprises such as Baosteel operate like rhinos in places like Africa and Latin America, where they focus on making strategic acquisitions of natural resources and tend to be very large relative to the local economy. And they occasionally coordinate with government-backed commercial and development banks in these deals (another type of rhino). Similarly, Western-based multinationals often act like rhinos when going after the "must-win" markets of China and India. In all cases, the rhinos drive large flows of dollars without strict, or at least strict short-term, financial return requirements.

Continuing the analogy, real rhinos in the wilderness have symbiotic relationships with tick birds, the small white birds that ride on their backs, eating ticks and warning the rhinos of danger. In return, the birds have a safe place to stay, because no predators attack rhinos, and they receive free transportation.

Being a "bird on a rhino" is one of my favorite investment strategies in government-skewed economies. It entails making small investments in scalable, low cost-of-growth companies that directly benefit from, and often help, the commercial and government rhinos. They are also called "5 to 20" investments because they can go from $5 million to $20 million rapidly.

China's financial sector includes some good recent examples of the "bird on a rhino" approach. The financial sector is evolving quickly with the recent addition of credit cards, wealth management, insurance, and securities subsectors. The sector is also teaming with rhinos, such as the state-owned banks, state-owned insurance companies, multinationals, and many others. Huge investment dollars are flooding into the sector at the current time.

One such "bird on a rhino" investment in this sector was undertaken by a friend I'll call Mr. Lee. He invested in a communications platform that could connect commercial banks with smaller networks of independent ATMs, mostly in outlying regions. The investment was small and the service highly scalable, with a low cost of growth. Most importantly, it benefited directly from the actions of the large government-backed banks (it was a bird on a rhino). Immediately after investing, Mr. Lee could offer the large banks ATM access in areas in which they did not yet have it. Unsurprisingly, all the banks jumped at the chance to expand their ATM networks, and all quickly contracted with the company. One large bank offered to buy the company. The value of Mr. Lee's small company jumped dramatically (5 to 20) based on the contracts.

This deal had all the basic qualities of a value point investment (see Figure 5.4). Mr. Lee found an opportunity to add value to both the investment (through several bank contracts) and the banks (offering them a regional ATM network). He targeted a large inefficiency—the capability gaps in the rapidly evolving financial services sector. He contacted the state-owned enterprises early on, invested surgically, and effectively made his returns at the time of investment. He also did not need to control the ATM company (minority share is OK), because the bank contracts gave him enough control for a secure investment. All in all, he entered with a healthy margin of safety, minimized the downside and maximized the upside.

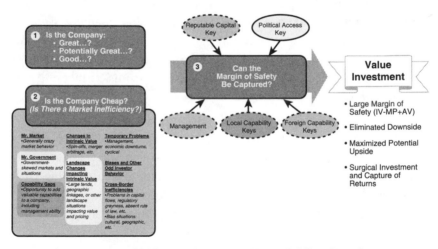

Figure 5.4   "Bird on a rhino"—Shanghai Financial Services Company

However, the dominant factor was the government-skewed economics. Between government-backed banks, regulatory committees, and tightly controlled foreign banks, the entire development and evolution of the Chinese financial services industry are under political influence. Secondly, political access was the critical component in terms of securing the bank contracts and the value-add at the time of investment.

Occasionally, and in greatly entertaining fashion, the rhinos battle it out, as in present-day Macau. The rhinos of Macau are the foreign- and domestic-invested casinos. Western-invested and -operated casinos such as the Wynn and the Sands, as well as locally owned casinos, are competing for Chinese gamblers by pouring tens of billions of dollars into their facilities and offering luxurious services and facilities. The net result is a massive influx of money, people, construction, and other activity in a small city in the space of seven years.

This situation has all the qualities of an attractive investment environment. There is a large economic trend (a rising casino town). There are large capability gaps. And there are large cross-border inefficiencies. Moreover, Macau by definition is a government-skewed market in which casinos are licensed by the local government (a shifting mix of Beijing and Macau political interests) and land is tightly controlled on the small islands. Visas and other requirements for staff and just about everything else are government-controlled. It is a political environment from top to bottom.

Enter MKW Capital, a private equity firm that builds and buys scalable investments benefiting from casino growth and competition—often "bird on a rhino" strategies. For example, casinos need thousands of employees (the Las Vegas Sands Corporation has 28,500 employees), and Macau now has more than 30 casinos. So MKW opened the first online human resources company based in Macau and immediately contracted with many of the major casinos, adding large value rapidly at the time of investment. This approach also took advantage of cross-border inefficiencies (Western human resources companies don't know much about Macau, and vice versa) and capability gaps (casinos need staff with specific skills), both of which I have argued are a type of market inefficiency. Their investment rose quickly on the backs of the competing rhinos. MKW also launched a locally based advertising company which directly benefits from the fiercely competing casinos that, unsurprisingly, spare no expense in this area. Multiple other "bird on a rhino" investments followed, and MKW quickly became known as the smartest investment group in Macau.

Strategy #2: Limited-Competition Situations

In the Macau scenario just described, the casinos were initially a politically limited-competition situation. Prior to the opening of the market, Stanley Ho had an effective monopoly for more than twenty years. Post-opening, the licenses remain controlled by the Macau authorities and are given to only select companies or individuals. Sheldon Adelson's first Macau Sands Casino greatly benefited from the limited competition at that time. Opened in 2004 as a day trip destination across the border from China, the $240 million investment returned its capital and quite a bit more within only a few months. Although the licenses are no longer as strictly controlled today, there is a reason why Stanley Ho, and several of his children have casinos in prominent locations.

Another example of politically limited competition is Saudi Arabia, which has historically had nine banking licenses. Owning one of these licenses in the cash-rich oil kingdom was a guarantee of high profits. Prince Waleed's first major investment in Saudi Arabia, after years of smaller, high-return real estate investments, was the acquisition of United Saudi Commercial Bank, at that time the weakest of the Saudi banks. Following a rapid turnaround, it returned to profitability, and Waleed became one of the Middle East's major players. (This could be described as the bird taking over the rhino.) This also foreshadowed his 1991 investment in Citigroup three years later.

Limited-competition situations can take many forms, but they are overwhelmingly government-created and therefore are infused with politics. PetroChina is China's biggest oil producer (the world's second-largest company by market capitalization) and dominates the sector by size and political authority. Land and prime locations in places like China and Russia are effectively limited competition and are politically allocated (ie., Vincent Lo in Shanghai). Telecommunications networks usually are limited to two to three in a country and are politically controlled. And so on.

The challenge in pursuing this strategy as a value investor is acquiring such limited-competition companies. While long-term uncertainties are typically the primary problem in developing economy investing, in this case, it is deal access. A few of these companies are publicly listed and minority ownership can be acquired, but most are smaller and privately held. This is where offering to invest with a compelling addition to value is critical (that is, the search for the opportunity to add value). Pursuing this strategy usually means relying heavily on political access.

Live by Politics, Die by Politics

For foreign deal-makers, a political advantage often declines over time

Political access can be somewhat tricky if you are a foreigner and going long-term. It can be a very strong advantage in terms of getting some deals. In many situations it is a requirement for getting *any* deals. But political access for foreigners tends to be a particularly short-lived advantage.

For example, most search engines in China, Russia, and many other countries are both dependent on foreigners and highly political. This tends to put the local governments in the difficult position of balancing the foreign technology they need with the control of information they want.

Thus, when Google entered China in 2005, it was in a fairly strong political position. Approximately 100 million Mainland Chinese users were already searching online in various forms (the online population is now approaching 400 million), and Google had fairly unique search engine technology. To some degree, the government needed Google at that point. In a reasonably strong position, Google agreed to filter search results but avoided many of the joint venture and technology transfer requirements other foreign companies had faced. However, as time passed, Google's political position grew weaker as domestic competitor Baidu increased its capabilities. Google's technological expertise was no longer perceived as quite so necessary. In a highly political situation, its political strength was declining.

At a 2009 dinner with a Google executive in London, I made one of my better predictions: that Google would likely fail in China. Google was politically weak in a mostly political competition with Baidu. I predicted that it would be forced out, be forced to sell into a minority position in a state-controlled company, or be kept at a minority market share while the local competitors grew in strength. My argument was that the use of political access by foreigners tends to be strong in the short term but weak in the long term, particularly in hypercompetitive and hyperpolitical industries such as state capitalist search engines. Third-place search engine Yahoo! had already sold its China operations in 2005 to local competitor Alibaba. In March 2010, Google preemptively and very publicly exited China (sort of).

It is unclear what other decision Google could have made. In rapidly developing economies, foreign players can be very strong at certain key points, but political access is hard to sustain in an ongoing competition. For real estate or fixed-asset investments, a short-term advantage is usually sufficient. Once ownership of a building is acquired, it is pretty difficult to lose it. You need a political advantage on the day you buy the building. But for operating entities in highly competitive industries, such as Internet companies, it is difficult to survive with a declining advantage.

The case of Dubailand offers an interesting contrast. This massive Disneyland-type theme park under development in Dubai has similar political aspects. As originally planned, it will eventually cover 104 square miles, contain 24 separate projects (including an indoor ski dome and a Tiger Woods golf course), and cost $65 billion. The project is overwhelmingly strategic, with the objective of bringing 3 million tourists into Dubai. As with most every major strategic and symbolic project in Dubai, it is controlled by the Royal Family and is very political.

However, operating a theme park requires fairly specialized knowledge, and at the time the deal was negotiated, foreign theme park operators were in a strong position. The risk of a public failure of such a high-profile project would have been the primary consideration for the government developers. Additionally, theme parks have large up-front capital costs and high, ongoing, fixed costs. So as the market and demand ramp up, which is always the big unknown in emerging markets, large operating losses are likely. Euro Disney had this same early operating-loss problem after opening in France, which, as a developed market, had far less uncertainty in its demand projections than Dubai.

All these concerns would put an experienced foreign operator in a strong negotiating position with the government. The challenge, therefore, is how to utilize this strong political value-add in the short term and not get stuck in a weakening position in the long term (like Google did). In the Middle East, my typical approach is to target the returns on fixed assets and then take a private equity-type approach for high fixed-cost operating assets.

In the case of Dubailand, a foreign partner could have easily negotiated ownership of the ancillary fixed assets, such as adjacent hotels and residential towers, which would be both secure and profitable after being acquired (a traditional value investment). And for the riskier operating asset, the theme park, they could have put in place either a no-risk management contract (10% of revenue), preferred equity or an equity stake with an initial public offering (IPO) or sale set for two or three years in the future. Then, as their political value-add declined over time, they would still have control of the fixed assets and no risk on the operating assets.

Additionally, the absence of strong local management and local competition in Dubai meant that any political advantage would likely be much more sustainable than in China or Russia. Again, understanding the investment landscape is critical to plotting the investment strategy.

In this context, it is interesting to watch the current negotiations between Shanghai and Disney about creating a Shanghai Disneyland. The Shanghai Disneyland project, announced in November 2009, is set to cover only 3.86 square miles and will cost approximately $5 billion. The smaller size greatly reduces the risk of operating losses or a possible perceived failure of the project. Plus, it does not have the same strategic objective of bringing tourists into the country as Dubailand. Disney appears to be in a fairly weak political position already, and I would be on the lookout for a much larger, domestically owned theme park to be announced in the near future.

The key takeaway for foreign investors and deal-makers is that when you use primarily political access, it is important to determine if this is a long-term or short-term advantage. The fatal mistake is to try to maintain a political advantage as a foreigner in an industry with primarily operating assets and significant local competition. Foreign-owned Internet companies in China are an example of this. The government involvement that helps you at the time of entry can also hurt you later. Live by the sword, die by the sword.

Political Access by Locals

For local investors and deal-makers, political access can prove to be surprisingly resilient and profitable. In 2007, I penned an internal Kingdom Holding memo titled "Access Isn't Enough" about the changing nature of competition for Middle Eastern investments. For 30 years, Prince Waleed's company, Kingdom Holding, has had uniquely strong political and commercial deal access across the region and in other emerging markets, and it has used this access to great success. But in 2005 and 2006, private equity firms started to enter the region in force, with more than 30 Middle Eastern private equity firms being launched and more than 70 private equity funds being raised. These firms began operating with a partnership model, superior industry specialization, and more readily deployable funds, in stark contrast to the traditional Middle Eastern family office (one politically connected boss and two or three chief slaves).

I questioned how Kingdom Holding could compete for deals against teams of analysts who could both make decisions and deploy raised funds faster. We had superior access, but the winning formula seemed to be access plus specialized expertise. It appeared that access was no longer enough.

This turned out to be one of my weaker assessments. Most of the new private-equity firms were satellite offices of international firms and struggled to get access to good deals. A few firms such as Amwal Al-Khaleej built successful businesses by fusing private equity-type management expertise with politically connected owners, but most struggled. However, political access remains overwhelmingly the strongest deal advantage in the region. The dynamic, which I did not predict, was that in many emerging markets, getting a deal at an attractive price requires access to closely held deals. Any open-deal or open-bid situation attracts too much capital in markets where good deals are few and capital is plentiful. Great returns in the Middle East are still mostly about getting access to closed deals. Being a little stronger politically (or in other forms of access) continues to make all the difference.

There is one final comment on political access and government-skewed markets. The benefits in politically infused markets overwhelmingly stem from the fact that a free-market system is more efficient and, therefore, often a more difficult place in which to make abnormally high returns. Political economics create companies and industry structures that can be very profitable. They also enable investors to use political advantages when structuring deals. You can benefit at both the company and deal levels.

But this also means investors can be dependent on continued political largesse. Obviously this can change. If the government can make you rich, it can make you poor. Similarly, if it can create an attractive industry structure, it can create an unattractive one. This strikes at the key question of this book's approach of how to be long-term and value-focused in uncertain and unstable environments. Again, the solution is to build an investment strategy based on where and when you add value.

Let me reiterate my original point about value point versus traditional value investing. You can see I am targeting the areas that most traditional value investors most strenuously avoid. I am presenting a value strategy for the opposite extreme. Instead of focusing on capturing a margin of safety for Hong Kong-listed shares of PetroChina, I focus on capturing and stabilizing a margin of safety for private illiquid assets in highly politicized markets. This does not mean this is the best target (although I do find these assets to have the largest mispricings), but if you can do these types of value-added private deals, everything else becomes easy by comparison and you can go almost anywhere.

6

The World Is Biased

Investors need an arsenal of advantages if they are to operate successfully in a world of colliding markets and actors. Solid financing and expertise are important. As discussed, political access can be a strength. A third, less obvious, but increasingly important advantage is reputation.

In developed economies and with traditional value approaches, an investor's reputation is certainly critical and helps one become an attractive buyer. In more uncertain and unstable environments, however, this "buyer of choice" effect becomes much more powerful. An investor with a strong reputation not only has preferential access to otherwise inaccessible deals, but also can often act *as the solution* to the very regulatory grayness, weak legal systems, and political and cultural differences I have cited as challenges. As uncertainty grows in an environment, so does the power of reputation.

It is one of the peculiarities of global investing that reputation has such amplified power, particularly in private negotiated deals. For example, if a Chinese state-owned enterprise (SOE) such as Founder in Beijing and a private American company such as Sutter Health in California are interested in partnering or collaborating in healthcare projects, there are likely very compelling business reasons for doing so. But in practice, such deals rarely happen due to both real and perceived risks. One is a private company, and the other is a state-owned enterprise. One is in a Western rule-of-law liberal democracy, and the other is in a state capitalist system. And of course large cultural and language gaps exist. The deals just tend not to happen.

But, in such a situation, the participation of a highly reputable investor or company can often make all the difference—and effectively become the solution to all these problems.

Weak rule of law, frequently changing regulations, lack of transparency, poor governance, limited minority shareholder rights, and unstable markets are all red flags and real risks—and investor apprehension is both prudent and warranted. Dealing with these very real increases in uncertainty is the central challenge to moving into global investing.

But also without question, many (most?) investors today are dramatically overstating these risks. The behavioral finance issues related to crossing borders and entering fundamentally different investment environments are not only large but seem to be growing. The worldwide landscape today is covered with investors behaving oddly.

The starting point for understanding much of this current behavior is to separate the real risks from the perceived ones. We can manage the real risks with the approach outlined in Chapter 2, "Rethinking Value in a Global Age": We eliminate the downside uncertainties in the current and long-term margin of safety, we quantify the risk, and we invest surgically. For the perceived risks (all the fears, lack of comfort, language barriers, and so on), we can acknowledge them in ourselves and then take advantage of them in others. Paraphrasing Warren Buffett, when others are fearful, that is the time to be greedy. This chapter and the next are about how to do this.

It turns out that colliding markets create lots of new biases. And reputation is my weapon of choice for taking advantage of them. Hence, in terms of negotiated deals, I consider this the second value key—reputable capital.

Note that Figure 6.1 classifies all these real and perceived "cross-border" risks as *cross-border inefficiencies and mispricings*. These are mispricings like any other—a deviation of price from true value—but they also can create significant hurdles to cross-border capital flows. Both the company mispricings and hurdles to capital flows can be targeted with a value approach.

That reputation has value in such situations should not be surprising. Deals and investments have always taken place in environments ʰere the rule of law is limited, from the American West in the ᵗo the Middle East in the 1980s, to Russia today. People just tend to do business with people they trust—family members, friends from grade school, and so on. And lots of marriages between the children of business partners occur. Relationships and reputation are the common solutions to increased instability. And if you're trying to do deals with new business partners, it usually requires building very close relationships with them (there is a reason why everyone goes out drinking together after every meeting in China and Russia). In many ways, Western investors have become overly reliant on enforceable contracts and the rule of law—and have somewhat lost their past abilities to build solid long-term trusted working relationships.

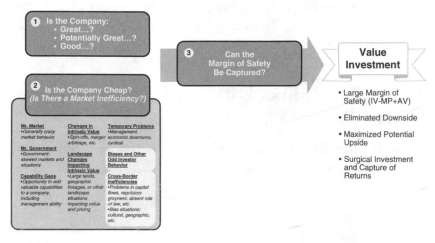

Figure 6.1   Biases and cross-border inefficiencies and mispricings

The most extreme cases of cross-border inefficiencies arise in deals between two emerging-market companies, such as China-to-Saudi deals. I call these "porcupine deals" because they resemble two porcupines trying very carefully to kiss. In these cases, rule of law, regulatory clarity, proper governance, and other standard controls are largely missing on both sides of the deal. The geographic, cultural, and language gaps are much greater. Even finding Arabic-to-Chinese translators for the meetings can be difficult. So when the two parties discuss potential deals, they encounter real structural problems, large perceived risks, little to no trust, and no professional or personal relationships to overcome them. In such situations, a highly reputable investor can enter and enable the deal to happen. Prince Waleed has referred to such situations as "openings." He has been very successful in targeting a number of them, including Middle East and North Africa (MENA)-USA, MENA-Africa, and MENA-China.

At the start of this book, I argued that investing in a new global century requires letting go of our view of the last one. This was an analytical argument about the need to rethink our value strategies, but it was also a psychological argument. It has a lot to do with recognizing our own psychological issues when confronted with fundamentally different investment environments. Although capital and trade have gone global fairly easily, direct investing remains overwhelmingly person-to-person. The increasing collision of markets and actors is creating a fairly fascinating new subtopic in behavioral finance.

The Room Looks Different Depending on Where You're Sitting

Cross-border bias impacts pricing, and risk is often a matter of perspective

Establishing the cost of equity is one of the more interesting calculations in global investing. When companies or investors from the West try to decide the cost of equity for an investment in a country such as Russia, this figure becomes the catchall for every bias and fear. Western investors might consider an investment in U.S. retail to have a 10% cost of equity but a similar one in Russian retail to carry a 20% to 25% cost. This calculation becomes particularly interesting when a deal involves partners from both the developed and developing markets, and everyone needs to agree on a common number. If you're operating worldwide, the cost of equity is often where the rubber meets the road in terms of behavioral finance.

For example, in 2004, Saudi Arabia opened a public bid for its second mobile telecommunications license. Mobile service is a business that functions particularly well in emerging markets. The networks are highly scalable and cell phones are now relatively cheap. Mobile service tends to be good at quickly capturing revenue from large populations of low-income consumers, often scattered de geographies with limited infrastructure. A good example is China Mobile's recent extension of service to the countryside (China's lowest-income population). In 2007 alone, their users increased by almost 100 million, from 332 million to 414 million, mostly from this extension to the countryside. And with the advent of prepay service, the billing and nonpayment problems of developing economies can also now be managed fairly effectively. Plus, governments often issue only two or three licenses, so it is one of those government-skewed markets with artificially limited competition. You can actually get a competitive advantage from the government regulation, the network effect, and the local economies of scales—a competitive advantage *tri fecta*. As a result, mobile service companies in developing economies are businesses everyone is trying to get into.

As the second Saudi mobile license was put up for auction, Prince Waleed became interested and started putting together a joint venture to make a bid. Given the technical and operating requirements, many of the local bidders looked for European partners and Kingdom Holding Company decided to partner with Spain's Telefonica. But this meant that Kingdom Holding and Telefonica had to jointly determine what price to bid for the license, and this raised the cost-of-equity question.

Viewed from Spain, Saudi Arabia is a risky market. It's far away. It's not the most pleasant place to be. Nobody speaks Spanish. The cost of equity could be 15%, 20%, or 25%.

However, Prince Waleed has been doing business in Saudi Arabia for 30 years and did not consider it geographically or politically risky. In fact, many investors with experience in the Middle East consider it to be one of the safest, most stable places to do business. It is worth noting that during the recent financial crisis, Spain was designated as one of the financial PIGS (Portugal, Ireland, Greece, Spain) while Saudi Arabia was barely impacted. The cost of equity for Saudi companies doing business in Saudi is more like 10% to 12%. What is the right cost of equity for a Saudi–Spanish venture?

The mobile license was eventually awarded to Etihad-Etisalat, the United Arab Emirates (UAE) mobile operator. Its high bid had a lot to do with how it viewed Saudi Arabia as a strategic market. But the fact that the highest bid was made by a regional company is telling. Similarly, a Kuwaiti Mobile Telecom Company (MTC)-led consortium later won the bid for the third Kingdom of Saudi Arabia (KSA) mobile license in 2007. How risk is perceived by local versus foreign companies is an important question. This is also a reminder that in emerging markets, public equities and open bids attract too much attention and capital. Hence, value point's focus on privately negotiated transactions, in both private and public equities.

In global investing, how things look really does depend on where you are sitting. There can be dramatically different perceptions of risk between Spain and Saudi Arabia in a way you would never see between New York and Texas, or between Canada and the UK. By separating these risks into the real and the psychological, we begin to uncover the actual stakes in a particular investment.

The Disproportionate Bias of Western Investors

Western investment approaches to perceived "risky" markets tend to follow a common pattern. Either investors and companies avoid developing markets (they avoid the risk by avoiding the market), stay in public stocks, or stick to short-term plays. Western interests notoriously (in my point of view) shy away from longer-term private investments, which unfortunately is where most of the value opportunities are. And when they do enter a private partnership, they typically take a noncommittal position (franchise fees up front, minimal capital at risk, exit, or IPO in two years). All of this runs counter to what I believe is Graham/Buffett's greatest lesson: that you acquire wealth through the long-term growth in economic value per share.

In a 2010 discussion, the newly appointed head of international investments at Apollo Management described how the firm was struggling with the question of how to break out of its current situation of having 90% of its investments in the United States and Europe, when the firm's long-term goal was to balance its portfolio between international and domestic markets. This meant going into developing markets. It also meant dealing with a U.S.-based investment committee whose members had little experience outside of Western markets.

The more common approaches to this going global problem typically include the following:

- Making short-term investments in overseas public markets. This is not a bad first step and is one I recommend in the global investment playbook detailed in Chapter 12. It expands one's circle of competence and can position an investor to later move into private opportunities. But as mentioned, emerging-market public markets are often considered the "dumb money," so this approach has its own risks. And most overseas public markets are still characterized by too few companies and too much money.

- Buying Western or Japanese stocks that have significant exposure to developing economies. This is fairly logical, but it can also result in swapping a perceived developing-market risk with a real increase in uncertainty. Most multinationals break out little detailed information about their developing market activities.

- Investing in the inputs, particularly natural resources, for high-growth economies. China is usually the primary target of this strategy. It is one of the largest sources of global growth and is very low in domestic resources.

- Investing in a fund of funds between the developed and developing economies, thereby connecting global capital with local investment talent. Again, this is a possible first step to direct private investing but seems a bit indirect.

All of these methods strike me as conspicuously contorted and awkward attempts to stretch out from what is already comfortable. In the West, if you like a company you just buy it. Why such complications elsewhere? As the investment world gets more global, more and more Western investors seem to be either contorting themselves or reflexively throwing more and more opportunities into the "too hard" bucket. These perceived risks, particularly a feeling of "foreign-ness," are powerful and surprisingly resilient.

This is ironic, because value investors are supposed to be the experts at identifying biases. But clearly, significant psychological biases exist in the investor community when going global. It is often possible to predict how a Western investment group will act or where it will pursue deals simply from the cultural backgrounds of its staff. If a group has employees of Chinese descent, it typically expands to Asia and seems to end up in Hong Kong. If it has employees of Indian descent, it gravitates to India. And if it has mostly employees who don't speak a second language, it seems to end up in India, Dubai, or Singapore. The pattern is conspicuous. At what point does a circle of competence become an excuse to stay with what is comfortable?

The strategies presented here are a departure from and almost a reaction to this pattern. It's a back-to-basics, or back-to-Graham, approach in which you return to Graham's original methods, take out a blank piece of paper, and start from scratch.

From this, my conclusion is that the most attractive wealth-creation opportunities in a new global age are *direct, value-based, long-term investments that capture growth in per-share economic value*. It is the strategy that appears to be the most lucrative and to offer the greatest number of opportunities. Ironically, it is also the strategy that most Western-based investors seem to fear the most.

Reputation Lets Your Capital Punch Above Its Weight Class

Four ways in which reputable capital can help investors

For investors hunting for deals in a global landscape, capital with a good reputation is a real strength. It can create advantages at the deal level and occasionally add value at the company level. So I have designated reputable capital as a second value key, as shown in Figure 6.2. Not only can an investor use this to get preferential access to deals, he or she can also add value to them and take advantage of many of the mentioned biases. If your reputation is strong, your capital will be valued more. It's that simple.

GE, which has arguably one of the world's best corporate names, is a good example of the value of reputation in global investing and deal-making. GE Money, the consumer finance arm, has been particularly successful at making direct investments across Asia, the Middle East, and Eastern Europe. Recent investments and deals have included local banks and retailers in Turkey, Spain, and the UAE.

And they are very much in demand in other emerging markets, such as Africa. If you are a medium-sized company, in Kenya or Latvia, an investment from international brand name GE, the company of Thomas Edison, is very attractive.

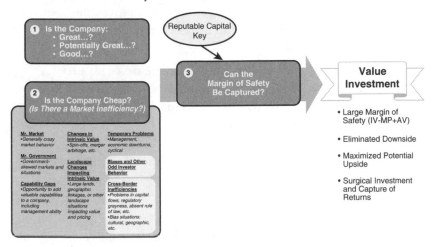

Figure 6.2   The reputable capital key and cross-border inefficiencies

Another recent example is Warren Buffett's 2008 investment in Shenzhen-based BYD, China's largest maker of batteries and possibly one day, electric cars. BYD is one of those stories that wakes up Westerners to how much the world has changed in the last ten years. Founded in 1995 by Wang Chuanfu, the company grew to 100,000 employees in less than 15 years. And it has achieved a dominant and defensible competitive position in batteries. It commands more than 50% of the global market share for cell phone batteries, which I suspect was more important to Buffett than its cool but technology-dependent electric cars.

But BYD is also a tightly held company, run and primarily owned by its founder. Chairman Wang has openly stated that he agreed to sell part of the company only because of Buffett's unique reputation. Even then, he denied Buffett's request for 25%, and agreed to only 10%. It was a classic Buffett value investment, but getting access was mostly about reputation.

In terms of the uncertainty language presented, reputable capital as a value key can have the following uses:

1. **Increased access to deals.** As in the GE and Buffett examples, this is the most common use and is an amplified version of being perceived as the buyer of choice.

2. **Decreased negotiated entry price.** Occasionally, you can secure a lower price on an acquisition or an investment stake—a "reputation discount"—but a good reputation is mostly about limiting the number of competing bids.

3. **Greater intrinsic value for the asset or company.** A reputable company buying into a target can occasionally increase the target's value. News Corp.'s recent investment in Rotana, a Middle Eastern media company, will likely increase Rotana's economic value due to the impact that News Corp.'s reputation will have on attracting artists. Such a reputable partnership also likely won't hurt if the company IPOs next year in Dubai.

4. **Potential advantage when competing for deals.** This type of advantage works on both sides. Not only do reputable investors have an edge, but a highly reputable emerging-market company typically is in a very strong position when dealing with foreign suitors or partners.

These advantages can be seen in the value framework shown in Figure 6.3.

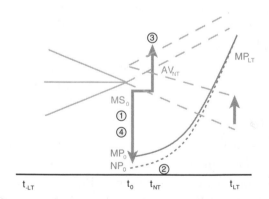

Figure 6.3   The uses of reputable capital

The most impressive example I know of the use of reputable capital was in the 1990s, when Prince Waleed was one of the most liquid investors in the world. He conducted billions of dollars of high-profile negotiated investments in Western companies, including Citigroup,

Euro Disney, the Fairmont, the Four Seasons, and Canary Wharf. These deals, typically in the hundreds of millions of dollars, were happening almost every month at certain points. His approach was to buy into companies he described as "on their knees" or "down but not out" and to use his capital as his "ultimate weapon." In such distressed situations, the combination of capital and a very good reputation can be powerful in negotiated transactions. It was during this period that Waleed started to be widely described as both a "white knight" and a "Western bargain hunter."

You will note that in these discussions I frequently mix *company advantages* and *deal advantages*. A Saudi mobile service company likely has significant competitive advantages. Warren Buffett has deal advantages relative to investors with lesser reputations (effectively, everyone). Recall from Figures 6.1 and 6.2 that I always ask three primary questions about the quality of the company (#1), the price (#2), and the deal structure (#3). In this chapter, the reputation and the behavioral finance questions raised mostly impact the price (#2) and the deal structure (#3). The investor biases and cross-border mispricings as well as occasional "reputation discounts" are about getting a low price. The increased access and increased intrinsic value are about getting the deal and stabilizing the margin of safety. In the following chapters, this distinction between deal advantages and company advantages will become more important.

How to Create an Emerging-Market ATM

Reputable capital + political access = a powerful investment approach

Reputation and political access can be used separately with fairly good results, but when they are used simultaneously, the results can be truly impressive. In fact, the generated cash flow can sometimes be so great that it creates what I call an *emerging-market ATM*—a simple structure that just shoots out cash.

One example of an emerging-market ATM that is truly impressive in both its scale (and cash flow) is Prince Waleed's one-mile skyscraper in Jeddah (see Figure 6.4). Although the exact height of the tower is still being decided, it will likely reach well above .62 mile and possibly to 1 mile. This would make it approximately four times the height of the Empire State Building and twice the height of the Burj Dubai/Khalifa, currently the world's tallest building.

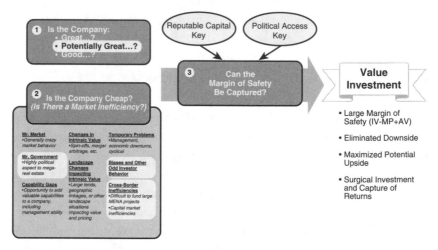

Figure 6.4   Waleed's one-mile tower

The mega-tower will be the centerpiece of a more than $10 billion real estate development occupying 3.2 square miles of land in northern Jeddah. The development is nothing less than the creation of a new modern city. It is the type of project that in many ways has come to symbolize the abilities and grand ambitions of the developing economies and their players.

Waleed's new city will occupy an entire peninsula on the Red Sea. Boats will be able to berth in a newly constructed Sydney-like harbor that will be excavated in the center of the development. Multiple skyscrapers and bay-front communities will line the new inland bay and the waterways that will bisect the development. On the Eastern inland side, visitors will enter via a grand skyscraper-lined thoroughfare similar to Park Avenue. And at the end of the thoroughfare, located on the harbor's promontory point, will be Waleed's one-mile golden Kingdom Tower. As far as I know, Waleed's new city is the grandest and most ambitious real estate development ever attempted.

A skyscraper of this magnitude raises some interesting design questions. In terms of buildings, it is a new animal, not just two or three stacked skyscrapers. Vertical transportation becomes more and more of a problem the taller you make the building, and entering and leaving the tower can easily take 30 minutes. Usable space is also an interesting question. At the base you can have 24,757 square feet net usable area per floor, but this decreases to 11,840 square feet by the 200th floor. So the top floors become less appropriate for office space and more appropriate for residential space. But this raises the question, do people really want to live 3,280 feet up in the sky? However, given the huge total volume, couldn't we build in large public spaces such as museums, parks, and shopping centers? As the project team went through the design process, we realized that the tower was starting to resemble a city in the sky more than a building.

Viewed this way, the "city in the sky" project offers interesting possibilities such as creating a museum in the clouds (Waleed is currently building a new wing for the Louvre in Paris), or putting multiple hotels in the building, or thinking about floating parks and lakes. It also creates unique problems such as rerouting air traffic from the nearby airport (the tower pokes into the airspace) and realizing that any fire escape plans may require giving people parachutes.

But this is a value investment from start to finish, and it's a fairly spectacular emerging-market ATM. Prince Waleed used both political access and reputable capital to buy a large piece of land, received approval to build an iconic tower (very political), and then pumped a huge amount of value into it at the time of purchase. The announcement about Waleed's intention to build the world's tallest tower caused the land price to surge.

From a distance, this project looks like a real estate development. But looking closer, one realizes Prince Waleed was operating as a solo investor and had no real estate company. In fact, he was doing something the local real estate companies could not. Using little besides reputation and connections, he was turning a land investment of hundreds of millions of dollars into a project worth billions. He was operating a value investor using primarily reputation and political access. The project is mostly an emerging-market ATM.

It was political access that enabled the purchase of such a large piece of land and secured the permission to build such large, iconic structures. And it was reputation that enables him to solve the secondary problem of obtaining the approximately $10 billion of capital needed for the development. In the U.S., this would have been difficult. In the more inefficient capital markets of the Middle East, it should have been next to impossible. All the factors previously discussed came into play: lack of trust, fuzzy contracts, side deals.

Waleed's unique reputation with real estate buyers, international investors, and local subdevelopers gave him access to required capital. In fact, Middle Eastern investors have been eager to put money into the project. Waleed's reputation became the solution to both the domestic and cross-border capital market inefficiencies.

The truly impressive part of this deal is that the whole thing was put together by a handful of people sitting in an office. During this period, *Middle East Economic Digest* published a ranking of the top ten real estate companies in the Middle East and Kingdom Holding made the list. I suspect the editors would be surprised to learn that the entire real estate division consisted of only a couple of people. It was really a value-added investment, consistent with Graham's Method.

It is important to note the low-cost nature of an approach built on connections, reputation, and capital. There are no physical assets to speak of, no specialists or teams of employees. These deals can often be done with one or two people in a single office, and the cash flows can be spectacular. The ATM seems to print money out of thin air.

Waleed looked at a variation on this same emerging-market ATM real-estate strategy in Shanghai in 2008. The proposed Shanghai development also included a one-mile skyscraper and the primary advantages brought to the deal were the same—political access and reputation. But the inefficiency targeted in this case was the much larger and much more political cross-border gap between Saudi Arabia and China.

For about five years, an unconsummated love affair has been going on between Saudi Arabia and China. The two countries are natural allies: One needs oil, and the other has lots of it. Officials on both sides, unsurprisingly have been looking for ways to build a closer relationship. But so far, their relationship has been limited to high-level summits and a few joint ventures between Saudi and Chinese state-owned enterprises.

The problem, in essence, is insufficient trust and history. Significant cultural and language barriers, as well as regulatory grayness, exist on both sides. And there is little in the way of working history or personal relationships with which to overcome these problems. The Middle East also suffers from a perpetual lack of skilled human capital, where virtually no business executives have any China expertise or experience.

The proposed Shanghai skyscraper project spoke strongly to the major political interests and to this persistent cross-border "gap." The idea was to do a large, symbolic project that would require truly unique political access—possibly a proposal from the King of Saudi Arabia to the President of China—and very large dollars, likely tens of billions. Not only would it be difficult to get a symbolic tower approved, but for the economics to work, the project would need a lot of surrounding land that could increase in value and offset the expected negative return from the $2–3 billion tower itself. The politics were both the problem and the advantage.

Assuming that the Saudi government could overcome the political hurdles, the next target would be the cross-border inefficiency between the Chinese and the Middle Eastern capital markets. Over the past 20 years, Middle Eastern governments and private groups have invested well over $500 billion in both the U.S. and Europe. But, as of today, very little GCC investment capital has gone into China. In fact, it is conspicuous and telling that while China has been one of the largest growth stories of the past 20 years, the GCC heavyweights, some of the world's largest investors, have almost completely sat it out. Opening the petrodollar floodgates, between the GCC and China is the holy grail of cross-border financing and is at least a $200–500 billion opportunity. But it would take the right group with the right project and the right connections to do it. Waleed's reputation applied to a highly political and very large real estate project could potentially be the solution.

This initial concept led to government meetings across Shanghai and Beijing to vet the idea. The most memorable of these was a meeting with the Shanghai Expo development group, the government group that oversees the 3.72 square miles of land being used for the 2010 Shanghai Expo. The expo site is actually the perfect location for such a project. It is in Pudong, close to Liujiazui and on the river. And they had already put in the basic infrastructure and connected it to the subway system, likely 30% to 40% of the project costs. After the 2010 expo, the site would be 80% empty, and they had no set plans for development at that time.

For the first 20 minutes of the meeting, it was clear that the expo management thought this project was ridiculous. The idea of a 3,280-foot tower was unheard of in China. But after hearing about the likely involvement of the Saudi Arabian government and a similar project underway in Jeddah, the expo management began to take the project seriously (many of Prince Waleed's projects begin with a process of explaining that you aren't crazy). In fact, the expo team immediately figured out the math and asked if 70% of the land would be enough. Basically, they recognized the value being added to all the adjacent land and wanted to keep part of it.

This project eventually got shelved as the 2008 financial crisis erupted. However, Prince Waleed quickly pivoted and moved forward with an even grander emerging-market ATM located 30 minutes outside of Riyadh. This real estate project, although lacking an ultra-high skyscraper, will likely cover 27 square miles, making it roughly the same size as Manhattan. The vision is to create a massive master-planned desert city and oasis that contrasts nicely with the rather drab state of Riyadh (think Scottsdale versus Phoenix). In the initial phases, it will likely contain 14,000 homes, a Four Seasons resort, and an adjacent personal camp for the Prince covering 1.16 square miles.

The investment strategy in all of these is the same: Use political access and reputable capital to surgically add huge value to a project, thereby turning both government-skewed markets and cross-border capital inefficiencies into capturable value opportunities. The key (really, the only) assets being used in these deals, which total more than $20 billion, are political access and reputable capital.

Such emerging-market ATMs can be seen regularly across the developing world. They are usually noticeable for the large cash flow they throw off and the investors they launch onto the world stage. And as the economic wealth of these developing countries increases, these types of negotiated deals are growing larger and more spectacular.

I suspect the reader now feels I have walked him/her quite a long ways off into the tall grass. Certainly building one-mile skyscrapers in China and the Middle East at first glance appears a long ways off from stock picking in the U.S. But going from Graham to Buffett to Waleed, and from traditional value investing to value point, is not really a trip at all. In practice, it is still a few investors sitting in a room following one consistently applied value strategy. Both Waleed's one-mile skyscraper and Buffett's BYD purchase can be simply laid out on the graphic presented.

And the feeling is important. There is something surprisingly resilient about geographic and cultural preferences. Buying a company in Texas from New Jersey just feels more comfortable than buying one in Kenya. But are geographic, cultural, and language factors really significant in your circle of competence? If you can value an insurance company in the U.S., can't you confidently value one in Africa? (By the way, insurance companies in developing economies are fantastic.)

A colliding world is full of such biases. But if you stick to Graham's Method, pursue a consistent value strategy, and stay within your circle of competence, it all becomes fairly easy and comfortable. And as a value investor, isn't the tall grass where you really want to be?

7

The Profits and Perils of Reputation

Both reputable capital and political access can create advantages for investors at the deal level, but they are somewhat intangible. And similar to intangible assets at the company level (brand value, goodwill, etc.), they can produce a very high return on equity. Two or three people with laptops, business cards, and connections can structure very lucrative deals—an "asset-light" type of deal-making.

However, this same "intangibility" also makes reputable capital and political access the most vulnerable in difficult environments. If you can compete for deals with no real concrete assets, so can your competitors. Just as brands and intellectual property can be copied much easier than a factory or building, so can deals done with these sorts of intangible advantages. As value keys, reputable capital and political access are both the most compelling and the most perilous.

Building advantages at the deal level is a topic Graham did not discuss at length in his writings. But for those of us value investing globally, access is almost always question #1. Getting preferential access to private investments or private investments in public equities has a large impact on deal flow and pricing. In Buffett's writing, deal advantages are also not discussed much, but clearly he enjoys a significant advantage in this area. That he can sit in his office and wait for the phone to ring, as opposed to actively bidding for deals, is a sign of a uniquely powerful reputation.

This chapter details various value strategies that rely on these types of intangible deal advantages. They are responsible for some of the most spectacular successes and failures of the last five years.

Institutional Investors on the Frontier

Reputable capital and political access are key assets for famous investment firms going global

Real estate investors and private equity firms are going east in search of growth. And although they sometimes use other capabilities, they are most often deal-makers using expertise, reputation, and capital. In this, they offer good test cases for reputable capital and political access strategies. Private equity firms in particular are good cases because, outside the West, they have shrunk their standard "leveraged buyout through distressed turnarounds" playbook to primarily growth equity. And most often they limit themselves to minority stakes in pre-IPO companies. In practice, this type of private equity looks a lot like traditional value investing with an overwhelming emphasis on discounting projected growth back to current intrinsic value. And also like global value investing, they face the same challenges with deal access, current uncertainty, long-term uncertainty, weakened claim to the enterprise, and foreigner disadvantages.

Looking at the successes and failures of these firms' global initiatives is illuminating.

Morgan Stanley Properties Rises and Falls in Shanghai

Morgan Stanley Properties opened its Shanghai office in 2006 with grand ambitions. The firm announced it would invest across all property types—publicly traded and privately held real estate companies, direct real estate assets, and direct developments. Having made its first investment there in 2003, a full Shanghai office and team were more of an acceleration than a new initiative. And by all accounts, the firm had some very successful initial years. It acquired multiple properties in Shanghai, including prominent commercial developments and redevelopments near Huaihai Road. And it comfortably pulled ahead of the local operations of Citi Property and Carlyle Group real estate.

But significant developments quickly buffeted, if not derailed, Morgan Stanley's ambitions. The first was that China discovered it no longer needed foreign capital for real estate; in fact, too much local capital was going into the sector. Second, Morgan Stanley encountered a surge in local competition. Local private equity firms, large real estate companies, private investors, various state-owned enterprises, and just about every other type of Chinese company started getting into real estate.

Morgan Stanley found itself less and less competitive at the deal level, particularly in sectors such as residential housing. Even in commercial development and redevelopment, where the firm's reputation and expertise gave it a bigger edge, it still faced serious challengers. After all, how do you compete for deals as a foreigner if the competition is mainly about reputation, capital, and political access? Within only four years, Morgan Stanley Properties Shanghai found itself in the situation you never want to be in in China—a foreign company with no clear advantage in an intensely competitive industry.

With state capitalist rules tilted against them, no real strong advantage to help win deals, and intensifying local competition, it was only a matter of time before a serious blow arrived. This appears to have now happened with the emergence of renminbi-denominated (RMB) funds. Companies using RMB funds have significant advantages, such as faster transaction approvals and an easier ability to access local debt. Not only has Morgan Stanley lost its main advantages in the face of intensifying competition, but its access to international funds is now almost a disadvantage.

This situation is not unique to Morgan Stanley Properties. Real estate investing in developing economies is mostly a competition for deals fought with reputation, capital, expertise, and political access. Most foreign real estate companies in hypercompetitive China now lack any significant advantage.

You'll recall how different Prince Waleed's approach was to Chinese real estate. Instead of trying to compete within the mainland market, he leveraged his reputation into a cross-border situation where it was more effective. He also focused on completing one or two very large deals where political access could be deployed more powerfully at a single point in time. This is in stark contrast to trying to play across the field and in every deal type long-term.

Currently, many foreign private equity firms are ramping up their operations in the Chinese mainland. Kohlberg Kravis & Roberts (KKR), Bain, and many others are migrating from Hong Kong into Beijing and Shanghai. But they will likely face the same key questions as the real estate investors. Reputation and capital currently are strong advantages at the deal level in private equity, but will they last? They are certainly much larger than any of the local private equity companies, and the major Chinese companies have not yet entered this space. But is there any reason to think they won't? At this point, reputable capital plus political access in the hypercompetitive Chinese market appears to be a necessary but not sufficient strategy—particularly for foreigners.

The Carlyle Group's Entry into the Middle East Leads to Gradual Success

The Carlyle Group entered the Middle East in 2006 with a similar splash. It opened a large office in the Dubai International Financial Centre, hosted a regional conference, and flew in British Prime Minister Tony Blair to speak. It was an impressive event, and most of the major families and investors from the region attended. But as the partners gave an overview of the company's history, there was really not much the attendees did not already know. Most had been targets of Carlyle fund-raising for decades.

In the midst of this event, a senior Saudi family head, who shall remain unnamed, stood and asked a pointed question along the lines of, "Why do you think you can succeed here? What do you do that we cannot?" It was a somewhat ornery but also fairly penetrating question. After all, the Middle East was not a new market, and the local companies and families had well-established systems for local deals. Plus, everybody had money. What exactly was Carlyle doing that they could not?

Middle Eastern players have been doing large deals, both locally and internationally, for a long time. They are quite comfortable buying real estate assets and doing private equity-type acquisitions in Europe and the United States. Cities such as London, Paris, and Marbella have extensive Middle East-owned real estate. And locally, the many family offices and conglomerates have been buying and selling assets easily, if not quickly, through well-established and mostly closed networks for decades. I've watched well-connected local investors sell tens of millions of dollars' worth of apartments in one late-night meeting over tea. Local cement factories and other industrial assets can sell in a day or two. If all Carlyle was bringing were capital and reputation, those were two things local companies already had in abundance.

The Carlyle Group's Middle East effort was not only competing with well-established family-type offices, such as the Olayans and the Rajhis, but it was also facing a host of newly formed local private equity firms, such as Abraaj Capital and Amwal Al Khaleej. The fight for private equity deals quickly became a fight between deal access— mostly political access—and specialized abilities and expertise. But everybody had a good reputation and lots of capital, and an active deal-maker could easily visit all the region's major cities in about four days.

Carlyle and the other international private equity firms quickly gravitated to deals where they could use their superior technical ability and international partnerships. Local firms quickly focused on political and family connections. And some, such as Amwal Al Khaleej, paired a private equity management structure with a network of politically connected owners.

The saving grace for Carlyle has turned out to be that most Middle Eastern investments are joint ventures between local companies and Western capabilities, such as brands, products, technologies, and management. It is a region with extensive overseas customers (oil, natural gas) and fairly limited local capabilities. Many, if not most, deals are cross-border, and that gives international firms such as Carlyle an advantage. In effect, Carlyle's reputation enabled it to be a recognized player from the minute it opened its Dubai office. But to remain competitive, the firm had to draw on other strengths and quickly recognize the need to do so.

I earlier presented a simplistic worldview in which I argued that most of the Middle East is godfather capitalism that is neither self-sufficient nor really that competitive. In such an environment, a strategy of political access plus reputable capital is likely enough to compete long-term. Drawing on foreign partnerships and capabilities helps as well. With this type of "asset-light" strategy, Carlyle can likely do well in Middle Eastern limited-competition godfather capitalism in a way it likely could not in hypercompetitive Chinese state capitalism.

Kingdom Zephyr Thrives on the Large, Developing African Continent

Kingdom Zephyr Africa Management, run by Tom Barry and Kofi Buckner, is a pan-African private equity firm based in South Africa. It was originally created through a unique joint venture between Middle Eastern investors and Western private equity professionals, both of whom were interested in broadly targeting Africa. Prince Waleed, who had been investing in Africa since 1996, represented the Middle Eastern investors, and Zephyr Management, L.P., which had been investing in Africa since 1995, constituted the private equity management. The resulting company, Kingdom Zephyr, has focused on growth equity, and its portfolio companies now cover the continent, including everything from turnkey power developers and small-scale consumer lenders to insurers and banks. It is an example of a foreign private equity firm using primarily reputable capital to thrive in a developing economy.

Unlike the Middle East and China, Africa has a significant lack of capital, an absence of particularly strong domestic competitors, and persistent cross-border inefficiencies. Adding to these challenges, investor bias toward Africa is very high. If German firms are somewhat hesitant to invest in Saudi Arabia or India, they are really hesitant to invest in Uganda. But the region is growing, prices are cheap, and really only 10% or so of countries have significant political problems.

In this sort of large geography, Kingdom Zephyr is in a likely sustainable advantaged position. It has a reputation that enables it to access both international and Middle Eastern capital. It can access deals anywhere on the continent. And it now has a strong deal history across industries, with no obvious impediments to industries going forward. As a strategy, it is leveraging reputation and capital in the short term while building scale and expertise in the long term.

All these situations boil down to the basic challenges for global value investors described in previous chapters. How do you get access? How do you deal with current and long-term uncertainties and instabilities? How do you deal with weakened claims against the enterprise? How do you overcome the foreigner disadvantages? In certain environments, these problems are larger than others. In most of these cases, it was deal access that was the primary challenge.

Reputation was a critical advantage—at least initially—in every case. However, investors who failed to realize that reputational and capital advantages can be lost over time encountered far greater difficulties.

Hong Kong, Dubai, and the Path of Least Resistance

A strong reputation can also create capital bridges

Reputation is more than a key for accessing deals in developing economies. It can also enable capital to move between disconnected geographies and investment groups. For example, Prince Waleed is seen not just as a reputable partner, but also as a bridge to Middle Eastern capital. Although he gets a warm reception almost everywhere, he gets a particularly enthusiastic welcome in places such as Kazakhstan, Kenya, and Mongolia. In these places, Middle Eastern capital can make a tremendous difference, and he is seen equally as a businessman, a prince, and a potential doorway to Middle Eastern petrodollars.

The importance of reputation in cross-border deals is an interesting quirk of global investing. We have become used to the idea that globalization makes money move fairly easily around the planet. Public markets, derivatives, commodity exchanges, and multinational banks have created a deeply interconnected financial system. Certainly, we are getting used to the increasingly frequent financial shocks that this interconnected system seems to deliver. But private deals are still done person-to-person and face-to-face on the ground. For large direct investments to happen between the U.S. and China or between the Middle East and Africa, there must be trust between partners. Going from domestic to global investing, trading seems to become more high-tech, but direct investing seems to become more hands-on and personal.

Asia Alternatives Management LLC, a fund of funds, offers an interesting example. It was founded in 2006 by Melissa Ma, Laure Wang, and Rebecca Xu and is based equally in California, Hong Kong, and Beijing. Asia Alternatives positioned itself as a solution to American institutional investors struggling to invest in alternative assets in the developing Asian economies (China, Vietnam, India, and so on). They positioned themselves as a trusted and reputable intermediary and a solution to this cross-border capital flow problem. The group quickly raised two funds and is now managing $1.65 billion.

In a sense, Hong Kong itself serves as a reputable capital bridge between Mainland China and the world. As recently as ten years ago, economists, public officials, and investors worried that Hong Kong would decrease in significance following its 1997 reentry into China. However, with Hong Kong sitting at a collision point between state capitalism and international capitalism, mainland companies found raising international capital much easier through private or publicly traded Hong Kong subsidiaries. For example, when China Resources Land, a $3 billion mainland Chinese conglomerate, wanted to raise foreign capital for mainland real estate development and acquisition, it launched a new Hong Kong subsidiary, Harvest Capital, for this purpose. Founded in 2006, Harvest, run by Rong Ren, launched both a $346 million international fund through Citigroup and a $500 million Shariah compliant fund for the Middle East through DTZ. Being based in Hong Kong and having reputable management and partners enabled them to become a capital bridge to the mainland. They rapidly raised an additional $1.2 billion in funds since.

In the Middle East, Dubai has played a similar bridge role to Europe and the U.S. As recently as 2003, it was uncommon to hear of significant European or American capital entering the Middle East. There were no headlines about The Royal Bank of Scotland Group (RBS) buying large amounts of Dubai's debt or GE making major private investments in Abu Dhabi. Local capital had similar difficulties moving freely within the region. Qatar investors were somewhat hesitant to invest in Dammam. Saudi investors were hesitant to invest in Lebanon. Money would move, but it was slow and inefficient.

Dubai changed this by establishing itself as a financial hub and by bringing investment professionals, bankers, and lawyers into the region. Dubai firms provided not only a trusted capital bridge to move money but also the brainpower to do it. With Dubai's rise, money began to move more freely (perhaps too freely) both within the region and between the Middle East and the West.

On an unrelated note, Dubai's rise as both a capital bridge and a service center for professional talent has had some interesting effects on the Middle East economies. The region is severely unbalanced, with the oil wealth in the Gulf Cooperation Council (GCC) contrasted with the poorer but more educated populations of Lebanon, Jordan, and Syria. As talent and money began to move increasingly freely throughout the region, countries such as Jordan and Lebanon increasingly found themselves losing their professionals to the GCC.

This situation came up in an exchange I had at the palace of the King of Jordan. King Abdullah and Queen Rania held a meeting at their home to discuss the state of Jordan's healthcare sector and to brainstorm possible initiatives. Improving healthcare, particularly private-sector healthcare, in a developing economy typically requires a sufficient and rising gross domestic product (GDP) per capita, a critical mass of healthcare professionals, and an effective regulatory framework. Jordan can put the right regulations in place, but the average GDP per capita is likely too low to support a full private healthcare sector at the current time. Compounding this problem is the fact that their professionals, who are particularly well educated, keep getting stolen by hospitals and insurance companies in the GCC.

Queen Rania asked whether Jordan could train more hospital managers and other professionals thereby leveraging Jordan's greatest asset—its educated population. This idea got the most support. In a bad turn of phrasing, I countered by claiming that if Jordan trained more staff, "someone like me" would simply fly into Jordan and hire them away. It would basically be a subsidy for Saudi healthcare. I believe the queen's exact reply as she wagged her finger at me was, "See, it's you. You are the problem!" I'm still hoping she was joking.

These sorts of cross-border bridges, whether at the company or geographic level, are all ultimately about reputation. The critical mass of reputable investors and institutions in places such as Hong Kong and Dubai is enabling capital to move in a way it has not previously. And in the process, we global investors have perhaps inadvertently answered an oft-discussed politico-cultural question: How do you reconcile deep but incompatible cultural traditions in a global world?

Many nonbusiness books have argued that the Middle East cannot really reconcile its deep cultural and religious traditions with the modern world. There is not a lot of common ground between the traditional Saudi-Wahhabi views of a desirable society and those found in Hollywood movies (or in much of Los Angeles in general). Similarly, it is questioned how Chinese state capitalism can reconcile itself with the requirements of international capitalism, such as free press and transparency. These sorts of questions contain an implied assumption that such differing politico-cultural viewpoints must increasingly interact and reconcile.

Both Hong Kong and Dubai demonstrate that such differing systems do not actually have to interact directly, let alone reconcile. The path of least resistance is to build parallel systems with cross-border bridges. Leaving on a plane from Riyadh to London, the women immediately uncover their hair, and the men all start drinking Johnny Walker Black. (It is rumored that on a per-capita basis, Saudi Arabia is the world's largest market for Johnny Walker Black.) Chinese business leaders work in one style in Beijing and then put on different suits and attend meetings with Western and Japanese bankers in Hong Kong. In all these cases, it turns out that walking between different worlds and ways of living has proven to be fairly easy and comfortable.

"Danger: Alligators. No Swimming. Survivors Will Be Prosecuted."

Never overestimate the life span of a reputational edge

This warning, sent to me by a friend, is reportedly from a sign next to a Florida river. It pretty accurately captures the feeling many foreigners have when doing business in China, Russia, and similar places. The competition is brutal. The rules are against you. And if you do manage to succeed, you will be punished (or, more likely, the rules will be changed on you).

Ten years after China joined the World Trade Organization (WTO), foreign life insurers have less than 6% of the market. Foreign property and casualty insurers have less than 1%. Citigroup and the other foreign banks constitute less than 2% of the Chinese banking market by assets and less than 5% by most other measures. In contrast, Goldman Sachs is arguably the most successful foreign financial firm in China. And it has recently come under significant media criticism for precisely that—for being too successful during difficult times. Survivors will be prosecuted.

These types of difficult environments are good test cases for reputation-based investment strategies. If a deal strategy based mostly on a reputational edge can work in China and Russia, it can work anywhere.

Chinese domestic management capability is improving and competition can emerge rapidly. In terms of competition, certain industries can be truly ruthless environments. You don't go to Kenya to compete in long-distance running, and you don't go to China to compete in industries such as restaurants and real estate. The combination of hypercompetition and a tilted playing field can be particularly brutal on foreign entrants.

However, per the central thesis of this book, this is not a criticism of the Chinese or Russian economic environments, but of strategies that fail to account for fundamentally different systems. Remember that the overriding concern of many such systems is economic growth, development, and advancing the living standards of their people. This is not necessarily the same thing as providing an equal playing field or being terribly concerned with private investment returns. How and when a reputable capital strategy is likely to succeed has a lot to do with understanding the environment.

Russia is generally less discussed but offers similar stories of the profits and perils of a reputable capital strategy. Additionally, we can see significant investor bias against Russia at the current time. But such bias can be an opportunity if you have the right strategy (i.e., you can eliminate the uncertainties and strengthen your claim). Russia's current focus on growth and modernization creates some fairly attractive opportunities for cross-border deals by reputable investors. The uncertainties can be eliminated through deal structuring against these objectives, and the impractical claims problem can be dealt with through tactics such as equity swaps.

The next two cases detail examples of both the profits and perils of relying mostly on reputation and capital advantages in such difficult environments. I detail the experiences of two very capable companies, Coca-Cola and Danone Group, which both entered China as foreign deal-makers using primarily this approach.

Both companies operate in consumer products—Coca-Cola in beverages and Danone in bottled water and dairy products. And entering China's growing market was a straightforward strategic decision for both companies. China is a "must-win" market for any beverage company with worldwide ambitions. Additionally, China's consumer-products market is largely free of the political forces that are woven into many of its other industries. Joint ventures are not required for market entry. Both acquisitions and joint ventures can be done with foreign majority control. Technology transfer is not much of an issue. At first glance, the Chinese consumer market appears free of many of the issues that Western companies often struggle with in state capitalist systems.

The beverage industry also has few specialized capabilities. True, Coke has its secret formula, but certainly other companies can make cola. Most successful brands are somewhat replicable, and there are few technology breakthroughs. The competitive advantages lie primarily in creating local economies of scales in the fixed assets (distribution, bottling) and captive customers (frequently used brands and products). But for all the surface similarities between the two companies, Coke and Danone had very different experiences in China.

Reputation and Capital Were Not Enough to Save Danone's China Venture

Groupe Danone gets wiped out in Hangzhou

French Danone entered the Chinese market in 1996 through a joint venture with the Hangzhou Wahaha Group, at that time a struggling beverage producer that had evolved out of a public school. Wahaha was emblematic of many domestic companies in the 1990s' nascent consumer market of Mainland China. It was quasi-government. It had launched a series of unsuccessful projects. It was struggling to find successful products while being severely limited in both capital and management ability.

Enter Danone, which had lots of capital and the right capabilities. Investing $70 million with another foreign partner, Danone (and foreign partner) secured 51% ownership of five joint ventures with Wahaha. Danone provided both needed capital and internationally successful products, and Wahaha provided needed local distribution and sales. Forbes characterized it as a "showcase joint venture" (see Figure 7.1).

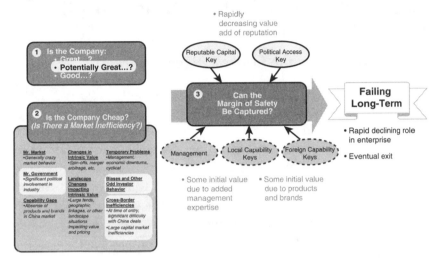

Figure 7.1   Danone Group in China

The deal effectively targeted Wahaha's need for products, management, and capital. But it took Danone's reputation to enter the Chinese market at that time and secure a joint venture with Wahaha, which turned out to be the ideal partner in many ways. Although there are large numbers of beverage companies with similar capabilities, it is unlikely that many other groups could have gotten such a deal at that time. I argue that it had as much or more to do with reputable capital than with the companies' products.

In fact, the Wahaha-Danone partnership would fulfill all expectations and grow into the largest beverage producer in China, ultimately containing 39 joint ventures.

Unfortunately, Danone's reputation, capital, and management prowess were not enough to keep the deal together. Within ten years, the joint venture fractured. Danone publicly accused Wahaha of creating copied products in separately owned companies under the Wahaha brand. Wahaha accused Danone of hampering its ability to succeed in the hypercompetitive China market. Lawsuits were filed starting in 2007, and Danone exited entirely in 2009. Before discussing the reasons for this, let me first summarize Coke's different outcome.

Coca-Cola Rides Its Reputation to 1.3 Billion New Customers

Coca-Cola wins in the future's biggest market

Some accomplishments in business really are impressive. The iPhone is truly a fun device. Being able to pay my New York Internet bill from my laptop in New Delhi really impresses me. I'm still not sure how Starbucks has convinced me to pay $4 per day for coffee. And Coca-Cola's successful targeting and capture of 1.3 billion new Chinese customers is one of those business stories that is more impressive the more you know about it. You cannot find a village anywhere in China that doesn't have Coca-Cola. Even the small makeshift roadside stands and random individuals selling from the backs of their bicycles usually have Coke. You also have to give Coca-Cola special praise for arguably the cleverest name of any Western product in China. Not only is "Kou ke ke le" pronounced just like "Coca-Cola," but it also translates to "can drink and make you happy" (approximately).

Coca-Cola entered the Chinese market in 1978 through an agreement with China National Cereals, Oils, and Foodstuffs Corporation (COFCO), at that time the largest state-owned enterprise in the food industry. In the initial agreement, Coca-Cola was given permission to introduce its products into select cities and tourist areas, which was a fairly big step in 1978 China. It also built a sales force, provided bottling equipment, and constructed bottling factories, with the first factory completed in 1980 in Beijing. Over time, Coca-Cola built a wholly owned company for its products in China and partnered with multiple bottling groups (Swire Coca-Cola, COFCO Coca-Cola, and Coca-Cola China Industries Limited [CCCI]) for distribution. Coke's standard separation of its concentrate/marketing activities from its bottling/distribution activities proved critical for navigating the Chinese market over the long term. The bottling joint ventures involve a complicated and evolving mix of government agencies and Hong

Kong-based partners. But the concentrate business remains firmly under Coke's control at its Shanghai headquarters. This type of hybrid structure is discussed extensively in later chapters.

At the time of the deal, the approach was primarily based on political access and reputation. In 1978, every Chinese industry had government involvement, so partnering with COFCO was necessary to gain market access. Coke also provided management and products, but companies all over the world had similar capabilities. Even more than Danone, I argue that it was Coke's political access and reputation that enabled it to be the first foreign company to open the door to China.

And over the longer term, Coke did several things that Danone did not. First, it kept effective control over its management and operations, primarily through the separation between concentrate/marketing and bottling/distribution activities. Second, Coke rapidly built brand awareness and captured a large customer base. In Buffett's language, it captured a piece of Chinese "consumer minds." This is in contrast to the Danone-Wahaha enterprise, in which Wahaha sold products under its own name.

The lessons for global deal-making from Coca-Cola and Danone are that reputation and capital can be very effective at gaining access to deals even in the most difficult of markets, and that is sometimes enough. Both Coca-Cola and Danone entered deals using reputation and capital in a way that was an effective but short-lived advantage for both. That left them only two possible strategies:

- **They could have planned for an early exit.** Recognizing that they were in a weakening position, both could have arranged an IPO for their China operations. This is the strategy many private equity firms use in certain industries in China and Russia.

- **They could attempt to rapidly build an entrenched position,** such as strongly branded products, a large captive customer base, or local economies of scale. This is basically a race against the clock. You have to build a more sustainable and defendable competitive position before your current advantage declines. And this is somewhat difficult in basic product categories such as beverages. It is much easier to do in technology or cross-border situations.

Note that both of these cases depended heavily on three factors:

- **The type of landscape.** State capitalism is very different from godfather capitalism or international capitalism. Additionally, whether that environment has low or high management capability and competition can have a large impact. Danone's approach would have likely been successful in Abu Dhabi or India.

- **The type of enterprise.** Operating or "light" assets are harder to defend but have a higher return on equity. Fixed or "heavy" assets such as real estate are easier to defend but, absent an exit transaction, they have more difficult economics over time.

- **Timing.** Entering the market or asset at the right moment and understanding your likely timeframe for survival (short-term versus long-term) is critical.

You have probably noticed that I have blurred the lines between direct value investing and more strategic cross-border deal-making. Clearly, Coca-Cola and Danone were focused on a strategic objective and not a value strategy. But in practice, many of the issues in negotiated deal-making are the same whether done with a strategic or value approach. Coca-Cola and Danone were both primarily struggling with how to access an opportunity and then how to deal with a weakening claim to the enterprise.

This blurring of the lines between traditional value investing and more value-added deal structuring is central to value point. In the basic framework, this is reflected in Question 3: Is the margin of safety capturable and sustainable? Getting a yes answer to this question in the short-term and long-term (and thereby eliminating the long-term downside uncertainty) often requires deal structures and strategies similar to those seen in the Coca-Cola case.

Emerging-Market Shenanigans

Political access and reputable capital deals are prone to shenanigans

Many emerging-market businesses and entrepreneurs long ago realized that foreign and multinational investment dollars are often much larger than the profits they can make with their actual businesses. As a result, over the past 20 years, a very sophisticated and complicated set of structures has evolved for fleecing foreign investors out of their capital. The complexity and creativity of the fleecing techniques is actually quite impressive.

All this falls under the fairly entertaining topic of emerging-market shenanigans. If disreputable Western companies such as Enron fleece investors with accounting gimmicks (accounting shenanigans), disreputable developing-market companies do so through clever deal structures with foreigners. And foreign investors who are overly reliant on reputation and capital are particularly vulnerable to this problem.

A common assumption throughout this book is that in many economic systems, investments that directly or indirectly rely on the rule of law and contracts, let alone minority shareholder rights, have additional uncertainties—and therefore unknown risks. Contracts can be broken. Political winds can shift. I know of one Middle Eastern company that, after partnering with an overseas group, simply stopped answering the phone when they called. And investments relying on "intangible advantages" such as political access and reputation are the most susceptible to the various emerging-market shenanigans. As discussed in the next chapter, the more tangible advantages (technologies, customers) are much less susceptible to these problems.

The topic of emerging-market shenanigans could likely be a book in its own right. And the list of investors who have fallen prey to some of these shenanigans is long and prestigious. The following sections present two of the more common ones.

Shenanigan #1: The Long-Term Squeeze-Out

I have presented a few examples of situations in which foreigners invest and then are slowly pushed out of the venture. This results from a changing power relationship between the parties over time, although it usually appears on the surface as a dispute about something else. A fight of some sort is provoked. A regulation is changed. Or a party is simply pushed aside and ignored, gets frustrated, and lashes out (creating a rationale for responding) or leaves on their own.

These sorts of squeeze-outs are described at length in Tim Clissold's book *Mr. China*, which chronicles the adventures of Jack

Perkowski and his $500 million China fund. In deal after deal, he ran into trouble post-investment, finding himself in a weak position and struggling to keep control and ownership of his investment. In most cases, he was squeezed out, pushed aside, or ignored by the local partners.

Mr. China is actually a good Rorschach test for global investing. Western investors and deal-makers reading the book always comment on how badly the local partners behaved. However, developing-market investors always comment on how naïve the foreign investors were. I tend to side with the developing-market opinion in this. If you leave your front door wide open every day, eventually someone will enter your house and take something. If you make passive minority investments in China or Russia using the strength of your reputation, but with no real legal protection, there is a good chance you will get ripped off or squeezed out.

The long-term squeeze-out follows from the weak or impractical claims against the enterprise and a weakening advantage over time. The Danone case, and the Shanghai GM case in the following chapter, are both examples of this approach. I find it rare to talk at a conference in the West without someone bringing up a Chinese or Russian "horror story" of this type.

For value investors, dealing with a weakening claim to the enterprise over time is a central question. Adding sustainable value is an effective solution, and my preferred approach, but is not always possible. Using equity swaps, public shares, and other more liquid structures can also be effective. If neither of these methods is available, one needs to make an honest assessment of the investment landscape and how likely such an event is. Reputable capital is usually enough in the short term or long term in environments such as Africa and the Middle East. It's usually not enough in Russia or China.

Shenanigan #2: The Profit Shell Game

Moving profits among associated companies, usually with different partners and equity-debt structures, is not a new shenanigan. Many of the original American industrialists were very skilled at shifting profits between their railroads, steel factories, supplier companies, and so forth. Typically, the idea was to use certain vehicles to raise capital for projects and then push the actual profits to different wholly owned companies. It's basically a shell game, in which you constantly move around the profits, and the outside investor or partner never chooses the right one.

A multipolar world is particularly prone to this type of shenanigan. The legal structures are vague, governance is weak, and reporting is haphazard. Many of the corporate structures are naturally interconnected and complicated: state-owned entities, publicly listed projects, family conglomerates, trading companies, and overseas holdings. And in global investing, partners are often geographically distant from each other and the projects. This last factor can give rise to the feeling that "Heaven is high and the emperor is far away."

When raising money or launching projects, disreputable businesspeople gravitate with surprising speed toward the idea of starting a second associated company at the same time. What if we start a supply company and give ourselves the contract? What if we just take the subsidiary public? What if we sell that one asset from our company A to our company B? And so on. The profit shell game has many permutations.

The recent arrival of public markets and IPOs in many developing regions has fueled the use of this type of shenanigan. Russia, Kuwait, Shenzhen, Dubai, Saudi Arabia, and many other places now have public markets that make this sort of profit shifting easier. These markets often have fairly weak regulatory oversight. There are often few institutional investors relative to the retail market. And many companies view the public market as something to be taken advantage of. On one side, you see companies going public in unusual ways such as floating a minority of shares, floating specific subprojects, or floating funding vehicles. But to be fair, on the other side, you have investors taking similar advantage of the situation by rampant insider trading and frequent manipulation of stock prices.

In a typical IPO profit shell game, a minority share of a company or a newly created project company (sometimes little more than a business plan) is taken public, and capital is raised. But the majority owners (those who control the project) then push the profits from that entity to their other companies, and the public vehicle sees few to no profits. The public entity eventually declines in value, and the majority owners buy it back from the public at a discount.

A debt-variation on this abuse-the-minority-shareholders strategy is to raise equity for a subsidiary or other controlled entity and then subsequently load it with debt (which you can do with controlling interest). Not surprisingly, the company cannot bear the debt burden, so it defaults and must re-raise equity in a distressed situation one to two years later. Usually this is brought on by a market downturn, which is not uncommon in developing economies. But the public and minority shareholders often can't afford to reinvest or choose to walk away, so the majority owners buy it back cheap. In the clever cases, the majority shareholders act as both buyer and seller. In the really clever cases, the majority shareholders also own the bank that provided the debt.

❈ ❈ ❈

These are two of the more common emerging-market shenanigans. Note that they mostly, but not always, require majority ownership or control, so foreign investors who buy in with large dollars for minority stakes are a common target. As a general rule, it's always wise to talk to someone's previous minority partners. You figure out pretty quickly who you're dealing with.

Public shareholders are usually the second most common targets. A third group are corporate debt holders. This is a newer phenomenon, because many developing economies have just started creating bond markets. Similar to the opening of the public equity markets, people are finding ways to take advantage of the immaturity of these markets and their participants. In 2010, Western investment banks, such as RBS, that owned Dubai World's corporate debt were surprised to learn that most of the projects were not viable under any capital structure and that they didn't really have a sovereign guarantee. This was not a planned shenanigan, but it worked out about the same.

❈ ❈ ❈

Reputation can be a very powerful and profitable deal advantage. And the more uncertain and unstable an environment becomes, the more effective it can become. But similar to political access, it is fairly intangible, thereby both enabling a higher return on equity (ROE) on one's time and assets but also being more susceptible to problems over time. It's profitable but somewhat perilous.

8

Capability Deals in Theory

During the 18th and 19th centuries, it was the United States that was the emerging market. Nineteenth-century British and European investors viewed the U.S. as a large rising market, but also as a somewhat distant and daunting business and investment environment. Even though they did not use the term "emerging market," business trades of that time are full of references to the "New World" and the "American frontier." Other common descriptions include "violent," "crude," and "constantly spitting brown tobacco juice" (from British novelist Frances Trollope).

For investors, America's rise in the 19th century to an advanced nation can be viewed as a process of European and British capabilities migrating into a large new market. English law, manufacturing expertise, the printing press, foreign capital, and especially professional management were brought to the New World from the Old through tens of thousands of mostly small deals and investments. It was the investors and deal-makers who seeded the New World with the Old.

By the mid-20th century, this mostly unidirectional migration of capabilities evolved into a more dynamic exchange of American, European, and Japanese capabilities. New York hedge funds and Silicon Valley tech companies took their expertise to London and Cambridge. The budget airline model migrated from the American Southwest to London and Southeast Asia. Automotive capabilities traveled from Michigan to Tokyo. And in return, Japanese anime traveled from Tokyo to Hollywood (picking up Jackie Chan and Hong Kong wire work along the way).

Now, at the beginning of the 21st century, we are witnessing a repeat of this entire pattern. Investors and deal-makers by the thousands are moving Western and Japanese capabilities into China, Russia, Brazil, India, the Gulf Cooperation Council (GCC), and many other developing markets. Russian exploration companies are contracting with European engineering firms. Singapore's Tamasek and Abu Dhabi Investment Authority (ADIA) are hiring British bankers. China is connecting its continental economy using high-speed trains from Germany, Sweden, France, and Japan. Analogous to the capability migration from the Old World to the New, we are now witnessing a capability migration from the Developed World to the Developing.

Although these capabilities can sometimes be accessed at a distance, investors and deal-makers usually build them into the local markets. Indian hospitals may ship in General Electric (GE) MRIs and Kimberly-Clark operating drapes, but the management is now local. The hospital itself is likely designed and constructed entirely by local companies, and the medical service payments are made by local insurance companies using locally hosted, and increasingly developed, software.

For value investors and deal-makers, a world seen through the prism of capabilities requires a shift in posture. It requires a departure from the standard strategy of evaluating relatively complete and stable companies and then investing from a distance. Global investors quickly discover that developing markets and local capabilities are in motion. Therefore, companies and competitive dynamics are similarly moving targets. If one hospital chain in India puts in a McKesson software platform or builds an open MRI center, that can change the competitive situation for every other hospital in the city. Much of global investing is about understanding competitive dynamics relative to migrating capabilities.

I have argued that global value investing gets easier with the broader philosophy of the "search for the opportunity to add value." Adding value makes it easier to capture value in such uncertain and changing environments. Capabilities are the most powerful way to add value quickly.

Capabilities are the big guns of value point. Whether it's a brand, a technology, a business model, a natural resource or other, capabilities are value keys that investors can use to open the door to investments and surgically add value. An energy investment group that has access to a deep bench of European or American technology (solar, turbines, wind, deep-ocean drilling, etc.) will be able to access even the most tightly held private assets in most places. Capabilities can also have an outsized impact on the other going-global problems— eliminating current and long-term uncertainties, strengthening claims to an enterprise and overcoming foreigner disadvantages.

Rethinking value investing and Graham's Method for a changing global world, one of my early conclusions was that value investing today is as much about build-and-fix as it is about buy-and-sell. Investments follow as much from business strategy as from valuation and price. And because business strategy is industry-specific, the right combination of capability keys for a deal is also industry-specific. Investing between Las Vegas and Macau is overwhelmingly about gaming, entertainment, advertising, and human resources capability keys. For Carlos Slim, investing is about using his telecommunications and media capability keys to exploit opportunities in Mexico and the United States. Rupert Murdoch has chain-linked along his media capabilities (brands, publications, assets) from Australia to the UK to the U.S. (and now into emerging markets). Warren Buffett is exceptionally well positioned to extend insurance into India, the Middle East, and Africa (insurance scales nicely in lightly regulated, large-population, low-GDP-per-capita markets).

This chapter is a departure from the previous chapters' strategies, which focused on primarily intangible advantages such as reputation and political access. Capability-based strategies are the meat and potatoes of most global deals. They are also the real crossing-over point from value investing into more hands-on value point deal-making.

From the New to the Newer World

Global value investing requires understanding the movement of capabilities and how this impacts competition and profits

It may be in part myth, but the story goes this way: During the 1920s, some Dutch businessmen went prospecting in the newly formed country of Saudi Arabia. At that time, Saudi Arabia was a large and mostly empty desert kingdom, populated mainly by small villages and desert-living Bedouins. The government was run from a mud palace in Riyadh, and the House of State often consisted of a traveling caravan of camels. It is said that the small country's treasury was carried in the camels' saddlebags.

To say doing business in Saudi Arabia in the 1920s was an adventure is a fairly big understatement. The country was poor and uneducated and had one of the world's harshest climates—particularly the Empty Quarter, the large, unlivable stretch of desert that constitutes the eastern part of the country. It is rumored that at various points in the country's history, people were killed simply by taking them out and leaving them in the Empty Quarter. Argentina's Dirty War would later revive a variation on this tactic by flying people out and dropping them in the Atlantic Ocean.

What is known for sure is that the Dutch businessmen met with the young government of King Abdulaziz, the founder and first king of Saudi Arabia. And in 1926, Foreign Minister Prince Faisal (later King Faisal) traveled to the Netherlands on a diplomatic mission. Out of this, a joint-venture deal was struck that would create the first bank in what would shortly thereafter become the world's oil capital.

The joint venture made simple business sense. The country's residents kept their money in goats and camels (as assets) and in saddlebags (literally). The businessmen had banking expertise and the ability to create a relatively modern private bank. It was a deal based on capabilities. In 1926, they launched Saudi Arabia's first bank, called the Netherlands Trading Society, which acted as both a private commercial bank and the central bank for the country. This bank would eventually evolve into Saudi-Hollandi bank, still one of the country's top banks.

Twelve years after the launch of Saudi Arabia's first bank, oil was discovered in the Kingdom, and similar Saudi-foreign bank joint ventures followed quickly (Saudi-British Bank, Saudi-American Bank, Saudi-Fransi Bank). Such capability-driven joint ventures still dominate the Middle East business and investment landscape. Not only banks but virtually every Middle East business is a similar combination of local assets and Western capabilities.

This original Dutch stake in the Saudi-Hollandi bank was later bought by ABN AMRO and eventually was caught up in the 2007 Royal Bank of Scotland Group (RBS)-Barclays bidding war for that bank. While Barclays and RBS were fighting to acquire ABN AMRO, Prince Waleed and other Saudi investors were vying to acquire ABN AMRO's 40% stake of Saudi-Hollandi. Saudi banks are coveted assets, particularly when oil is more than $80 per barrel.

For investors and deal-makers on the ground around the world, very little discussion occurs about globalization, interconnected financial systems, and a "changing world order." Most of the discussion is about capabilities and their impact on competition and economic value. Most deals happening today between the developed and developing world, or between the New and the Newer World, are still quite similar to this long-ago deal between Dutch traders and Saudi royals.

At a 2010 New York conference, ConocoPhillips' CEO and Chairman James Mulva described its growth strategy as 50% organic and 50% inorganic, with most of the inorganic growth coming from these types of capability-driven deals. ConocoPhillips needs access to exploration, which often means building partnerships and other cooperative agreements with state-owned enterprises that control such resources. ConocoPhillips' strength in such resource deals is that it has technology that many developing economies need. These types of "resource for tech" capability deals are as common today as they were 100 years ago. Direct investing in much of the world often gets boiled down to these sorts of simple capability-driven deals.

Viewing the investment world through a prism of capabilities, three significant trends are apparent:

- Capabilities are migrating.
- Capabilities are consolidating.
- Business models are being transformed.

Capabilities Are Migrating with Increasing Speed

Emerging markets are not quite the same thing as developing economies. In emerging markets, the middle class is, hopefully rapidly, rising. Newly ascendant middle-class consumers are abandoning buses and bicycles and buying their first cars. They start to consider products such as braces and veneers for their teeth and services like auto detailing for their cars. This can result in unusual experiences in places such as Kunming, China, where you might get invited to go to the new drive-in theater (a 1950s-type car culture is all the rage in some places), and 20% of the adults will be wearing braces.

Thus far, the emergence of these markets and the advancement of their economies have gone hand-in-hand with an inbound migration of mostly Western capabilities. This process can be fairly inspiring, such as seeing the first private tertiary hospitals get built in second-tier Indian cities. (A note to my old friends from medical school: Private pediatricians now make more in Mumbai than in California.) Sometimes the inbound migration of capabilities can be a bit ridiculous, such as the recent opening of a massive Louis Vuitton building next to Sukhbaatar Square in Mongolia. The store, offering Mongolians "chic nomadism," is located approximately 300 feet from where General Sukhbaatar's horse famously urinated during a 1921 rally.

In smaller, godfather-type economies such as Qatar and Indonesia, this capability migration occurs primarily through joint ventures, technical arrangements, management contracts, and franchise deals. For example, Saks Fifth Avenue has franchised its Middle East operations. You can find a 7-Eleven store on almost every block in Singapore and Hong Kong. And Citigroup, prior to its 2003–2004 much-too-public withdrawal from Saudi Arabia (and subsequent effective blacklisting from reentering), had a very successful management agreement with and a 20% ownership stake in local Samba Bank (previously Saudi American Bank). Given the fairly limited local management abilities and competition in these types of countries, such arrangements tend to be long-lasting. The Saudi-Hollandi bank deal has lasted over 80 years.

In the larger developing economies such as China and India, this migration of capabilities usually is accomplished by cross-border development deals happening in parallel with domestic development. In China, foreign joint ventures in automobile manufacturing such as Shanghai-GM have been launched in parallel with purely domestic automotive companies such as Geely Automobile. Sometimes this parallel approach can occur within the same company. This naturally leads to issues regarding technology transfer and complaints of legal and illegal copying. A reporter for the *Wall Street Journal* in China recounted to me the story of one foreign company that was so tired of its technologies being copied that it created internal designs for a bogus, nonworkable machine. Within a few months, a local competitor had the designs and began trying to manufacture the machine. The competitor was even bold enough to go to the company to ask for help when it couldn't get the machine to work.

Sometimes capabilities migrate without any sort of cross-border deal or arrangement. Many of the leading companies in China, India, the GCC, and Brazil are copies of successful Western companies. Baidu is a copy of Google. Air Arabia is a copy of Southwest Airlines. Successful business models migrate as rapidly as capabilities. I know of one Macau group that flies to Las Vegas, looks at the various businesses around town, and then flies home to Macau and launches copies of them. Currently, Singapore is currently copying Macau's casino businesses in similar fashion.

Across the board, this migration of capabilities into developing economies is driven by powerful business rationales. For Western companies, these rapidly developing markets often represent their best, and sometimes only, opportunities for revenue growth. Some, like Coca-Cola, succeed. Other Western companies go after developing economies as a type of "Hail Mary" strategy when they are in weak or declining positions at home. Sometimes this works, such as T.G.I. Friday's and Hooters restaurants, which have conspicuously great locations in places like Beirut and Shanghai. However, more often this type of desperate emerging-market strategy fails, resulting in a phenomenon best summarized by Joe Studwell when he stated that China is the place "where American elephants go to die."

For local governments, this capability migration has a similarly powerful rationale. In smaller cities, such as Wuhan, Bangalore, and Brasilia, importing foreign capabilities is the fastest mechanism for growing the local GDP and advancing the standard of living. As Henry Kravitz has said about the China market, "They need everything."

For local companies, Western capabilities can create an important advantage in less advanced but often ruthlessly competitive local markets. Technologies, exclusive products, Western brands, and other capabilities can become competitive advantages if *you* have them and a competitive threat if your *competitor* does.

For example, in late 2010, Chinese car manufacturer Geely Holding purchased Swedish Volvo from its American owner, Ford Motors. The $1.5 billion cash and debt purchase (with Chinese PEs in the '60s to '80s, few foreign acquirees will accept Chinese stock) was widely described as part of the increasing Chinese outbound mergers and acquisitions (M&A) trend. And Geely Chairman Li Shufu has stated that the acquisition will "strengthen its presence in the U.S. and European markets." But according to Peter Williamson of Cambridge Judge Business School, the Volvo acquisition appears to be a deal focused not on international expansion but on bringing foreign capabilities back into Volvo's domestic market. It appears to be a capability deal, with Geely mostly focused on winning in the growing Chinese mainland market (Geely's 2009 revenue had increased 228% year over year). Plus, with Volvo losing $2.6 billion over the previous two years and 13-year-old Geely's revenues only at $14.1 billion, I would be surprised if Geely didn't quickly shut down Volvo's international operations and move everything to China. Geely has already announced a new factory in Beijing for Volvo models. Whether this will be a base for increasing international or domestic sales will be an interesting question to follow.

However, this migration of capabilities is not all positive for Western companies. Since 2006–2007, emerging economies such as Morocco and Mexico have increasingly started reaching out to China and India, instead of the U.S. and Europe, for new capabilities. Chinese products such as cars, cell phones, and white goods are in many ways more suitable to these low-GDP-per-capita environments than American and European products. Cheap Chinese point of sale (POS) machines are more suitable for small retailers in Latin America than National Cash Register Company (NCR) or IBM machines from the U.S. In addition to being cheaper, they are more suitable for environments where infrastructure, education, and distribution may be limited. Stand-alone solar panels that can heat an individual apartment's water supply are common across many emerging markets and increasingly are coming from China. Compact, low-energy Haier washing machines are similarly becoming widely used in Africa and Latin America. These emerging-market-based companies have realized they possess advantages in reaching low- and moderate-income customers in other developing nations.

Within this trend, an increasing source of profits for developing-market companies is turning Western technologies into commodities and then exporting them internationally. Although GE turbines or Qualcomm CDMA (Code Division Multiple Access) chips are the core technologies in power generation and non-GSM (Global System for Mobile Communications) mobile service, a lot of the surrounding technology has already been commoditized by Chinese and Indian companies. Huawei, the Chinese telecommunications equipment manufacturer, produces most of the equipment for mobile service networks. Unsurprisingly, it uses its large scale and low labor costs to offer this surrounding equipment at a low price. Huawei already has opened centers and offices in Stockholm, Dallas, Jakarta, Bangalore, Moscow, and Ireland. As a result, mobile service providers in Kuwait might buy their core GSM or CDMA technology from the U.S. or Europe but virtually everything else from Huawei, now the world's #2 telecommunications manufacturer. Of Huawei's $21.5 billion in revenue in 2009, $3 billion came from the Middle East alone.

You can see a similar capability migration in the power-generation business. Companies might buy their turbines from GE but purchase all the ancillary equipment from Indian and Chinese companies. For those of us watching capabilities move across borders, the question of whether to draw from the U.S. and Europe or from China and India has changed in the last several years.

Capability Consolidation Follows Migration

Moscow supermarkets are mostly owned and operated by Moscow companies, and St. Petersburg supermarkets are mostly owned by St. Petersburg companies. This type of geographic fragmentation is common in certain types of industries, but also at certain stages of economic development. The economic integration of a country or region and the consolidation of its industries requires, among many other things, rising wealth, sufficient infrastructure (which requires lots of capital), and favorable government policies and management. China is particularly good at deploying infrastructure (total highways reached 40,389 miles in 2010, with about 3,106 miles added in 2009), and you can see a rapid consolidation across most industries in China today. In contrast, India is grappling with the realization that chaotic government and an inability to improve infrastructure is fundamentally limiting the country's growth, particularly relative to China.

For investors and deal-makers, if capability migration is the first step, capability consolidation is the second. Not only do you have capabilities migrating in from developed economies, but you also have capabilities migrating within an economy. High-quality, technically proficient banks and hospitals unsurprisingly start to consolidate, and regional banks and hospital chains emerge. In industry after industry, you can see a process of initial development, followed by consolidation, leading to captured efficiencies, and then ultimately to competitive distance for the market leaders. Chinese M&A is currently transitioning from the inbound development deals of the last decade to a new wave of domestic M&A.

Consolidation, like migration, is driven by competitive considerations. The initial competitive drive to capture new capabilities is followed by a competitive drive to capture operational efficiencies and build scale.

However, for the investor, both fragmentation and consolidation can be your friend. We can do direct investments at both stages of the process with a value approach. I know of one investor who, while operating in a highly fragmented unmentioned country, effectively built a carry-trade around beer distribution. By setting different payment terms in different, largely disconnected regions, he was able to capture a carry city by city as he distributed the beer. The drawback of such fragmented economies is that you sometimes have to worry about things like bandits and highway robbers (true story).

Capabilities Enable Business Transformation

Moving a factory to Vietnam or a call center to Manila is something that the West pays attention to. Whether it's because it has an actual impact on employment or because it's a good way to scare people (and that's a good way to sell newspapers and get votes) is debatable. But outsourcing and offshoring are two strategies that are surprisingly well known in the U.S. public, media, and government circles.

Offshoring and outsourcing are capability strategies. They are a subset of a much larger and more important strategy: *drawing on worldwide capabilities to transform business models*. As the worldwide mix of capabilities continues to evolve and migrate, you can leverage them into new types of business models and attack established competitors. How much of the success of Walmart's low-cost retail business model is due to its use of low-cost Asian manufacturing capabilities?

Within the West, transformative business models are most commonly the result of a new technology or the falling cost of an old technology. The emergence of Internet commerce (a new technology) and the falling price of the DVD (an old technology) enabled Netflix to create a transformative business model that brought down market leader Blockbuster. Not surprisingly, shipping cheap DVDs from a central warehouse has a far higher return on invested capital (ROIC) than building, stocking, and operating stores across the country. But this sort of transformative business model is within a developed economy—American technology changing an American competitive dynamic. I am focused on leveraging the changing mix of worldwide capabilities into mostly local business models.

The most important characteristic of a multipolar world is that many of the rising systems are fundamentally different. They are new animals in terms of economics, demographics, and government—and also in terms of the business capabilities they add to the world mix.

China and India, given their large scale, low labor costs, and low-income domestic consumers, have fundamentally new types of capabilities. Leveraging these resources into American retail enabled Walmart to decimate competitors across the country.

Using low-cost emerging-market capabilities to transform Western industry is just one approach. Drawing on global capabilities to transform industries *in emerging markets* is far more interesting. Remember, I am an investor looking to structure an investment, not a multinational thinking about strategy and operations. I am looking for tools to access closely held deals, to overcome foreigner disadvantages, to strengthen my claim to an enterprise, and to hopefully add rapid value to the asset value or earnings power value of a company.

We see such emerging-market business transformations frequently. To much fanfare, Western casino moguls such as Sheldon Adelson and Steve Wynn entered Macau following its 2002 reopening. But they did not just replicate Las Vegas in Macau. They reconsidered the gaming and entertainment business models. No longer limited by American labor costs, construction costs, or revenue models, they reimagined what a casino could be. Whether it is America's reliance on technology to make expensive staff more productive or Saudi Arabia's reliance on low-cost Asian labor and Western management to compensate for weak domestic human capital, it is important to be aware of how many of our business models are based on what was previously possible. If I can get government permission to master-plan an entire city and can access much cheaper construction, why can't I build a profitable one-mile skyscraper? Why can't I increase our casino staff by 300% in Macau? What impact would that have on a luxury service business?

For example, in 2007, the $2.4 billion Macau Venetian resort opened with 3,000 rooms and gambling and casino services on a scale never before seen (total gaming space exceeds almost 550,000 square feet. Not only does it have the world's largest gaming space, it also claims to be the largest building in Asia and the second-largest in the world (after the Boeing Company plant in Washington state). Plus, by drawing on staff from Asia, Australia, and the West, they have increased both the scale and the service levels of the casino business. The Venetian is a reimaging of the casino business model based on assembling a best-of-breed combination of global capabilities. This has not gone unnoticed by nearby Singapore, which in 2010 opened its first casino, the Marina Bay Sands, in response. In its first 6 months of partial opening, the truly spectacular $5.5 billion facility logged more than 5 million visits.

With this same transformative approach, Middle Eastern developers pioneered a new field that caught the world's attention: mega real estate. The developers took advantage of uniquely emerging-market capabilities: low labor costs, active government involvement, low construction costs, foreign customers, and an ability to master-plan very large areas. With this they transformed hotel, real estate, and convention center business models. Why can't I make a sky-scraper that rotates? Why can't I build multiple harbors and water-ways within my development and put the hotel under water? In fact, why can't I build palm-shaped developments out into the water and double the city's coastline?

Although Dubai's recent debt crisis has resulted in some blanket criticism of its mega development projects, it would be wrong not to recognize how much the country has redefined what is now considered to be a premier real estate project—and how much success it has had. As a business environment, it is more dynamic and much nicer than most American or European cities. Plus the advantage of a bankruptcy after a real estate binge, particularly with excessive leverage, is that the fixed assets remain. The buildings and infrastructure are still there. We know what Dubai built with its excessive borrowing; where exactly did all that money go in Greece? If they had the choice, I suspect the European Union (EU) would likely abandon Greece and adopt Dubai.

The Madinat Jumeirah development, located on the Dubai coast between the well known Burj Al Arab sail tower and the first (only?) completed Palm Island is an example of mega real estate as a type of transformative business model. In addition to being a fairly spectacular development, the Madinat is also a particularly effective attack on the European corporate conference and retreat business market. Large and medium-sized European companies frequently host corporate conferences and retreats where they might send employees to hotels and conference centers for a weekend or even weeks. In European cities such as London and Paris, this can be particularly expensive, and going to cheaper locations outside the city centers is just not that exciting. However, sunny Dubai is a short flight away, and the large hotel and shopping complexes in the Madinat offer a facility, level of service, and price unmatched by European hotels and centers.

Designed by Mirage Mille, the Madinat's facility is the type of mega real estate project that typically shocks Western visitors. Its design vision was to re-create life along the historic Dubai Creek, including waterways, wind towers, and a souk. It's a compelling value proposition to foreigners: More than 600 hotel rooms are typically 30% occupied by large European companies holding conferences and retreats (the remaining rooms typically are occupied by Middle Eastern and Russian tourists). Similar to the Venetian, it's a transformative business model that uses a best-of breed combination of capabilities: lower cost, larger scale, sunny location, higher service levels, and iconic architecture.

This view of the world as a sea of migrating, consolidating, and occasionally transforming capabilities is a bit strange for a value investor. But such capabilities play a central role in the rapidly evolving competitive dynamics of developing markets and cross-border situations. It is a crossing over from investing to more hands-on deal-making and using capabilities. Such deals can almost be thought of as corporate raiding in reverse. Instead of buying companies to break them up or sell off assets, we buy companies to add assets. But as detailed, the advantage of developing economies is that this can be done in a surgical fashion that meets all of Graham's criteria.

Most Capabilities Are Local

The movement of capabilities is driving increasing localization

Sitting in a Kunming café one night, I chatted up a local businessman who had just joined a local auto service start-up. Being somewhat of a one-interest person, I began digging into his business. The company was being positioned as the first servicing and detailing business for luxury cars in the Yunnan Province. He cited the increasing numbers of Lexus and Mercedes being purchased by people in this quiet (relatively speaking) part of Western China. The strategy was to capture these luxury car owners by offering frequently used repair and detailing services at specially created centers in the major nearby cities, such as Lijiang, Dali, and Chengdu.

Although there are glamorous dreams of globalization, this Yunnan auto service company is a far more accurate symbol of the future. The company will repair and detail luxury cars made domestically and sold locally. The facilities will be of international quality and use highly trained local staff. It is run by local MBAs, many of whom are serial entrepreneurs in the region. It is symbolic of globalization in that it is a local service business of international quality run for local customers. Its strategy of building local economies of scale and a captive customer base with frequent visits (a sustainable competitive advantage) is the same approach you would see in the U.S. or Europe.

If you spend enough years on the ground looking at companies around the world, a fuzzy but consistent macro picture emerges. Going geography by geography, industry by industry, and company by company, the investment world looks mostly local, albeit with some interesting interactions (capital, trade, capabilities) among the different localities. There are certainly industries where the competition is truly worldwide (cars, cell phones, laptops), but these are the minority and often have the lowest profits. (For the value-crowd, the less competition the better, so we are especially wary of global indutries.) Looking at companies' fundamentals around the world, it is overwhelmingly about competitive dynamics, and this results in a mostly local or multilocal worldview.

A mostly local worldview is a stark contrast to most globalization talk today, especially "the world is flat" idea. Thomas Friedman's argument is that globalization has made the world a more level (that is, flat) playing field and that there is now increasing competition between companies in previously unconnected geographies. This is clearly true for a handful of industries, such as information technology and automakers—and it reflects the worldview of many multinationals.

But as a value person, I am interested in a worldview based not on competitive possibilities, but on competitive strengths. It's not whether a company in India can compete with a company in the U.S.; it's whether that company can win (and whether it can win consistently over the long term). The defining dynamic of the global age is not communication, it is competition, which is overwhelmingly about local strengths, such as captive customers and local economies of scale. Hospital CEOs, bankers, and lawyers in Shanghai simply don't worry about what's going on in New York. The largest distributors and retailers in Bangalore are not threatened by Walmart in the U.S., and vice versa. I ask the reader, in your particular business, be it healthcare, broadcasting, media, book publishing or whatever, how concerned are you about Brazilian, Chinese, or Indian competitors? Is your world flat? Or is it mostly the same as it's always been? Much of the globalization talk falls into this type of situation—compelling in theory but not really seen in reality (or in the data). To practitioners, the business and investment world is overwhelmingly local. It is truly ironic that, after 500 years, "the world is flat" has been restored to its previous position as the most widely held false idea of its time. (On a side note: I am editing this section in a New York Starbucks in February 2011 and Thomas Friedman has just walked in. A little spooky.)

And for value-focused investors, the world looks even more intensely local, because we are always hunting for those rare companies that have a sustainable competitive advantage. In this sense, the more protected a company is from global competition—the more local it is—the more we like it. It is much easier for a company to achieve a dominant and stable market share in a smaller market, say, the Yunnan province, than it is in a global market. Ironically, the global migration of capabilities described, far from making the world flat, is driving, if anything, an increasing localization of competition.

Crossing the Governance Rubicon

Value-added deal-making can mean crossing into management issues

Ben Graham's principles solidified value-based thinking in generations of investors: A company has a true value, and you don't buy until you really know where it is relative to price. However, I think his career of reading financial statements and stock picking from an office also solidified in investors' minds the idea that this is how value investing is done. Investments are surgical but also in many ways are hands-off and at a distance. Shareholders are at one level, and management is at another. Nonmanaging shareholders are sometimes involved in the significant capital allocation decisions (spin-offs, dividends, share buybacks) but usually not in ongoing business or operational decisions. Developed economies have a natural and structural separation between the capital structure and the company, between owners and management—and between the topics of finance, value, and capital and business, operations, and customers.

This is not the case in most of the world today. Global investing and deal-making often require crossing the divide, the "governance Rubicon," between shareholders and management.

Many of the going global problems discussed reside at this governance divide. Accessing investments can be difficult. Minority shareholders can be powerless. Claims against the enterprise can be weak or impractical. Foreign owners can be at a disadvantage. Most of these issues sit at the intersection of management and ownership.

I have argued that the broadest approach for overcoming these problems is to both capture and add economic value. It is not the only solution and, certainly, traditional value investing approaches work quite well. (I actually use both traditional value investing and value point together.) But I find it can solve most of these problems in one surgical move and, therefore, open up a whole new class of assets for investment. But adding value means adding economic value (mostly), and economic value is built mostly *at the business and operational level*. So adding value means crossing the governance Rubicon and getting more involved in the operations of the business.

This is actually quite natural in most developing economies or cross-border situations. Owners and managers are often the same people. And when they are not, no real governance or agency theory formally separates them. The same underdeveloped regulatory and governance structures that make investing more difficult also make being operationally active easier.

Private equity firms typically are more comfortable with this situation. They are used to jumping into the operations of a business with a surgical mindset. Kohlberg Kravis & Roberts (KKR) has its 100-day plans. Cerberus has its turnaround strategies. There are well-known approaches for improving management, helping companies expand, and driving productivity increases. It is the traditional value community that seems less comfortable crossing the governance divide.

Global value investing starts to look a bit like private equity with the investors actively involved in operations. However, private equity in these same markets also starts to look more like value investing, because the standard leveraged buyout (LBO) and debt-financing tactics are usually unavailable or impractical. My experience is that most of the investment strategies converge to a mix of unlocking and adding value. And sooner or later you cross the governance Rubicon and discover that adding economic value to a business lets you comfortably invest in a way that meets Graham's original principles.

Value Point's Deep Well

Capability keys are the deep well of value-added deal-making

Value investors are obsessed with competition. It determines the company's profits and most of your returns. But the competitive situation can change rapidly, particularly when few barriers to entry exist or when the company is in a rapidly evolving industry or environment (ie., many of today's markets). A competition obsession turns out to be a fairly useful affliction in such situations, as well as in global investing in general. One could easily explain globalization, and this entire book, as an aggregate of local competitive dynamics. Competitive considerations and pressures are the key driver of virtually everyone's behavior (companies, government, investors) in every market.

As discussed, competing successfully as a business in developing economies usually means building or acquiring the right mix of capabilities: a luxury brand, a regional sales force, professional management, local financing, a European technology, Asian manufacturing. If Hewlett-Packard (HP) has moved its service centers to India, Dell likely needs to do so as well. If an Indian coffee shop has franchised Starbucks, a competing local coffee shop probably needs a similar franchise. In some cases, such capabilities can create a real competitive advantage (exclusive brands, advanced technology, a unique resource). But in most cases local companies need to continually move up the development curve simply to stay in the game and make sure a competitor doesn't pull ahead in scale or operating efficiencies.

Within a capability worldview, capability keys (such as brands and technologies) are very effective tools for value-added deal-making. They are effective because they speak directly to these competitive pressures and anxieties at the company level. Similar to the political access and reputable capital keys, they open the door to investments and add value.

However, unlike the previously mentioned more "intangible" keys, they can have a more direct impact on the balance sheet and income statement. Injecting a new capability, such as a factory or a product line, into a company (whether by franchise, joint venture, merger, or something else) can add a tangible or intangible asset to the balance sheet. And depending on the type of management, this can be translated to the income statement over time. Value-added investing is about impacting the AV, EPV, or DCF in the near term. We can also impact the relationship between EPV and AV by leveraging in management as a capability. This can be effective in targeting situations in which the earnings power value is less than the asset value. Recall from Chapter 3 "Value Point," the discussion of the interrelationship among earnings, assets, management, competition, and capabilities.

Because the worldwide mix of capabilities is constantly changing and evolving, capability keys provide endless opportunities for investors. Capabilities are the deep well of value point and can be used to target capability gaps, as shown in Figure 8.1.

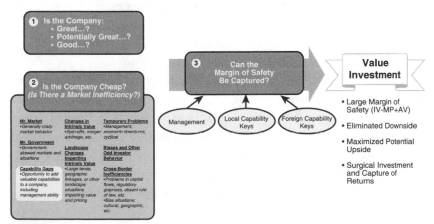

Figure 8.1   Capability keys and capability gaps

For example, a Four Seasons management contract is a capability key that can add significant value to a hotel, real estate, or service apartment project almost anywhere in the world. Luxury hotel properties in places such as Africa, India, and Russia are fairly attractive businesses as they benefit from a combination of low local labor and construction costs and luxury pricing. You can also sometimes create an additional upper pricing tier for foreign tourists, as local luxury and international luxury are not necessarily the same. The limitation is that they are "fixed asset-heavy," so the return on equity is lower. And luxury hotels in emerging markets also tend to suffer operating losses quickly during economic downturns.

But from an investor's point of view, the primary challenge with buying or building luxury hotels is acquiring the asset or location. A luxury hotel typically needs a prime location, which means acquiring either an existing hotel or vacant land in a valuable location. Such prime locations are almost always tightly held by families, companies, or governments. In places such as India and Egypt, such assets can be seen by their owners as not just assets but the family's lifeline and inheritance. An offer to buy a majority stake of a well-located hotel or plot of land is unlikely to be accepted—at least not at the reasonable or low price you want.

However, a capability key can change this equation dramatically. Offering to buy a minority stake in such a hotel and to transform it into a Fairmont or Four Seasons is an attractive offer. The brand elevates the hotel to international luxury status and opens the business to a new class of Western luxury hotel customers. This capability often also improves marketing, management, and reservations and operating systems. Recall the cases discussed in Chapter 3, where EPV > AV, EPV = AV, or EPV < AV (refer to Figure 3.7). In this situation, we can likely increase the value in any of these three scenarios. In fact, the most attractive situation might be where EPV < AV, because we are confident that a management contract will correct that problem as well as likely increase the overall asset value. As will be discussed in Chapter 12, "A Global Investment Playbook," "potentially great" companies (such as fixer-upper hotels) are often more attractive investments than currently great companies.

In addition to increasing access and increasing value, a capability key such as a luxury hotel management contract can give the investor stronger long-term control. He or she can acquire only a minority share and still have sufficient claim to the enterprise through control of the contract.

A luxury hotel management contract can actually add value to an entire real estate development. If a foreign investor with a Four Seasons contract and a local developer jointly bid on land in a prime location, the Four Seasons name would effectively brand the entire real estate development at a luxury level. Not only would this be perceived as a more attractive bid by the seller (often the government), but it would also drive value into the development's residential units, service apartments, and shopping centers. This creates lots of possibilities, such as phasing the development with different pricing or selling the luxury residential units in the first year.

Recall that in Chapter 3 I expanded the definition of a market inefficiency by adding a third term for added value. Traditionally, a market inefficiency is the difference between true value and market price (a mispricing of an asset as it currently is). It is common for investors to try to expand the margin of safety by redefining the intrinsic value upward, say by digging into more intangible assets or incorporating more speculative future growth. Or they might attempt to expand the margin of safety by incorporating in what an industry expert might pay for the whole company.

However, I have argued that our real challenge is not to hunt for smaller and smaller inefficiencies as we go worldwide, but to address the increased current and long-term downside uncertainties. Measuring intrinsic value in these environments is difficult enough without further and further refining its definition. If we can deal with the uncertainties, the inefficiencies are quite large and don't require ever finer definitions. The added value deal-making approach lets us both target the larger market inefficiencies and enables us to tackle the uncertainty problems. In the equation in Figure 8.2, you can see that we keep these factors separate from the estimation of the current intrinsic value as is. In this case, a gap in a company's capabilities (a capability gap) that the investor can fill can be considered part of the market inefficiency in the second term.

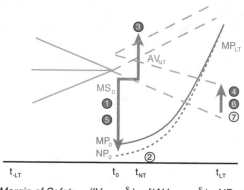

$$Margin\ of\ Safety = (IV_{t=0} - \delta) + [(AV_{t=NT} - \delta) - NP_{t=0}]$$

Figure 8.2   The uses of capabilities

Unlike the previous two value keys, capability keys are mostly about crafting a compelling business strategy—not a financing or acquisition strategy. While previous keys show us how to access deals and capture existing inefficiencies, capability keys are more about adding value. They are also far more sustainable. Capability keys can help an investor in seven ways (see Figure 8.2):

1. **Increased access to deals.** Capability keys are particularly effective at opening the door to private investments in developing or cross-border situations.

2. **Decreased entry price.** Similar to a "reputation discount," a capability key can often result in a discount. Additionally, if a key such as a Four Seasons contract will increase the value of an entire real estate development, one can argue for a deep discount on the hotel property itself.

3. **Increased economic value of the asset or enterprise.** Whether the capability increases value by earnings, tangible assets, or intangible assets, the impact on the value of the investment can be significant at the time of the investment (usually an increased asset value), in the near term (management increases EPV relative to AV), and in the long term (EPV).

4. **Eliminated long-term downside uncertainty (a stabilized margin of safety).** This is one of the most important differences between capability keys and political access or reputable capital keys. Many capabilities can add sustainable value, which can eliminate the future downside uncertainty. Note that this remains the primary objective when operating with a long-term value approach in uncertain and unstable environments.

5. **Create advantages when competing for deals.** When competing for a deal, a capability key beats no capability key almost every time. Even if two bidders have capability keys within the same industry, some capabilities are better than other (Four Seasons is more valuable than Hyatt).

6. **Strengthened claim to the enterprise.** A capability key can create a long-term operating partnership, which is more stable than just a financing relationship. It decreases your dependence on contracts and various shareholder rights. This is very important in some situations.

7. **Increased defenses against nonmarket forces.** This can be important in many state and godfather capitalist systems. Control of strategically important foreign expertise and technologies can be a good defense against political and other nonmarket threats.

Using value keys to craft business strategies is the core of value point and of expanding the value tool kit to more hands-on deal-making. The deal architect uses various keys to build a compelling business strategy that adds so much value to all parties and the company itself that the deal is a no-brainer for going forward. Because worldwide capabilities are always changing and creating new competitive pressures, this is the deep well for such deal-making. In the next chapter, I present various strategies for this in practice.

9

Capability Deals in Practice

When you walk along Century Avenue in Liujiazui, Shanghai's Wall Street, it is hard not to be impressed by the level of activity. The buildings and parks are flooded with newly minted bankers, financiers, and lawyers (also "my people"). There are cranes on almost every block, and new companies are opening and closing almost every week. The chaos is thrilling.

Located halfway along Century Avenue is the newly completed 692-foot Hines building, now named the 21st Century Tower. It contains a 187-room Four Seasons Hotel, 430,556 square feet of Grade-A office space, and 65 Four Seasons private apartments. In 2009, a minority owner of the project wanted to sell his stake, and I was investigating to see if it was a possible Kingdom Holding investment. Prince Waleed is already an owner of the project through the Four Seasons. Buying the minority stake and acquiring the naming rights seemed like a possibly clever way to acquire a Kingdom Tower on the next Wall Street.

Located just down the street from the Hines building is the Bank of China tower. Waleed and several Saudi associates own several hundred million USD of the Bank of China through an initial public offering (IPO) allocation in 2006. Along the river in the other direction is the Citigroup skyscraper, another Waleed holding. Looking across the river on the Bund you can see the newly renovated and reopened Peace Hotel, which is now managed by Fairmont, another Waleed holding. In the notoriously difficult Chinese investment landscape, you can pass four Waleed properties in a 10-minute walk.

This raises one of the initial questions in this book, which is, how is he doing this? How is it that so many investors struggle to go worldwide, while Waleed, from his small office in Riyadh, seems to walk so effortlessly across geographies and industries? Even into difficult environments like China?

A big part of the answer is his "deep bench" of Western capabilities. Drawing on his Western portfolio and relationships, he can leverage capabilities into private deals. In China, he was able to launch a fairly powerful three-pronged investment approach made up of his Western holdings expanding into the mainland, his ownership of an emerging-markets hotel vehicle, and his ownership of both Bank of China and Citigroup.

Waleed also started out as an emerging-markets investor and understood investing in places such as the Middle East and China 20 years before it became an important investment question. In the late 1970s, he began his career by opening a small prefabricated office on a Riyadh side street and doing local deals with little capital and no assets. He started off as an investor in an environment with no public companies, little rule of law, fuzzy regulations, no market information, and little reliable management. He toiled away for 10 years, gradually going from a fairly unknown prince to one of the Middle East's leading investors. He was profiled in *Forbes* for the first time at age 33.

Only in the late 1980s did Waleed begin to seriously enter the developed economies. Only then did he really start to develop deeper expertise in areas such as public markets, multinationals, global strategy, formal governance relationships, reporting relationships, and rule-of-law environments. His first major Western investment was his 1991 distressed acquisition of Citigroup, still his most famous. Following this with a string of high-profile Western investments—the Four Seasons, News Corp., Euro Disney, Apple, Canary Wharf, Saks Fifth Avenue, the Fairmont, the Plaza, Motorola, and on and on—he quickly became the largest foreign investor in the United States. But people tend to forget that Western investing was really the second act of his career and that he was also actively investing in the Middle East and Africa all during this period.

The third act began in the late 1990s, when Waleed seriously returned his sights to the emerging markets: Africa, the Middle East, and Asia. Ironically, it was his then-extensive Western holdings that gave him his biggest advantage in many of these markets.

At the beginning of a global investing age, Waleed was in the enviable position of being very comfortable in both developed and emerging markets—and having a deep bench of Western capabilities and relationships to draw on. Unsurprisingly, he has been a flurry of activity, continually traveling to everywhere from Mongolia and Kazakhstan to Africa and South America. He perhaps better than any other private investor understands the power of reputation in many cross-border situations, the value of political connections in some systems, and the impact of the right strategic partners—say, GE or News Corp.—on deals. *Forbes* aptly nicknamed him the "Prince of Deals."

This chapter is about capability deals in practice. It's about how to use capabilities to access and construct deals with a significant and stable margin of safety. If the overall presented strategy is a combination of Graham's value thinking and the deal history of various global investors, this is the crossing-over point from the former to the latter.

On a side note, Waleed recently announced two such capability deals that are worth pointing out:

- In April 2010, Qatari Diar, a wholly owned unit of the Qatar Investment Authority, purchased a 40% stake in Fairmont Raffles "for a combination of cash and other considerations." The deal was reported to be $847 million, made up of $467 million for the 40% Raffles stake, $105 million for the hotel contracts, and $275 million for an unnamed hotel property. The transaction was announced by Prince Waleed, who, prior to the acquisition, was the majority shareholder of Fairmont Raffles with 58%. It's basically a capability deal straight out of the Prince Waleed playbook. Qatari Diar's subsidiary QD Hotel & Property Investment can now steer Qatari hotel management contracts to its new partner, Fairmont Raffles. In one move, Fairmont got access to Qatar's tightly controlled real estate and hotel market and reshuffled some of its assets. It was a cross-border deal based on valuable capabilities.

- In February 2010, Rupert Murdoch's News Corp. purchased part of Prince Waleed's Rotana Group, the leading Arabic media and entertainment group. This was another capability deal. Prior to the transaction, Waleed was the second-largest owner of News Corp. and the largest owner of Rotana. News Corp.'s extensive capabilities can add real economic value to Rotana's regional media and entertainment business. Immediately after the deal was made public, Waleed also announced plans for a Rotana IPO within 2 years, saying, "We need to brand the company very well before going into an IPO." This was using reputation and capabilities to add economic value and then an IPO to further monetize it. In a January 2010 interview on Fox News, Waleed also described his investment in News Corp. as an "alliance," as a "core investment that may never be sold," and as a "strategic investment." Per my framework, News Corp. is one of Waleed's best capability keys.

Waleed remains one of the greatest business stories never told. He created one of history's largest fortunes but has never undergone much external, independent analysis. In part, this is due to the lack of an independent press in the Middle East (there's no such thing as Saudi investigative journalism). It's also due to the fact that he has had only about 10 investment staff in 30 years, so firsthand accounts are limited. And because I'm a loyal guy, you won't read the "Waleed story" here. You'll note that all the information on Prince Waleed and Kingdom Holding in this book is limited to already-public information.

Winning Long-Term in Difficult Environments

Capability keys crack the China problem

I focus a lot on China, both in this book and in life. In terms of global investing, it is the largest developing economy by far—now the world's second-largest economy—and in terms of strategy, it's just a fascinating question. If you can crack the China problem and succeed as a foreign investor there, you can succeed anywhere. Per Takashi Miike's fantastically violent film of the same name, hypercompetitive state-capitalist systems are the *Battle Royale* of global investing.

Chapter 7, "The Profits and Perils of Reputation," recounted the experiences of Coca-Cola and Danone in Mainland China. Both had primarily reputation and political strategies that I have argued are usually short-term deal advantages in such an environment. Danone died fairly quickly, whereas Coca-Cola beat the clock and managed to build economies of scale in time. But this was also in beverages, which is an industry that changes very little when moving from international to state capitalism. Industries such as banking or oil and gas change much more dramatically.

A famous Warren Buffett quote is, "When a management with a reputation for brilliance tackles a business with a reputation for bad economics, it is usually the reputation of the business that remains intact." The same could be said about good investors meeting a difficult investment environment. Good management and excellent execution won't save you. In difficult investment environments, you need an overwhelming advantage from day one. Or it's better to steer clear.

The only strategy I know for consistent successful long-term private investing in China is to use capability keys. Purchasing public equities through the exchanges or by private negotiation can be done with traditional value investing techniques, but private, illiquid, long-term investments require capability keys. By assembling the right combination of capability keys, you can create an overwhelming value-add that enables you to access investments and overcome the uncertainty and control problems. However, you will also encounter many situations when even that is not enough, and you may need to exit early or steer clear.

The following sections detail three capability key deals in the Chinese mainland. All are within the automotive industry, and they cover a wide spectrum, from great success to great failure. They are not direct value investments but illustrate the dynamics of structuring value-added deals in such environments.

Case #1: GM's Precarious Success in Chinese Automotive

General Motors (GM) entered China in the mid-1990s. Per government mandate, it entered through a joint venture with a state-owned company, Shanghai Automotive Industry Corporation (SAIC). Over the following 15 years, the joint venture (Shanghai GM) achieved an impressive level of commercial success, but GM now finds itself in a precarious state of existence. As will be detailed, Shanghai GM is a case of good management executing effectively against a likely nonwinnable strategy.

In contrast to beverages, the Chinese automotive industry is an example of a fairly "state-capitalist" industry. The development of a domestic auto industry and domestic auto companies is a priority for the country and the state actors that have such a prominent role in the economy. In practice, the strategy is to import Western and Japanese automotive capabilities while simultaneously developing local expertise and operations. And because this is China, the competition can be fierce.

The political factors operate at three levels—national, local, and company. At the national level, the country has created a three-tier system for auto company operations. Wholly owned Chinese companies (such as Cherry and Geely) are given top priority, joint ventures with foreign automakers (GM-SAIC, VW-SAIC) are second, and wholly owned foreign companies are third. At the local and company levels, political factors generally impact the terms of contracts, staffing, and trade agreements.

At each level, the objective is to develop the industry and protect nascent domestic enterprises from much larger foreign competitors. This can lead to awkward situations in which local companies partner with foreign companies to access technological and management expertise. But they also want to limit their size and influence so that they are not pushed out of their own market.

Within this system, GM entered China through a 50:50 joint venture (foreign companies are limited to 50% ownership) with SAIC. The deal was a good example of using capability keys to add value rapidly. GM had a strong position due to its deep automotive expertise, products, and management—all of which SAIC lacked at that time. Plus, its Buick and Chevrolet brands had complete product series, with both small-volume cars and luxury middle-class vehicles. SAIC was an attractive partner given its capital, human resources, and access to a deep local auto supply chain. It also had government support in Shanghai and nationally.

The Shanghai GM venture was well managed, with no major conflicts or management changes. Over time the local partner (SAIC) gradually assumed more governing power, with greater localization of expertise. Three production centers and one tech center were established on the mainland. The consortium was also very effective at targeting changing Chinese consumer tastes, frequently replacing their cars with newer generations. As of 2009, Shanghai GM was the number two automaker in China, with more than 720,000 cars sold per year. By all accounts, the joint venture is a commercial success.

However, GM is still locked into a difficult investment environment, and this is slowly playing out over time. As a large state-owned industry group, SAIC can set up multiple auto joint ventures and has many subsidiaries and affiliates: auto component companies, testing and verification centers, logistics companies. This domestic strength is one of the reasons Shanghai GM has been successful. It also enabled Shanghai GM to be included on government procurement lists and enjoy other supportive policies. But this is also the problem. Year by year, GM's value-add is diminishing, and SAIC's is strengthening. And this is the big red flag for illiquid foreign investing in difficult environments.

In 2006, SAIC launched its own 100%-owned car business, SAIC Passenger Cars. Unsurprisingly, significant management and other levels of Shanghai GM transferred from Shanghai GM to SAIC Passenger Cars. This places GM in a precarious position. Will SAIC give preference to SAIC Passenger Cars? Will market share start to shift? What if they now ask to renegotiate the terms of the joint venture agreement?

Altogether, SAIC now has three competing passenger car companies: Shanghai GM, Shanghai VW, and SAIC Passenger Cars. But two are foreign joint ventures, and one is domestically owned. From the perspective of Chinese officials, this is very logical and pretty smart. It is an excellent strategy for developing a domestic auto industry and auto companies. But absent some new value-add by GM, it places GM in an increasingly precarious position. I suspect it is only a matter of time before car sales begin to shift to the domestic companies, or GM is forced into a more passive minority position, or both.

Note that I am again mixing direct investing and business development considerations. Clearly GM is not entering China as a direct investment, but rather as a multinational with a strategic objective. But compare this type of deal with a classic long-term value investment in an illiquid asset. You typically want to buy a "great" company at a good price, with a sufficient margin of safety. But in many developing economies, very few "great" private companies can be bought, so your best approach is often to very surgically build a "great company." You add value at the company level, like GM did, to create a great Chinese car company of which you then have ownership. But to get access, eliminate uncertainties, and strengthen control, you also need advantages at the deal level—and how sustainable these are is an important question.

GM in China exemplifies the struggle in executing even a strong capability key strategy long-term in an investment environment that is likely just too difficult. The precarious state of GM's position goes hand-in-hand with the success of the enterprise thus far. The early value-add at the enterprise level that created a "great company" is now slowly being overshadowed by both a threatened competitive position (domestic auto companies have a better government-given competitive advantage) and weakening advantages at the deal level. All this occurs despite outstanding management and execution. Note that in 2010, SAIC quietly purchased an additional 1% of Shanghai GM, giving it 51% ownership and control of the joint venture.

Case #2: Fiat Dies Quickly in Chinese Automotive

If GM is dying slowly in China, Fiat died almost immediately. It entered in 1999 through a similar joint venture with a state-owned entity, Nanjing Automotive. But in contrast to the GM joint venture, this partnership had problems from the start. The joint enterprise ended up offering only four types of passenger cars (Palio, Siena, Weekend, and Perla) and between 2003 and 2006, the yearly number of cars sold varied between 26,000 and 36,000, less than 2% market share. The joint venture ended in 2007 with Fiat recalling its management and selling its stake to its partner.

Although Fiat's capability key strategy was similar to GM's, poor partner selection and ineffective execution doomed the enterprise. For one thing, Fiat's partner, Nanjing Automotive Group, largely carries commercial vehicles, which are a poor fit with Fiat's passenger car lines. Its expertise and assets in commercial vehicles could offer little support to passenger cars. The Nanjing government is also considerably less influential than Shanghai.

Management was the other problem. Per the terms of the deal, Fiat oversaw manufacturing, and Nanjing oversaw sales, but this strategy never proved very effective. The four compact cars that management introduced were at odds with the Chinese focus on big size and luxury style. Even within the four models, few innovations were introduced. The additional fact that the company CEO changed four times in 7 years probably didn't help.

If the key takeaway from GM is that even a very strong capability strategy with effective execution is sometimes just not enough in a difficult environment, Fiat's takeaway is that it is better to walk away early when your only option is clearly a losing strategy (such as joint venturing with an inappropriate partner in a difficult environment). Sometimes ineffective management is a blessing, as dying quickly and getting on with other things is better than dying slowly and losing a decade of work.

Case #3: Bosch Succeeds in the World's Largest Automotive Market

In contrast to both GM and Fiat is Germany's Bosch, which enjoys a leading, stable, and well-protected 40% market share on the Chinese mainland today. It's a long-term direct and illiquid investment that is doing exceptionally well in the same industry.

Bosch entered the Chinese market in 1995 through a 50:50 joint venture—in this case with Zhonglian Automotive Electronics, a subsidiary of SAIC. The joint venture, named United Automotive Electronic Systems (UAES), produces not automobiles but the advanced engine management systems (EMSs), which are sold to local automakers such as Shanghai GM. This was a capability deal based on Bosch's technological leadership in the EMS field. By all accounts, the joint venture has been very successful, and UAES is now the Chinese market leader. In 2009, UAES annual sales reached 7.15 billion RMB. And far from weakening over time and in exact reversal of the Shanghai GM situation, Zhonglian Automotive sold an additional 1% to Bosch in 2008, giving it 51%.

The key differences with Fiat and GM are the strength of the capability strategy and the targeted industry position. Bosch's leveraged capability was a fairly unique advanced technology that it kept control of. In terms of the discussed framework, it is a sustainable capability key (it did not decrease or become localized over time).

Additionally, UAES uses Bosch logos in its sales, and the Bosch brand has become well recognized among Chinese consumers and within the Chinese auto industry. Bosch is slowly translating a strong and sustainable capability key into brand awareness, customer loyalty, and other business strengths that will make it very difficult to dislodge from the market. This is a case of a winning capability key strategy and effective management thriving long-term in a difficult environment.

Bosch's positioning in an automotive subsector was also critical. By entering a highly technical subsector that the major automakers depend on, it effectively turned the political forces from challenges into advantages, a state capitalism judo throw. The primary interest of the government is the development of domestic automakers that can make globally competitive cars. The government focus, which is a mixed blessing for GM, actually strengthens Bosch's position. China cannot make globally competitive cars without advanced engine systems.

Compare these cases with the Coca-Cola and Danone examples from Chapter 7. GM and Bosch are primarily using capability keys but also are targeting much more difficult environments. Coca-Cola used primarily reputable capital and targeted beverages, a fairly open industry sector. It is still unclear whether a foreign majority-owned automaker probably can succeed long-term in China. The competition is intense and the politics difficult. But this is not necessarily a bad thing if you understand the situation. A foreign investor in the automotive sector can still focus on illiquid investments but depending on the subsector may have to go short-term (sell after 3 to 5 years), accept an eventual likely minority position (not bad if it's public), or attempt to turn the political priority to an advantage by investing in an indispensable success factor for the domestic automakers (a critical supplier or distributor).

The language I am using is different, but these questions should be familiar to value investors. Graham wrote extensively about an investor's obligations at both the time of the investment and going forward as an owner. That a value strategy depends equally on the time of the investment and going forward. I have translated this into uncertainty language by arguing that the primarily challenge is eliminating downside uncertainty at the time of the investment and in long-term. But I have found that a clever investor can often achieve this with structured deal-making, even in the most difficult of markets. And the more value keys you have in your tool kit, particularly capability keys, the easier accomplishing this becomes.

Winning Short-Term in Really Difficult Environments

Know when you can't win, and switch from buy-and-hold to buy-to-sell

A third possible strategy is to switch from buy-and-hold to buy-to-sell, although this is a diversion from the central objective of this book. I still believe that the most attractive returns come from capturing growing economic value (per share) over the long term. So I have not focused much on short-term strategies, which are fairly well known. But when dealing with very difficult environments, it is worth pointing out the third option of buying with the requirement of selling in 1 or 2 years.

Telecommunications and media industries in state-capitalist systems are these kinds of exceptionally difficult environments. Unlike the discussed automotive examples, which were a mix of commercial and government interests, state-capitalist TMT (technology, media, telecommunications) is usually all government all the time. This is a situation where switching to buy-to-sell is likely the only viable option. The following sections summarize two cases of foreign investment in Chinese TMT.

Case #1: Rupert Murdoch in Chinese Media

Rupert Murdoch's Chinese investments have been well documented. Bruce Dover's book *Rupert Murdoch's Adventures in China* is particularly good reading. From buying Phoenix Satellite Television to launching some of the first Mainland Chinese websites, his attempt to enter the Chinese media industry was impressive in its pure dogged determination. But his aspiration of capturing a significant portion of the Chinese market was not achieved.

By any standard, Murdoch has outstanding capability keys in the media space. His portfolio of content houses and publishing/

broadcast platforms is already global. His failure to capture much of the Chinese market is an example of strong management and outstanding capability keys confronting a just-too-difficult environment. Significant, let alone controlling, long-term ownership of Chinese media assets is next to impossible for foreign investors. This situation is not unique to China. Foreign investors cannot acquire controlling ownership in media assets in most state-capitalist or godfather-capitalist systems.

The story of Rupert Murdoch in China is not repeated here. The key takeaway is that if Rupert Murdoch (and Google) can't do majority or significant minority buy-and-hold in Chinese TMT, it probably can't be done.

Case #2: Softbank Succeeds in Chinese TMT

In contrast, Softbank, a Japanese telecom and media company, has enjoyed significant success in China's TMT sector. It entered the Chinese market in the late 1990s with strong capability keys in the telecommunications and media sector, but with a buy-to-sell growth strategy focused on private investments.

Reviewing Softbank's investment history, one can see that it has positioned itself smartly along the development curve of the industry and has conducted a series of successful deals. In 2000, Softbank partnered with IDG to make a joint investment in search engine Baidu's second venture capital round. It was a standard growth equity investment but is notable for being successful in a space in which Rupert Murdoch and later Google would both fail. It's a straightforward buy-to-sell investment that leveraged their deep capabilities in the space at the right point in the industry's development curve.

Their 2004 investment in Alibaba was similarly successful. Softbank, which is one of the top shareholders of Yahoo!, invested $60 million and acquired 20% of Alibaba which resulted in a large return through Alibaba's 2007 Hong Kong IPO. This investment also had the additional twist of being leveraged into a new Japanese venture. They launched Alibaba.com Japan, a company focused on connecting Japan's small and medium enterprises with international suppliers. Their deal paired a short-term private pre-IPO investment in Alibaba in China with a longer-term capabilities deal in their home Japanese market. This type of cross-border capability deal is similar to Waleed's Qatar-Fairmont play.

The key takeaway is that buy-to-sell combined with capability keys can work well even in the most difficult of environments. And buy-to-sell can sometimes enable other cross-border buy-and-hold investments.

Foreign Versus Local, Capability Stampedes, and Global Wing Walking

Using capability keys surgically is somewhat tricky

Using capability keys in practice can be both powerful and a bit tricky. The goal is to extend value investing to more hands-on deal-making. In doing so, you dramatically increase the number of companies that can be targeted with a long-term approach. You also create a host of tools that can be used to address the access, uncertainty, and control problems. However, it is easy to get sucked into business development and ongoing management which is something you want to avoid. The objective is to leverage in a very surgical value-add at the company and deal level. It's like corporate raiding in reverse. The next sections discuss a couple of key points in this approach.

It Is Important to Distinguish Between Foreign and Local Capability Keys

I am currently investigating projects between the University of Cambridge and various Saudi Arabian companies. It's not a huge deal, but it's kind of interesting. The idea is to create Saudi Arabia's first internationally recognized MBA program. Combining Cambridge's educational expertise and reputation with Middle Eastern wealth is a compelling story. Cambridge, which reached its 800th anniversary a couple years ago, arguably is one of the world's top universities. Saudi Arabia is a young country by comparison but commands a powerful strategic position in the world economy.

Creating a joint graduate school of business is an easy-to-understand capabilities deal. It's also one of those situations where flying

between historic Cambridge and Saudi's desert capital has me won-
dering a bit about the path my life has taken. I am a long way from the
physics lab.

But even within very compelling capability-driven deals, who is
foreign and who is local is always important. And the Cambridge-
Saudi deal highlights an important distinction within the capability
keys—that they can be subdivided into foreign and local types.

We've discussed how Western capabilities are migrating to developing economies, but some of these capabilities will become
localized, and others will not. For example, the migration of Western-
(and Hong Kong-) trained investment bankers into Shanghai was a
localization of banking capabilities into the country. Investment banking divisions were created, and young local associates were trained. If
the Western-trained bankers later go home, the capability stays.
However, Cambridge University degrees in Saudi Arabia will remain
foreign capabilities indefinitely. They cannot be replicated by local
competitors, and if Cambridge decides to leave, the capabilities (such
as a prestigious Western degree) leave with them. Foreign capability
keys can include foreign customers or contracts, technology, credentials, natural resources, and others.

This distinction between local and foreign capabilities is particularly important in highly competitive markets such as China and
India. Localized capabilities can be rapidly copied and any competitive advantage rapidly diminished. Foreign capabilities tend to have
more sustainable value at both the company and deal level. Bosch's
use of advanced engine systems out of Germany is, to some degree, a
foreign capability key strategy.

When looking at an investment in a particularly daunting environment, the mental image I stick to is one of wing walking. Wing
walkers, the acrobats who walk on the wings of biplanes at air shows,
really have only one rule. You never let go of one pole until you have
your hand firmly on the next one. In difficult environments, I never
let go of one value-add until I have my hand firmly on the next one.
Many of the examples in this book are about foreign companies
entering a market, doing well, and then getting blown off the wing a
couple years later. Foreign capability keys tend to be the most sustainable advantages.

Draft Stampedes When You Can

The local-versus-foreign capability distinction is also important when a developing market is exhibiting a "capability stampede." As a significant new capability is brought into the market or a new industry sector opens up for private investment, the large companies and investors all charge after the opportunity (yet another permutation of Mr. Market). The big animals stampede in that direction, launching joint ventures, cutting deals with Western partners, and bringing in new capabilities. For example, the Middle East and India have both witnessed a stampede into private healthcare in the last 5 years. As the private sector opened up, lots of new private hospitals were launched, and lots of new capabilities flooded into the regions (hospital managers, billing systems, insurance underwriting).

The problem is that although 20 new private hospitals can arrive in Bombay in 2 or 3 years, the consumer market for private healthcare services may take 5 to 10 years to really emerge. And the regulatory structure is almost never in place in time, which is important in hospital operations and insurance pricing. Such a lack of regulations is typically good for the insurer but bad for the hospital. The net result of such stampedes is most often weak demand, oversupply, written-off capex (capital expenditures), and difficult politico-economics.

However, as always in investing, one person's problem can be another's opportunity. The trick is to benefit from bringing new capabilities into markets and also to benefit from those who stampeded and are now struggling. My general approach is to draft the stampedes whenever possible.

For example, about 7 years ago a university stampede occurred in Saudi Arabia. The government began issuing licenses for private universities, and every prince wanted his own university. By 2002–2003, it was rumored that more than 20 major universities were in various stages of development, most in the $100–200 million investment range. (I ended up killing the proposal for a $200 million university for Prince Waleed.) And in classic stampede fashion, the capabilities and infrastructure all arrived much earlier than a significant market demand for private higher education. Supply was high, and demand and pricing were low, particularly with the government still offering free university education (it's hard to compete with free). The billions invested in campuses across the country quickly became write-offs.

This created a drafting opportunity. In this case, the strategy was to use a foreign capability key such as a Western business degree about 5 years after the university stampede. At this point, a Western partnership can add significant value to over-built universities struggling to differentiate themselves amidst too much supply. And unlike universities, with their large campuses and capital requirements, a prestigious business school has more attractive economics. They can charge higher prices, offer executive education, raise large endowments from companies and wealthy alumni, and they have few real capital costs (you don't need science labs or dormitories). By drafting the stampede, you both avoid the initial difficult economics and place yourself in a position to add significant value to lots of large and already financially committed players.

Lessons from the Saudis

A few last takeaways on capability deals from the world's first cross-border investors

The first blessing for the historically desert-living Saudis was discovering 20% of the world's conventional oil reserves underfoot (technically, under sandal). This blessing is still going strong for them, much to the consternation of the historically educated but perpetually struggling Lebanese, Syrians, and Jordanians of the Levant.

The second blessing for the Saudis was that they were forced into cross-border investing 30 years before the rest of the world. Not only did they have far too much capital to invest in their small domestic markets, but they also realized early on that they were at a very large disadvantage when going into foreign geographies. They were far away. They faced language and cultural gaps. And they did not have the technical abilities of U.S., UK, and European investors. They understood the "foreigner disadvantages" previously discussed very early on. They struggled but eventually found tactics for being successful when investing across borders. They became the world's first successful cross-border investors.

Based on this, I have compiled a short list of takeaway lessons on cross-border investing and capability deals based on my experience with the Saudis.

Lesson #1: A Foreigner and His Money Are Easily Parted

The framework presented is simple but is a surprisingly good predictor of success and failure. Is the company good or great? Did you get a cheap price? And, most importantly for going cross-border, is the margin of safety *capturable and sustainable*? This third question is all about having advantages at the deal level, both initially and sometimes in the long-term, eliminating uncertainties, and strengthening your claim to the asset. If you don't have a strong advantage at entry, a little alarm should go off in your head. Did all the local investors already pass? Am I the dumb money? And if you are in a difficult environment with a declining position, all the alarms should go off. A long list of prestigious investors and multinationals have fallen prey to such cross-border situations. I am surprised how frequently the same bad strategies are tried. Value investing's number one rule is to never lose money. The global version of this rule is to be hypercautious about the very effective tactics for separating foreigners from their capital.

Lesson #2: Never Try to Date the Prettiest Girl in School

Everyone who goes to India wants to meet with Reliance. Going to Abu Dhabi, everyone wants to meet with ADIA. To China, with CIC and CICC. These companies are prestigious and great partners, and they serve the best tea, but they have lots of suitors. Most investors are far better off focusing on smaller and less famous companies for investments. Avoiding the really pretty partners also has a big impact on pricing and how much value-add you bring to the table. The big, famous companies just don't need much from anyone.

Lesson #3: Be Clear if You Are Dating or Marrying

The level of commitment of parties often varies significantly when crossing borders. Many companies are willing to franchise their brands or operating capabilities with foreign partners but not much else. These are limited-commitment arrangements. Other companies are interested in equity and long-term operating partnerships. It's good to be clear about such interests at the start. A common source of conflict when going cross-border is when one partner wants to marry and the other wants to date.

Lesson #4: Make Your Friends Before You Need Them

Cross-border deals are rife with behavioral finance issues. Flying in and closing a deal quickly is very rare. You need communication and/or a commercial relationship over time to build trust between parties. And from these relationships over time, deals and investment opportunities will eventually emerge. Building relationships, and your reputation, before you actually need them is critical.

Lesson #5: Think Like an Industrialist

If you have a critical mass of capability keys, you will find there are opportunities almost everywhere. Rupert Murdoch can leverage his media assets into deals in Qatar, Africa, Europe, and the U.S. Waleed's hotel empire can continue to expand to virtually every major city in the world. This sort of almost industrialist approach to value investing tends to be a helpful mindset. And as will be detailed in the following chapters, capability keys can be amplified when combined with reputable and political access.

Lesson #6: Don't Get Caught Up in Geographic Strategies

If you think of investing in terms of capabilities and surgical approaches to capture or add value, the world begins to look mostly industry-specific. Geography tends to be a second thought. If you have gaming capabilities or expertise (human resources, travel, media, entertainment, gaming), you tend to be in Macau, Singapore, or Las Vegas. If you have mining capabilities (drilling, logistics, exploration), you tend to end up in Africa, Latin America, Canada, or Australia. Petrochemicals are in Russia, the Gulf Cooperation Council (GCC), and Texas (I always feel somewhat sorry for people who work in this field). But the more you think about capabilities and expertise, the more industry-specific the world looks.

Additionally, a strongly geographic focus can lead to questionable investment strategies. Certainly the U.S., China, and India are large markets that can support focused regional strategies, but is Mexico really large enough, with enough deals, to support a dedicated private equity strategy? Does combining Mexico with all of Latin America in a regional strategy really make sense? There are plenty of examples of firms doing types of deals they shouldn't and expanding into geographies they shouldn't just for the sake of a regional footprint. Going global, I focus overwhelmingly on industry-specific strategies. That tends to get me to the right places and keep me out of things I should avoid.

Lesson #7: Capabilities, Like Capital, Are About Timing

You need to deploy your capability while a gap still exists and while the capability can capture the most value. A carmaker entering China today would have few capability advantages. However, companies such as UAES and Softbank are continually adding capabilities and staying at the front of the development curve of their industry. Similar to deploying capital in downturns, timing is important in capability deals.

Lesson #8: Never Go Hostile as a Foreigner

Nationalist, cultural, and religious tensions—and all the other human fault lines—are always just below the surface. Going into a geography as a foreigner and doing hostile acquisitions or other aggressive actions can easily become consumed in such issues. I follow a structurally positive strategy of both searching for and adding value. Going hostile is not part of the investment thesis. It works well as a strategy but it also tends to keep me out of hostile situations, which is a good idea in itself if you're the foreigner.

That is more or less the extent of the theory in this book: a value-added strategy to complement traditional value investing. In the next chapter, we put it all together and focus on particularly large, aggressive "go for the jugular" deals that combine all the keys at once into hopefully ridiculously large return investments.

10

Global Tycoons, Value Tanks, and Other "Go for the Jugular" Strategies

New investment frontiers don't open up that often. And certainly the world will globalize only once. It is a very rare, possibly singular, occurrence for so many new markets around the world to suddenly open up—and at the same time, for so many investors to be so hesitant. This is one of those times when ambitious people should go as big as they can as fast as they can.

This chapter is about going for the jugular. It is for people who think, like Prince Waleed, "I knew from the beginning I wanted a global empire." It pulls together the theories described in previous chapters and presents a series of strategies, vehicles, and habits for truly ambitious global investing.

Global Tycoon Investing

Applying multiple value keys to undervalued companies with multiple inefficiencies can create particularly large returns

Per Graham, a company worth $100 million purchased for $50 million is usually a good investment. The lower the price, the better the returns become. If an investor adds value at the same time, those returns get even better. The idea is to buy a $100 million company for $50 million and quickly increase its value to $150 million. Value point investors strive not only to push down the price as much as possible, but also to add as much value as they can.

In a special subset of value point deals, all the value keys (political access, reputable capital, management, and local and foreign capabilities) are used together on a company that is beset by multiple problems and inefficiencies (mispricing, investor bias, capability gaps, a lack of political access, and so on). If value point is about adding value, the idea here is to add value with a bazooka. We want a good or great company with a massive inefficiency and a massive value-add.

I refer to these as "five keys" strategies (see Figure 10.1), or "global tycoon investing," because powerful deal-makers have an outsized ability to construct such deals. In one meeting, a piece of land in Dubai can be bought cheap and turned into the world's largest theme park. Ten new tertiary hospitals can be launched as brownfield acquisitions in ten second-tier Indian cities. A distressed bank can be purchased at a steep discount and immediately merged with a leading one. A $10 million investment can go quickly to $50 million in smaller operating companies. $100 million can go quickly to $500 million in larger deals. The economics of such deals can be seen in Figure 10.2.

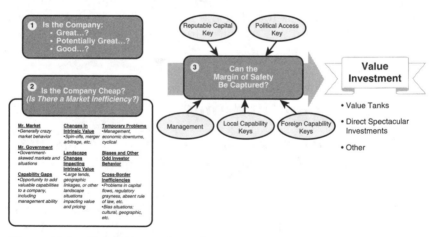

Figure 10.1   Global tycoon investing

For all the ambition, such investments can be strangely anticlimactic in execution. Extensive business analysis ends up as a simple deal being presented to several, often quite different, partners. If done well, the presented deal adds such value to each participant that everyone immediately says yes. The more powerful the added value, the more the deal becomes a no-brainer.

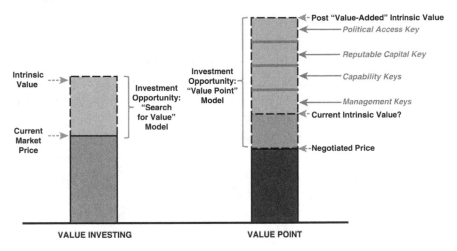

Figure 10.2   Global tycoon economics

Rethinking from Good to Great

Distinguishing among good, potentially great, and great companies in uncertain terrains

For nine chapters, I have been inartfully dodging a critical question: What kind of companies do you target when going global? This is actually Question 1 in Figure 10.1. And it is answered somewhat differently in different investment environments. Real estate mogul Sam Zell might target construction and housing companies when going from the U.S. into Brazil. KKR might target innovative entrepreneurial companies when going into India. What is a good or great company is the central question.

Warren Buffett speaks of putting companies in three buckets: good, bad, and too hard. But bad and too-hard companies are pretty easy to recognize in practice. It's the various degrees of good to great that an investor can agonize over.

You run the target company through your various investment filters. Does the company have a share of the consumer mind, such as Starbucks in the United States or Jay Chou in China? Is it sustainable (Coca-Cola: yes; Lady Gaga: no; Chipotle: likely)? Is the company at risk from generic products (beer: no; soap: yes)? Can a technological change significantly impact the company (BYD's electric car business:

yes; BYD's battery business: no)? How will the company do under really adverse economic conditions (luxury hotels in Dubai: not so good; health insurance in India: quite well)? And so on.

Running target companies through the standard qualitative and quantitative filters, the "bad" and "too hard" companies get rejected fairly quickly and confidently. It's distinguishing between good and great companies that is the challenge. And there is the struggle to specifically define the "just not good enough" line at which you grudgingly pass on a company you really do like. This is the situation where having a pleasantly ornery partner, an in-house devil's advocate, to kill off your "not quite good enough" ideas can be really helpful (greetings, Mr. Munger).

In the developed economies, there are various definitions of good and great companies for a long-term value approach. Recall my Buffett "Great Company" Corollaries from Chapter 2, "Rethinking Value in a Global Age." I claimed that a great company has a competitive advantage or some other characteristic that not only eliminates the current and future downside uncertainties but also maximizes the potential gain in per-share economic value.

But is this the same thing as a great company in India? Does a different landscape or set of regulatory rules change what makes a great target company? Do the increased uncertainties, instabilities, and other differences change what you look for in a company? A company with significant fixed assets might be far more defendable in a limited rule-of-law country. But don't such fixed assets also mean a lower ROE? Does the ability to add value or the existence of much larger mispricings change what constitutes a great investment? Does applying Graham's Method *de novo* in fundamentally different environments lead us to fundamentally different definitions for good to great companies?

Ben Graham, investing in a time of limited information, great depressions, and world wars, might have argued that a "good company" is one with verifiable assets or earnings. Modern value investors, investing after a period of more than 50 years of relatively stable economic growth in rule-of-law liberal democracies, might assert that a good company must have an attractive return on capital. Whether measured by return on invested capital (ROIC), return on equity (ROE), or a similar measure, good companies are generally regarded as those that produce large earnings relative to the amount of capital required. Buffett might define a good company as one that is easy to understand and that has honest management, an above-average return on capital, no big capital needs, and some degree of franchise. However, Prince Waleed, investing across developed and developing economies, would likely say that a "good" company is one that is global (having a presence in many countries), has trustworthy management, and has a premier brand.

Narrowing from "good" to "great" companies, the viewpoints begin to vary much less. Buffett would likely say that a great company has a sustainable competitive advantage. Waleed would likely say that a great company is one-of-a-kind and nonreplicable. In any case, a great company should already have clearly compelling financials: usually a high and stable return on invested capital, a low cost of growth with an ability to self-fund, and a very long-term and protected competitive position (usually demonstrated in market share over time).

My point is not to very briefly and badly summarize the thinking of such great investors, but to point out that the difference between good and great companies is most often in the uncertainties and in the current and long-term per-share economic value. For the purposes of translating this to differing economic systems, I define good and great companies as follows:

- Good companies have relatively protected profits and/or distributable earnings. Most important is that the per-share economic value won't decrease from the time of the investment going forward. The goal is to protect the margin of safety that was the basis of the investment and eliminate the downside uncertainty.
- Great companies are good companies that additionally have the greatest potential for future gain in per-share economic value.

I assert that good and great companies are defined mostly by their uncertainties. All the various filters speak to such uncertainties. Good companies' value can't go down, and great companies maximize the upside as well.

That different economic environments impact what is considered a good or great company should not be surprising. The economics of an industry and a company's position within that structure are major factors in assessing the attractiveness of a specific company. If the newspaper industry traditionally had one local paper per major city, that industry structure was a big factor in the assessment of *The New York Times*. Value investors have always talked about good versus great companies within a specific industry and *within a relatively developed economy*. They just usually left off the last part of that sentence. But can't a company half in and half out of the Russian government with no effective competition meet these good-to-great requirements? Would you really call that a franchise? Or attractive industry economics? Or is it mostly about an attractive environment? If Saudi Arabia has a $200 billion influx of petrodollars per year, resulting in real economic development, can't that environment make many companies, even mediocre ones, good or great?

As the line between government and commerce blurs in developing economies, so do the lines between company, industry, and environment. The line between investor and deal maker also blurs. *A company can be good or great due to the company itself, its industry, its environment, or the investor's impact on.* So when I search globally, I am almost always looking for three situations rather than two:

- **Good companies + environments** such that the downside uncertainty is eliminated
- **Great companies + environments** where the upside potential is also maximized
- **Potentially great companies** where an asset can be rapidly structured into a great company

The company doesn't have to be "great" right now. It can be great when I am through with it. I can buy a "potentially great" hotel in Kenya and rebrand it as a Movenpick hotel, making it "great." I can identify an insurance company in a management-weak environment (such as Saudi Arabia), particularly if the earnings power value (EPV) is below the asset value (AV), and put in place a foreign management contract that improves it quickly (EPV equal or greater than AV).

It is in this "potentially great" category that Prince Waleed is arguably the world's master deal-maker. When he purchased his stake in Citigroup in 1991, it was a company on its knees, on the verge of bankruptcy. Only later would it become one of the world's leading banks. When Waleed purchased the George V hotel in Paris, now rated the world's #1 hotel, it was not even within the top 1,000 hotels. When he purchased 5% of Apple Computer in 1994, it was in a "down but not out" condition, and Steve Jobs had yet to return. When he purchased United Saudi Commercial Bank, it was the weakest of all the Saudi banks. In fact, going through Waleed's investments, from the Four Seasons, to Saks, to Canary Wharf, to the Fairmont, to DKNY, most were in the "potentially great" category when he bought them. He is sometimes referred to as the "prince of fallen angels," but it is really just one consistent value strategy.

Note how dramatically the term "potentially great" expands the number of companies one can target with a value approach. It expands the target list way beyond just underpriced and underperforming companies to a whole host of developing companies that in many ways characterize developing economies and cross-border situations. I argue that "potentially great" as an asset class is the most direct and logical application of value investing to the world's markets today. Also note how many targets this creates within the EPV versus AV cases shown again in Figure 10.3.

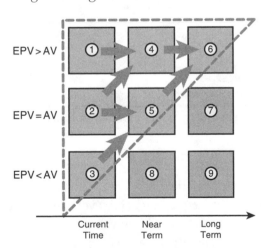

Figure 10.3 Good, potentially great, and great target valuation cases

Also note how "potentially great" fits into Figure 10.4. The left side of the chart describes a traditional value-investor approach: Find a good-to-great company and buy it cheap (the search for value). The center section illustrates the deal-making aspect of value point investing: accessing investments, adding value, strengthening claim to the enterprise, overcoming foreigner disadvantages, and actively stabilizing the margin of safety. It is this center section that enables an investor to not only target private investments but also to expand into "potentially great" companies. Not only can I now target the much larger market inefficiencies (value minus price) of today's colliding markets, but I can also actively create an opportunity (value minus price plus value-add). I can both capture and create inefficiencies. It's basically more hands-on, which is the most logical posture for more uncertain and unstable environments. Compare this fairly simple and logical posture to the contorted postures so many investors are using to stretch out to global opportunities.

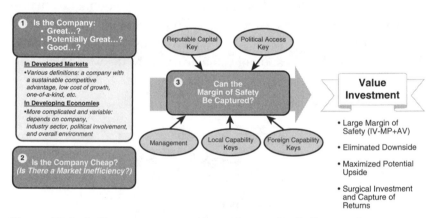

Figure 10.4   Is the company good, great, or potentially great?

A Note on Mergers

Much of the strategy described is about negotiated deal-making at the point of entry or acquisition. However, subsequent mergers are another potential method for adding value, particularly when a company is in the "potentially great" category. For example, Prince Waleed's mentioned acquisition of Riyadh-based United Saudi Commercial Bank in the late 1980s began as a typical value point investment. It was an investment in a bank that had suffered 3 years of operating losses (i.e., a down-but-not-out scenario). Waleed bought in and began restructuring and cost cutting, quickly reducing staff from 428 to 314. In under a year, the bank returned to profitability.

But what made the deal great was what happened next. Waleed merged the bank with Saudi Cairo Bank after separately leading a group of investors to acquire 33.4% of that bank. He followed this with a subsequent merger with Saudi American Bank (Samba), at that time 30% owned by Citibank. The end result was significant ownership of one of the Middle East's leading banks and a company that fits the "great" company definition. This was a series of transactions that quickly turned a "potentially great" company into a "great" one. It can also be viewed as investing along a capability consolidation trend (in this case, modern banking in the Middle East), as discussed in Chapter 8, "Capability Deals in Theory."

Waleed used a Western version of this same strategy with his luxury hotel assets. His $5.5 billion Fairmont Raffles merger in 2006 created a luxury hotel company with 120 properties in 40 countries, a "great" global company. However, this is a far cry from Waleed's initial purchase in 1994 of 50% of three of the five existing Fairmont hotels. Waleed described the deal as being about "burnishing a gem—the Fairmont name." I do not focus much on these types of merger strategies as they are much longer term approaches. We overwhelmingly focus on very surgical approaches where you make your returns at the time of investment.

Beware of Low Prices in Exotic Places

A final warning on cheap assets in exotic places. Virtually everyone who goes to Cancun or Cabo San Lucas ends up taking a look at real estate and ponders the idea of buying a beach home. After all, the weather is nice, and the beach homes just seem so cheap. Looking globally for investments, the same thing often happens. Companies in India and China seem so cheap, and the locations are somehow compelling in a way less exotic locations are not. Why not just buy a couple?

The reality is that most really cheap assets, including homes in Cancun and small companies in Mumbai, are cheap for the right reason: They're not worth much, and they're not increasing in value any time soon. Anything less than a good-to-great company, even when purchased at a very steep discount, is unlikely to return a profit. This is why I put company quality as Question 1 and price as Question 2. Quality is still the #1 issue.

"Value Tanks"

Building all five value keys into a focused investment vehicle is a powerful way to roll across borders and invest globally

For the past 15 years, Prince Waleed has been firmly established at the global tycoon level, having built a global empire and achieved effectively unlimited reach. While most investors struggle to go global, he struggles against limited bandwidth. In a colliding world with fairly spectacular mispricings, he simply has more options and opportunities than resources to execute against them. For every good-to-great investment he makes, there are probably ten he doesn't do.

One of his more effective solutions to this problem has been to launch focused investment vehicles that contain multiple value keys in a stand-alone structure. Because of the bazooka-type value that they can add to deals and their suitability to almost any environment, I call them "value tanks." They are particularly good at entering and investing in the established emerging markets.

An example is Kingdom Hotel Investments (KHI), a Dubai-based hotel acquisition and development group focused on the emerging markets of Africa, the Middle East, and Asia. Launched in 2000, KHI's primary business is to buy and build hotels and resorts in rising markets and then position or reposition them with Western hotel brands such as the Four Seasons or Fairmont. This is value-added deal-making between Western operating companies, local emerging-market assets, and Middle Eastern capital. And the resulting resorts have been fairly impressive, such as the Sharm El Sheikh Four Seasons and the Fairmont Mount Kenya Safari Club.

Kingdom Hotel Investments also makes periodic acquisitions of Western hotels such as the George V in Paris, the Hotel Des Bergues in Switzerland, the Plaza in New York, and the Savoy in London. Sometimes these are straight acquisitions, and other times they are renovation and repositioning plays.

Generally, KHI targets good, potentially great, and great hotel properties. A Four Seasons hotel in Damascus or a Movenpick in Beirut is a good company but not great. It has a lot of fixed assets, and growth is expensive. Plus, it doesn't deal with adverse conditions well, and economic downturns can result in significant losses.

Other investments have met the great and potentially great criteria. The Plaza Hotel in New York was a great company when purchased from Donald Trump. The George V in Paris and the Four Seasons Sharm El Sheikh were potentially great. All became one-of-a-kind assets with attractive financials.

Luxury hotels in developing countries have lots of the pricing issues and room for added value. First, they are hardly a favorite Western investor target. Even the Western hotel companies themselves are often hesitant to own such assets or invest directly in places such as Nairobi and Beirut. Middle Eastern investors tend to be even more hesitant about dealing with partners in Africa and China. So there is a lot of attractive bias by competing investors. Also, luxury hotels in developing markets have significant capability gaps that deal-makers can address, such as the absence of branded hotel management, operating systems, and access to Western tourists.

KHI attacks all these problems. First, the company can utilize fairly powerful political access with Waleed as its chairman. Waleed has long-term relationships with governments across Africa, the Middle East, and Asia, which are clearly important for securing prime land or assets for development. As Waleed travels and meets with government leaders from Mongolia to Kenya, he routinely looks for hotel opportunities, which are then forwarded to KHI.

Second, KHI has a strong reputation with companies and investors in both developing and developed economies. That means it can draw international investing partners to opportunities they might not have pursued otherwise. Deploying hundreds of millions of dollars from the U.S. into Africa is difficult. Deploying these amounts from the Middle East into Africa takes an exceptionally strong reputation. The Kingdom reputation solves these problems and acts as a catalyst for investments. KHI went public on the Dubai and London stock exchanges and serves as a bridge between international capital (particularly Middle Eastern money) and these emerging markets. Additionally, Western hotel companies generally become more comfortable investing in places like Beirut if Waleed and KHI are their partners. Per the framework, KHI effectively uses both political access and reputable capital.

Third, KHI can impact the management and operational issues that plague many developing market hotels, because it has exclusive management contracts with the Four Seasons, Fairmont, and Movenpick. This alone can add tangible value to hotels almost anywhere in the world. Buying a hotel or acquiring land in a downtown location is difficult, but when the seller knows that you will turn it into a Fairmont, things become much easier. Western brands and management ability can both reposition the hotels and add other operational advantages.

Using all five value keys, KHI is a focused investment vehicle (a value tank) that can add significant value to deals and invest virtually anywhere in the world (see Figure 10.5). Unsurprisingly, KHI has rapidly grown to 34 hotel properties in 17 countries across Africa, the Middle East, and Asia. In most cases, KHI hotels are the premier hotels in these cities. And the deal structures have the value equation one looks for: good-to-great companies captured with a healthy and sustainable margin of safety. With a mixed strategy of development and acquisition, they can target most of the cases shown in Figure 10.3.

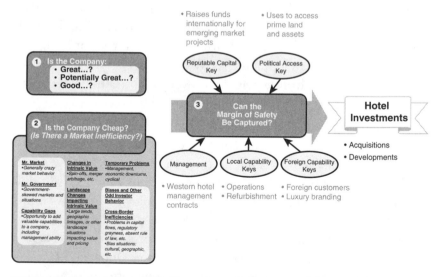

Figure 10.5   Kingdom Hotel Investments "value tank"

Another Waleed value tank is the previously mentioned pan-African private equity firm Kingdom Zephyr. Zephyr targets the high growth rates and low asset prices in Africa. The approach of Kingdom

Zephyr is similar to that of KHI. Target good, potentially great, and great companies in emerging markets—in this case, the African continent. Benefit from high growth rates. Take advantage of sizable market inefficiencies, particularly widespread investor bias against Africa, and buy the companies cheap.

Kingdom Zephyr as a value tank deploys all five keys, as shown in Figure 10.6. As mentioned, Prince Waleed has strong political access in Africa. Africa is considered the backyard of the Middle East. Past direct investments include a 17% stake in Senegal Communications and a 10% share of West African Ecobank. In terms of capabilities, Kingdom Zephyr can build strategic partnerships with both European and American companies in multiple industries. In this case, the capabilities are not so much in-house as an ability to put in place through partnerships. Again, reputation serves as a bridge to international and Middle Eastern capital. In February 2010, Kingdom Zephyr closed a new $492 million Pan-African Investment fund with commitments from private-sector investors, development finance institutions, and wealthy families in Africa, Asia, Europe, the Middle East, and the U.S.

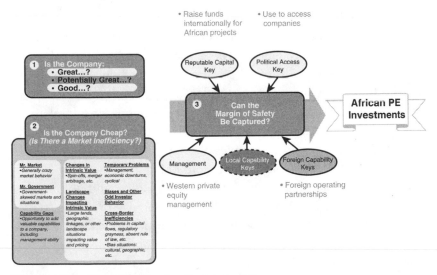

Figure 10.6   Kingdom Zephyr "value tank"

The result is a focused investment vehicle (value tank) that can access private deals and add value anywhere on the African continent. Their portfolio companies now include everything from producers of canned tuna in Madagascar to housing developers in Morocco and Algeria.

This is all fairly straightforward. The approach is to keep it simple so you can go big fast and focused. And you might have noticed that the two mentioned value tanks actually overlap and support each other. Waleed has two direct lines of entry into the African continent—his hotel and the private equity vehicles. These two lines also make it possible for him to initiate a third type of entry—"direct spectacular" investments, which are discussed in the next section.

"Direct Spectacular" Investments

Building all five value keys into one large, direct, and spectacular investment is a surgical way to cross borders

Waleed is often quoted as saying that he does something spectacularly or he doesn't do it at all. This is usually taken as a statement of ambition (which it probably is), but it is more important as a statement of investment strategy. An investment that is "spectacular" is, by its definition, rare and difficult to do.

Waleed is drawn to investments that the overwhelming majority of investors could not achieve. These usually result in his being the only real bidder at the table, a situation investors always like. Additionally, if an investment is "spectacular," it implies that it will be very difficult for others to replicate later. It results in one-of-a-kind assets that can command a premium over the long term and can have the type of "great company" economics one seeks. Therefore, in terms of investing and deal-making, doing something spectacularly means both focusing on great one-of-a-kind companies and minimizing competition for the deal. Striving for a spectacular project also creates a momentum that can be helpful when doing deals in difficult environments. As they say, it is often easier to accomplish the impossible than the merely difficult.

"Direct spectacular" investments are very large, bazooka-type value-add direct investments. You construct one large project that leverages all the value keys and takes advantage of multiple market inefficiencies. The returns are high and the approach is still surgical, with the investor coming in at one specific point. If focused vehicles are tanks, "direct spectacular" investments are long-range cruise missiles.

The previously discussed ultra-high Saudi-China skyscraper project is an example of a "direct spectacular" investment. As a symbol of both countries, such a cross-border project would require unique political access in both China and the Middle East. That is pretty rare. It would also require a reputable lead investor who could bring enormous amounts of international investment capital in a politically infused, limited rule-of-law environment. And because the facility would likely be positioned as an energy hub, bringing in the right strategic partners—such as PetroChina, Sinopec, Saudi Aramco, Sabic—would also be key. Such a "spectacular" project could be accomplished by only a handful of investors and, if built, would likely never be replicated. Thus, it fits the "direct spectacular" profile.

Note now this fits the value point framework. It's a potentially great company. It's cheap. The deal structuring of the various components and project phasing guarantees that the lead investor will do very well financially. The margin of safety is very large, the downside is eliminated, and the upside is maximized.

Another Waleed "direct spectacular" investment was his 2006 purchase of Bank of China's supplemental IPO shares. Following Bank of China's 2006 oversubscribed IPO, the bank decided to float a small number of additional shares it had held back. Waleed led a prominent group of Saudi investors in a bid for $2 billion of these shares. This large request to the Chinese government drew on the unique Saudi-China political relationship. It had a lot to do with political access. Waleed's reputation also connected the deep stores of Middle East and North Africa (MENA) capital to Chinese pre-IPO opportunities. And it leveraged his knowledge of China from Citigroup and his other portfolio companies operating there. Again, probably only a few investors could leverage such large MENA dollars and political access into such a Chinese opportunity and possibly succeed. The group was eventually awarded several hundred million dollars' worth of shares, making them one of the largest foreign recipients.

These two approaches, "value tanks" and "direct spectacular," are value-adding strategies that are particularly effective when investors cross borders and go global. They also reflect an investment style that focuses on coming from a position of almost overwhelming advantage in situations that most Western investors avoid. You add tremendous value at a specific point (ie., a value point).

Rethinking Good to Great Environments

With an environment focus, Macau and Liujiazui jump off the map

When Warren Buffett purchased PetroChina in 2002–2003, he was buying a state-owned monopoly with a market capitalization of $37 billion—and an actual value he had estimated as being at least $100 billion. The subsequent almost ten-fold investment returns were a classic value investment by its greatest practitioner.

But at second glance, the investment also seems a sharp contrast to Buffett's investments in companies like Sees and Coca-Cola. State-owned entities do benefit from politically limited competition but they also tend to be managed rather poorly, lack innovation, and be fairly risk-averse. Political risks are often the primary consideration of management. Is PetroChina really a great company like Coca-Cola, or is it an OK company in a great environment (a state-owned monopoly in a state-capitalist system)? Does the distinction matter if the resulting financials are similar? At what point is a great company created by the environment instead of the company or industry structure?

I find it to be a worthwhile exercise to occasionally start not at the company level but at the opposite extreme—the environment level. Instead of filtering companies for certain characteristics, I filter environments for factors that will either drive away price from value or produce abnormally high profits for even mediocre companies. I look for environment characteristics such as rising or falling wealth, political involvement, capability gaps, cross-border inefficiencies, and investor bias.

Viewing the world this way today, one environment that jumps off the map is Macau. Macau sits at the intersection of multiple previously unconnected cultures, countries, and economic systems. It is a true creature of an inefficient, colliding world. Chinese and Japanese gamblers coexist with Hong Kong bankers, Filipino laborers, and Las Vegas managers. Regulators range from the Nevada gaming authority to the Beijing government. And just for fun, all the legal documents must be filed in Portuguese, a legacy of Macau's colonial heritage.

Not surprisingly, Macau is a great investment environment with lots of mispriced assets amid spectacular economic growth. Since 2002, so many casino and hotel projects have been launched that they figuratively and literally dwarf the actual physical geography. A new land mass, the Cotai Strip, had to be created to accommodate the buildings. It's the kind of very large economic trend we like to see.

Additionally, cross-border inefficiencies and biases are everywhere. Western casino, entertainment, retail, and hotel companies, having made large financial commitments, are now struggling with Macau's changeable political landscape. Meanwhile, the Chinese government is struggling to manage the flood of Chinese capital and gamblers moving across the border. Everyone is trying to figure out consumers' still-evolving tastes. And all this seems intensified by the small geography in which everyone is forced to operate. If Biosphere contains all the world's ecosystems, Macau contains its different cultures, companies, and politico-economic systems. Meetings between various Chinese, Japanese, Western, Indian, and Russian professionals occur all across town in this strange global business, Biosphere.

Macau-based companies also have massive capability gaps. Casino owners need construction companies to build their projects and expert management to run them. The casino managers need advertising, human resources, and gamblers. The gamblers need banks, hotels, and, in the case of Chinese gamblers, loans. And everyone needs staff. The capability needs of this rapidly developing economy are a dealmaker's paradise.

Recall MKW Capital, which was mentioned in Chapter 5, "How Political Access Adds Value," as an example of the "bird on a rhino" approach. Within Macau's environment, their investment in an online human resources company, MacauHR, can be seen as an astute understanding of Macau's staffing problems (a capability gap). Their investments in hotel and tourism websites, such as Macau.com, and media companies, such as Aomen TV ("Aomen" is Chinese for Macau), clearly benefit from all of these environmental conditions.

Macau as an environment has all the characteristics—capability gaps, cross-border inefficiencies, and rapid growth—that make value-added deal-making easy and mispricing common. Good and even mediocre companies can end up with great financials. This is a situation where I would argue that a "great" company is defined mostly by the environment, and not the company or industry structure.

Another current standout environment is Shanghai's Liujiazui district. Situated in Pudong and designated as China's financial center, Liujiazui's ambition is to one day become the Wall Street of Asia. For investors, its current situation is very similar to Macau's:

- **Surging mainland cash is fueling a large trend.** As China's GDP continues to grow at 8% to 10% per year, the country's wealth (personal, commercial, and government) is increasing. Naturally, this is causing a large increase in the size of the financial services sector, which is increasingly centered in Liujiazui.

- **Growing numbers of financial transactions are occurring between China and the rest of the world.** Liujiazui is becoming a crossroads city for both domestic and cross-border, corporate and financial transactions. About half of Liujiazui's rapidly expanding Grade-A office space is currently occupied by foreign banks, legal firms, and investment groups, with the other half housing major Chinese companies. The result is an increasing of cross-border inefficiences.

- **The financial services industry is rapidly upgrading its capabilities.** About every six months, the government opens a major new financial product or service class. In 2007, after mutual funds were introduced, over 300,000 new brokerage accounts were opened per day for five straight days. Insurance companies recently received permission to begin investing up to 15% of their assets in overseas capital markets. In April 2010, stock index futures were launched. And in October 2010, trials for credit derivatives were announced. The rate of development is startling, and all of this creates large gaps in required capabilities.

- **The renminbi (RMB) is going international.** The Chinese government's increasing efforts to internationalize the RMB are particularly interesting for Liujiazui as a financial hub.

Cash-rich China is increasingly offering RMB-based loans as part of oil and other resource deals with other countries. For example, in 2010, China gave Venezuela an additional $20 billion in long-term financing, tied to future oil purchases—but it was based on the renminbi as the currency. The Chinese government has even floated the idea of a new RMB-based Marshall Plan to support the development of other emerging markets. The increasingly international nature of the RMB creates needs for new capabilities, particularly in overseas and cross-border situations.

The takeaway is that because the variation in the types of environments is much greater internationally than within developed economies, it is often a good thought experiment to consider first the environment almost independent of any specific company. You can note that the additional market inefficiencies I have introduced into the traditional value investing equation (cross-border inefficiencies, capability gaps, large trends) speak more to the environment than specific company characteristics.

Invest Like a Global Tycoon

Going big depends on focus, discipline, and daily habits

Asset management groups, international private equity firms, and institutional real estate companies tend to be sizable operations. Lots of staff and offices. In contrast, value investors tend to be more solo or small-team operators. For example, all of Prince Waleed's deals, with their grand ambitions and global reach, were put together with just four or five investment staff in a Riyadh office. This is possible because his deals are based on narrow value strategies that are applied with fairly impressive focus and discipline. It is simply impossible to go from $30,000 to $28 billion with a small staff without tremendous focus and discipline.

A look at what Waleed does in the course of a workday—and what he doesn't do—is instructive. The Kingdom Holding office has no analysts reading annual reports or traders watching Bloomberg terminals. It has no workrooms or cubicle farms. In fact, you witness startlingly few of the activities you would see in a private equity firm, real estate group, or large hedge fund. There is only the prince sitting behind his desk with several sofas in front of him, and three or four investment staff working down the hall. Throughout the day, he reads reports and meets with various political and business leaders. He discusses current projects and possible new opportunities, which are then analyzed by both the few internal investment staff and also some outside firms hired for that purpose, like McKinsey, Booz and Co., and Citigroup.

Waleed's process has a strict formality and discipline. There are no hallway meetings, and his schedule is managed to the minute. Presentations and discussion meetings are rapid and focused, typically 10 to 15 minutes. And those presenting must typically submit the relevant documents the day before—and can expect that Waleed will read them all and mark them up extensively in his characteristic green ink. Within the meetings, presentations usually last no more than 3 minutes before he jumps in and takes over the discussion (there is a certain art to speed presenting). And as you leave the office, there is always another group waiting to enter. There is a machine-like quality to the days.

This process never slows or stops. At night, the activity shifts to Waleed's palace. On weekends it continues at his desert camp. During vacations and business trips, it continues aboard his Boeing 767, on his yacht, or in boardrooms around the world. The people sitting on the sofa change, but this process of continuous meetings never stops.

All this activity represents Waleed's systematic global hunt for opportunities. What does the vice president of China need? How about Fairmont Raffles or Canary Wharf? How can we increase the value of this real estate project? If United Saudi Commercial Bank merges with Saudi Cairo Bank, doesn't that increase the value?

A simple equation is at the core of all this activity. And I think it is the same equation you see in successful value investors everywhere. If you invest only when you cannot lose money, time becomes your ally, and you must become wealthy—*if you keep doing it consistently*. A value-investing and deal-making approach, when combined with rigid operational focus and discipline, effectively guarantees wealth over time. In this, Waleed, Buffett, and Graham have an almost identical methodology. You search for value (unrecognized and added), eliminate uncertainty, quantify risk, and invest surgically—and big. Then just stick to it.

To operate over long periods of time with such focus and discipline, it helps to build an operational system around you that both amplifies and enforces consistency. The trick is to build discipline and focus into your daily habits. Scheduling strict meeting structures, limiting staff, limiting companies for review to specific types, and so on. I find you can often tell how successful an investor will be just by looking at his daily habits.

And on top of an operationally enforced and amplified discipline and focus, there is the additional power of an optimistic and positive nature. Whether achieved through an engaged, rational mind, religious faith, or other, an optimistic nature seems to be critical to the process. You have to be the one who sees value in a company when nobody else does. You have to be the one who doesn't give up on a deal when everyone else thinks it's impossible. You have to be the one who believes the distressed company can be turned around or that the parties can come back together even though everyone is frustrated and angry. I argue that the secret equation for becoming a Global Tycoon is the following:

value strategy + [focus + discipline + optimism] + time = wealth

The Best Deals Are Simple Deals

Keep it simple in complicated places

Successful investors frequently say that a good investment is one you can write on the back of a napkin. You keep it simple. I have always liked the version by physicist Niels Bohr, who said that he never understood an idea until he said it to himself in German, French, English, and Dutch. The idea is to look at an idea a thousand ways, but then boil it down to a few glaringly simple statements. So simple you can write them on a napkin or say them to yourself in multiple languages. My approach is a little different. I always convert everything to a physics or math problem, which basically makes it an uncertainty analysis, and then I boil the ocean. I do hundreds of pages of analysis on a given idea. And then I throw it all away, pull out a single piece of paper, and rewrite it in a few sentences.

This desire for simplicity in the value crowd is both a strength and a weakness. When it comes to investment strategy and execution, it is a strength. The more complicated the structure of a deal or investment, the more things that can go wrong. The more moving parts in the machine, the more things that can break. It's also why you aggressively front-load the investment with a margin of safety, so you are less exposed to difficulties and risks going forward. Simple deals also have the mathematical advantage that can then be put together in complex situations or combinations without propagating uncertainties. Simple companies with no uncertainties can be looked at in complex situations and combinations without increasing the uncertainties; the reverse is not true. This "keep it simple" approach is clearly important when moving to more complicated and changeable environments. Execution takes longer. Operational changes take longer. Contracts are harder to sign. Everything that can go wrong eventually does. The more complicated the environment, the more important it is to keep it simple. However, this desire for simplicity in the value crowd also leads to a tendency to oversimplify reality. People want to start talking in simple anecdotes about investing or markets or industries. It is equally important to simplify in strategy and execution and resist the urge to simplify in analysis.

In the last step, the napkin stage, I always make sure that the investment answers the three questions in a powerful way. The company fundamentals are simple and attractive, the margin of safety is impressive, and the deal advantages are overwhelming. It has to jump off the page.

This chapter is a mix of big ambition, value strategy, and tactics. Value tanks and direct spectacular investments are very effective tactical approaches for Western investors looking to cross borders. In the next chapter, I expand on such tactical considerations and focus almost entirely on ways to find deals and get them done.

11

It's Still About Price and Quality

I sometimes think investing is a slow, step-by-step, career-long process of experiencing all the things that can go wrong. You discover hidden liabilities in your investment. The company's products inexplicably start losing market share. A CEO quits or has to be replaced, and then the new CEO turns out to be no better. The economy retreats and revenue collapses, causing your high-fixed-cost companies to start bleeding cash and sending management and shareholders into a panic. Such reversals always bring to mind the counsel that elder surgeons give to anxious medical students: "Relax. All bleeding stops eventually."

There is something inherently punitive about the process of improving as an investor. Understanding an investment strategy is fairly straightforward, but it seems to take a lifetime of hard lessons before you can consistently find the narrow path from investment to return.

This chapter switches from frameworks to tactics to finding companies, structuring deals, and getting things done. From one side, I adapt some of Buffett and Graham's well-known investment advice to different environments. From the other side, I detail the tactics of some of the rising global investors.

But after all the theoretical and tactical considerations and permutations, successful global investing boils down to the same bottom line as traditional value investing: the need to capture the economic value of good companies at a discount. Returns are still about price and quality.

From Screening to Networking

The first challenge in going global is entering foreign markets in a smart way

How is it that U.S.-based George Soros ended up buying an airline on Hainan Island, China? How do you go from trading in London and New York to negotiating an airline deal in a southern Chinese city? Entering a new market, let alone a new country, a prudent investor is rightly cautious. And doubly so in developing economies, with all their quirks. Usually as you get closer to signing, an alarm goes off in your brain. What am I doing? Do I really want to buy into something illiquid so far away? Have all the local investors already passed on this? Am I the "dumb money"?

The first challenge any investor faces when going global is learning how to enter a market in a smart way. Being a foreigner, you almost always have serious disadvantages (less information, fewer connections, fewer local operating assets, etc.).

But as necessity is the mother of invention, investors have over the past decade learned to cross borders fairly intelligently. Doing so usually consists of three activities:

1. Building a partner network
2. Getting access to unique information
3. Creating a deep "capability bench"

These activities can collectively be described as going from *screening to networking*. Traditional value investing is usually about screening investments—filtering stocks against price/value algorithms, reading annual reports, and so on. Value point is about putting together a network through which you can locate investments, build partnerships, and structure deals. If the primary objective is to find an opportunity to add value, this often means understanding people and their needs in a way that cannot be done just by reading reports. But in both screening and networking, you still spend 90% of your time waiting for the right investment to come along.

Tactic #1: Building a Partner Network

Prince Waleed's frenetic lifestyle and hyperintensity are always remarked on by journalists who meet him, and I can attest that their descriptions are not exaggerated. He lives at a truly crazy pace—17-hour workdays, nonstop meetings and calls, as many as six televisions going at all times. On one trip, Arabian Business estimated that in a single day he met 573 people, took more than 200 phone calls, and sent more than 100 text messages.

His vacations are not much different. Waleed and the entourage pile into his 767 (soon to be replaced by a private Airbus 380 that may or may not have a swimming pool) and jet from country to country. At each stop, meetings are held with local government officials and business leaders. It is not unusual for these meetings to consume 13 to 15 hours in a given day, sometimes in three countries.

My favorite story, related to me by the prince's head of communications, had to do with a trip that covered Eastern Africa, South America, Los Angeles, various parts of Asia, and Paris all in one month. Since the trip included places where GSM cell phone service is not always available, the communications head had the task of moving satellites so that the Prince's cell phones would be uninterrupted throughout the trip. The net result was that a few Caribbean locations got GSM service for the day as Waleed passed through.

However, what is often missed is the logic behind all of this hyperactivity. The prince is continually building his *partner network* and has been systematically doing so for 20 years. He knows government officials—typically the president, king, or prime minister—in almost every major country. He knows the CEOs of most of the world's leading companies. He has built a unique and powerful global network of partners that he can mine for investments and deals. And if he decides to enter a new market, such as Hainan Island, he can reach out through this partner network, most likely entering the market through an old friend—say, the head of the provincial government, the CEO of a large local company, or the regional head of a multinational that is already there.

Tactic #2: Accessing Unique Information

The second intelligent market-entry tactic is to get access to *unique information*. If you are a foreigner, you need to assume that you are at a disadvantage relative to the locals in terms of information. Therefore, your standards need to be higher. You don't just need information; you need unique information.

Fortunately, getting unique information—not insider but unique—is fairly doable in developing economies and especially in cross-border situations. The markets are not very transparent and contain large information asymmetries. And often, the base data (government statistics, databases, transaction records) on industries and companies just doesn't exist. Things tend to be underdeveloped, and the general level of chaos often means nobody really knows things.

In these situations, having unique information is doable and can be a big advantage. It's hard not to make money if you're one of the few people with accurate consumer purchasing information in parts of China or Africa. This is actually quite similar to the situation in Graham's time when, prior to the passage of the Securities and Exchange Commission (SEC) Act, many corporations did not publish a lot of basic information. In Security Analysis, Graham estimated that only "half of our industrial corporations supplied this moderate quota of information."

During one of my first major real estate projects (approximately $200 million) in the Middle East, I asked for local real estate reports, only to discover that there were none. At that time, the region had few analysts or specialized real estate firms. It became clear that the base data didn't really exist either, as nobody reports accurate sales information to the government. I ended up hiring some former management consultants to gather independent data so that I could build my own market models on a large piece of land that the prince had purchased. This exercise had an interesting side effect. When word got out that Waleed was working on a real estate project, the price of that land jumped from Saudi riyal (SR) 19 per square meter to SR 28, increasing the total value by $43 million. I ultimately recommended that we hold on the project but definitely keep researching it.

It is actually much easier to enter Hainan than New York with unique information. All the characteristics of developing economies (lack of infrastructure, lack of laws, lack of reporting, autocratic governments) directly affect the quality and availability of information. Not only do government agencies rarely have the information, but the information they do have is often inaccurate or politically manipulated.

Apart from doing your own data gathering, I know of only three consistently accurate sources of information for developing and cross-border environments. The first is financial statements that have been audited by the big accounting firms. These firms are relatively powerful in these economies and can push back when the client tries to hide or falsify its numbers, which is not uncommon. Interestingly, you can now see this phenomenon migrating to the United States in the form of back-door initial public offerings (IPOs) by Chinese companies purchasing small but listed U.S. companies. The type of accounting firm they use (usually a small Chinese-owned accounting firm) is the tip-off in such situations. An important caveat is to be wary of the mentioned emerging-market shenanigan in which companies move profits between audited and unaudited (or weakly audited) companies. Unfortunately, although audited statements by the big accounting firms are accurate, the information they contain is widely available and therefore not too unique.

The second source is the commercial banks. They typically are conservative with their lending, both in types of products and approvals. They also have met the Basel banking standards, putting them several generations ahead of other local companies in terms of standards and reporting. They are sometimes the only institutions that really know what is going on in parts of the economy. And when a corporate scandal occurs in an emerging market, it is usually the local bank that brings it to light. With SEC and other regulatory-type bodies often underdeveloped, the commercial banks are most often acting as the local sheriffs.

Being able to see a developing economy's industries through a local bank is a tremendous advantage if you can get it. (Waleed frequently refers to banks as "the eyes into the economy.") It is likely not a coincidence that one of Waleed's first major acquisitions in Saudi Arabia was United Saudi Commercial Bank. His first acquisition in the U.S. was Citigroup. And his first major acquisition in China was

Bank of China. But for those of us who can't buy banks, this goal is accomplished by networking.

The third source is any direct consumer information. Banks are great for learning about a target industry, but they leave you blind in terms of consumer behavior. You can often learn more about inflation from contacts at a local supermarket than by talking to the local banks or government officials. Or about healthcare spending by talking to local insurance companies (the eyes into the healthcare system). I know one company that regularly sends people to the customs house just to see what is being brought into the country.

A fourth source is political information. It's not necessarily accurate, but it can be a big deal in places like China and Russia, where being aware of looming government changes can be critical. Of course, the temptation with unique information, particularly political, is to start speculating, trading in real estate and stocks. This is not something I think one should be involved in, but I mention it because it is common in so many markets today. In some unmentioned developing market exchanges, I sometimes think there is very little outside of insider trading and speculation. Just to reiterate, the described unique information approach is with the objective of leveraging unique information into constructing value-added private deals only.

Tactic #3: Creating a Deep "Capability Bench"

The third tactic for intelligent market entry is to create a deep *capability bench*. Ultimately, you need access to deals, and I have argued that capability keys are the best way to achieve that. However, most of us don't own lots of companies, so we access capabilities through strategic partnerships and operating agreements. Accessing good Eastern European bank or insurance projects likely means having a Western technology or business services partner and creating joint proposals. Creating a deep bench of such capabilities is key for intelligent market entry. If I have partnerships with gaming companies in Las Vegas, my entry into Macau is both easier and smarter.

To LP or Not to LP

A final note on becoming a limited partner (LP) in an overseas fund. Private equity groups from developing economies are continually meeting with Western investors about raising funds. And the pitch often includes the idea of using an LP position as a market-entry technique, a way of getting direct access to deals in developing markets. This approach may work well in some circumstances, but in my experience I have never seen it succeed in terms of building effective mechanisms for direct investment.

An approach that does appear to work well is investing as an LP in a developing economy venture capital (VC) fund of funds with follow-on rights. The wide spread in VC performance makes this a good way to target the high-performing VCs and then invest more in those few star performers (i.e., a heightened alpha approach). Or by investing directly in a VC fund, the follow-on rounds for most companies create opportunities for larger direct follow-on investments as well.

Picking Your Hunting Ground

The second challenge in going global is defining your advantages (and disadvantages) in an investment terrain

I have painted a simplistic picture of different landscapes and some of their inherent characteristics: their fundamental differences with developed economies, the additional challenges, the additional advantages, and so on. I have also argued that this is all fundamental to a colliding and multipolar world. In other words, it probably won't change anytime soon. But if you think about all the geographies, industries, transaction types, and my expanded definition of market inefficiency, there is really a lot of room for creativity in picking a hunting ground. Turnaround situations in weak-management godfather economies. Growth equity in state capitalist retail. Political access deals in cross-border situations. (I have a dream about launching an investment group in Washington, DC called Crony Capital.) Choosing your hunting ground is one of the areas where moving onto a global landscape increases your options by an order of magnitude.

Typically, you choose your terrain (industry, transaction type, amount of equity) and then search for the best deals. You pick your spot on the lake before you fish, and it is usually the first decision that bounds your possible returns. Not many groups doing middle-market U.S. private equity are making a 50% internal rate of return today.

However, this two-step approach creates a couple of problems when you start to go global. The first is that it assumes that you can pick your hunting ground and then just go execute. But choosing your hunting ground means identifying the largest opportunities *that can be captured*. It can mean finding unrecognized value and simply buying it. But it can also mean finding value that you can access and others cannot. It can mean finding deals where you have an advantage in getting the deal, often over entrenched locals. And most importantly, it means identifying deal types where you can stabilize the margin of safety over the long term.

The two-step approach doesn't capture the deal-making aspects of choosing your hunting ground. It doesn't consider what combination of value keys you are using and where those keys can create an advantage. The formula for choosing a hunting ground is "unrecognized + inaccessible value + created value." Medium-sized public companies in China can offer unrecognized but accessible value. Real estate in godfather capitalist Qatar can offer recognized but inaccessible value.

So quite a few additional factors come into play between the time you pick a hunting spot and then execute. We can effectively collect all these factors into an additional step in the process.

Step 1.5: Targeting Advantages (and Avoiding Disadvantages)

If the first step is choosing an attractive hunting ground and the second step is finding the best investments within that space, we can add a middle half-step for assessing where you have the strongest deal-making advantages in a given geography (see Figure 11.1).

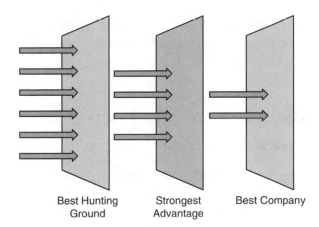

Best Hunting   Strongest   Best Company
Ground   Advantage

Figure 11.1   What is my advantage?

"Creating a deal advantage" is a catchall for many of the mentioned factors: accessing inaccessible deals, lowering the negotiated
price, creating defenses, strengthening the claim to the enterprise,
overcoming foreigner disadvantages. It's a combination of advantages
at the deal and company levels. Hunting where you can leverage
advantages can be very profitable (such as Saudi Hollandi Bank).
Hunting where you have weak or declining advantages can result in
rapidly collapsing investments (such as Danone in China). The main
point is that you should have a fairly strong answer to this question
when going global: What is my advantage?

Advantages are also about timing. A well-constructed deal that
brings in various capabilities can create a strong advantage at certain
points in time. For example, a foreign capability value key such as
insurance adjustment expertise can be an advantage in acquiring or
developing insurance companies in Africa today. But it may not be
much of a capability advantage 5 years from now. Reputation, capital,
and political access can be advantages in accessing real estate investments in Kazakhstan now and likely in the future.

This "What is my advantage?" half-step is particularly good at
predicting bad investments. And it captures the wing-walking phenomenon of investors entering foreign markets showing initial success and then quietly collapsing several years later. That foreign
investors frequently enter China and Russia with big public

announcements and later leave quietly (or never break out their losses in their financial statements) obscures this very common phenomenon.

Look Again Before You Leap

Be sure about short-term versus long-term advantages

Ultimately, much of value investing is about negotiated deal-making. It's about buying, building, or fixing a good, potentially great, or great company and getting in at a really low price. In practice, that's often about who is sitting in the room, who is strong, and who is weak. Or, as discussed in the preceding section, who has the advantage and who doesn't.

If you're doing such negotiated deals with one eye on the door (you're thinking short-term or buy-to-sell), it's pretty easy and can be done almost anywhere. Short-term strategies are numerous and profitable. All you need is a short-term advantage—just enough to get the deal done. You can focus on pre-IPO investments in high-growth countries. You can do short-term venture-capital-type plays in technical industries. Buy real estate or other fixed assets during an oil boom. Do contracting based on political access. There are quite a few options, and most Western investors do tend to stay short-term when going global.

I have argued that the largest opportunity is to go where few others are comfortable going—global, long-term, and mostly private investments (or PIPEs)—and to benefit from a company's growth in economic value over time. If you're in the room to stay, and you're negotiating an acquisition or development deal, how strong are you now? How strong will you be in 5 years? How do you maintain an advantage over time? Do you need to? After you have structured the deal and captured a healthy margin of safety in a good company at a great price, take a second and reconsider such questions. Look again before you leap.

In somewhere like India or the Middle East, I am quite comfortable with a short-term advantage at the time of the investment. In cross-border deals between, say, Asia and Africa, I am also fairly comfortable with a short-term advantage. It's usually enough. In hypercompetitive markets, particularly in state-capitalist countries, I want much more durable advantages that will protect my claim and my margin of safety well into the future. The two advantages that are particularly strong in the long term are *foreign capability keys* and *local economies of scale*. I'm sure there are many others, but these are the two I know best. Note that one is a deal advantage related to the claim on the enterprise and the margin of safety, and the other is a company advantage related to its strength relative to competitors. Having both is the best scenario.

The competitive advantage of local economies of scale is well known. Large scale, whether geographically or functionally, relative to the size of the market means that fixed costs are a smaller percentage of operating costs, relative to competitors. An auto servicing company that dominates a Chinese province spends less on marketing as a percentage of costs than a smaller competitor. Assuming that the company actively defends itself against entrants (it's surprising how often they don't), the company's market share and competitive advantage should persist and show up on the financial statements as a higher-than-normal ROIC. Achieving such economies of scale is occasionally doable at the national level and sometimes even globally. However, given the size of such markets it is much more difficult and rare, which is why I have argued that most attractive value opportunities are local.

In many cases, local economies of scale are not enough. I discussed in Chapter 9, "Capability Deals in Practice," how GM achieved significant scale in China yet still is likely to lose its market share or earnings. GM is both weakening in its claim on the enterprise and facing a competitive threat from new entrant Shanghai Automotive Industry Corporation (SAIC) Passenger Cars, against which it has no strong defense. In these cases, foreign capability keys are needed. The United Automotive Electronic Systems (UAES) case, also discussed in Chapter 9, was successful due to its proprietary technology, effectively creating a foreign capability key for UAES in China. This gives UAES a strong advantage at both the company and deal level. Other common foreign capability keys include overseas customers, credentials, and critical offsite services.

However, even in difficult environments, creative and clever deal-makers can usually figure out ways to build in and sustain an advantage. I mentioned at the start that Graham's Net Nets was essentially a clever way to eliminate the critical uncertainty. Structuring global deals is a lot about coming up with similarly wiley ways to eliminate key uncertainties.

One of my favorite examples involves a Saudi gentleman I met doing small, private investments in China. For many years, only a handful of us commuted between the Middle East and Asia, so we tended to meet at some point. This young man had built a strong track record doing small private deals out of a Beijing office. In contrast to the large private equity firms and multinational companies, he was using family money and just a few staff. His strategy was to look for small, growing, family-owned companies. In this, he avoided the large private equity deals, the explosive-growth VC-type opportunities, and the pre-IPO investments that are somewhat synonymous with emerging-market PE today. And unlike almost everyone else, he did not care about near-term liquidity. Instead, he looked for well-run family companies that were seeking $5–10 million.

By the time we met, he had enjoyed 5 years of successful investments with this approach. The question is, did he have an advantage? Did he need one? He was targeting companies that others were missing or were uninterested in, mostly because they did not offer the explosive growth, liquidity, or big PE opportunities others were looking for. Coming from a Saudi family office, he also understood family businesses—that they were not just businesses but the family's lifeline. By offering a long-term relationship, he ensured that they could grow their business safely and find funding for the next one. He was offering a relationship as an additional safety net. This is really an example of classic value investing in that he searches for mispriced value in "undesirable" companies. He avoids the crowds and goes where others aren't.

My point is that even the most difficult environments offer lots of workable approaches. Your advantage is an important consideration, but it often does not have to be as overwhelming as a foreign capability key. It can be structured into deals in lots of ways. I generally find that if you're in the room and focused on a long-term partnership with the objective of adding value to your partners and your project, you are 80% of the way there. In this case, a young Saudi investor with the right attitude was succeeding in the long term with a fairly soft advantage.

Before moving on, it is worth looking back at a few Waleed deals to identify the advantage. In 1991, he famously purchased a large stake in Citigroup. It is important to appreciate what an unusual investment this was at that time. An emerging-market investor buying a large piece of a major U.S. bank today would be very noticeable, but in 1991 it was really quite extraordinary. Waleed's advantage was mainly reputable capital, which was a powerful tool at that particular time. During this period, he acquired large positions in one Western company after another and has been seen ever since then as a distressed-value investor and a bargain hunter. But I don't think he was committed to this strategy. Instead, he was just using capital at a time when it offered him his strongest advantage. And he has done much fewer of these types of investments since. Were these investments a search for mispriced value or recognition of a strong deal advantage?

It depends on whether you think Waleed read the balance sheets and saw mispriced value. Or did he realize that he was in a position of strength relative to other parties in the deal? Was he thinking as a hunter of mispriced value or as a deal-maker in a position of advantage? I have argued that these are basically two sub-versions of the same global value approach.

In comparison, Waleed did not employ this strategy in China, even though such a capital advantage would have been much stronger there. But capital is a short-term advantage and China usually requires a long-term one, such as foreign capability keys or local economies of scale. Waleed's investments in China have overwhelmingly relied on his capabilities and political access, not his capital.

Filling Your Global Dance Card

Targeting companies and potential partners are both good starting points for going global

Parroting Buffett yet again, if you could invest in only 40 companies in your lifetime, which ones would they be? Which 40 would create the greatest economic value and let you capture the greatest wealth over time? Who would fill your dance card?

You probably can tell that I focus a lot more on certain types of companies than others: real estate projects, banks/financial services, entertainment/casinos, consumer finance, healthcare, and insurance companies. The last one is close to an obsession. Insurance is very attractive almost everywhere, particularly in large-population, low-GDP-per-capita, and low regulatory environments. And the technical requirements also enable a strong advantage and value-add by foreign investors ("technical but not technological" being my mantra in most things). As a foreign investor, insurance works out well at both the company and deal level. I consider the economics in insurance and the other sectors so attractive in developing and cross-border situations that they are always on my target list. And if I do not target them directly (some are too big), I go at them indirectly with "bird on a rhino" and other ancillary strategies. But these are the company targets for my global dance card.

However, you can also think about your dance card in terms of potential partners. Sands casinos would be a great partner in many places (family-friendly casinos in Dubai?). GE Energy Financial Services and GE's technology division could be fantastic partners for entering many markets. Dubai-based Emaar could be very strong in mega real estate projects in many developing economies—say, in Morocco. FocusMedia in China has tremendous scale in indoor media, which could be leveraged into various types of investments (Middle Eastern mega real estate, Indian healthcare). I generally hunt for a good-to-great company with attractive economics—or for a potential partner with impressive capabilities that can be used in other investments. You can come at the question of who should be on your global dance card from either the company or potential partner direction.

With a clear company and partner target list, you realize opportunities are everywhere. Why isn't Ralph Lauren in China? Why has Victoria's Secret barely left the U.S.? How will Marks & Spencer turn around its China initiative? Why are most Middle Eastern and African insurance companies still multiline, with healthcare not pulled into separate specialized companies? Note: Individual mandates have made healthcare 50% of many developing market insurers' income statements. What will Dubai and its state-backed companies do now that the "build it and they will come" real estate/tourism strategy of the past 15 years has collapsed? Who holds the eight Indian licenses for inbound cash remittances? Note: Expatriate cash remittances between Saudi Arabia and India are second only to those between the U.S. and Mexico. Attractive companies and partners are everywhere.

Moving the Castle to an Island

Some investments need to be more than competitive

A Columbia Business School student once asked Warren Buffett what he would want to know about a company or investment if he could know only one thing. Paraphrasing, Buffett's reply was, "Whether it has a sustainable competitive advantage." With a long-term value approach, it is not so much about identifying companies with abnormally high profits or returns on invested capital. It is about identifying companies that have profits and distributable earnings that are strongly protected from competitors. Protected profits (i.e., a sustainable competitive advantage) are the most important thing.

Such barriers to competition go by quite a wide spectrum of names and analogies: a competitive advantage, a franchise, a barrier to entry, "building a moat around your castle." My recent favorite example was in a *Wall Street Journal* column by *Dilbert* creator Scott Adams, in which he described his investment strategy as buying companies that he hates. Adams hates certain companies either because he must buy their products (oil companies) or because he cannot resist them (Apple, Starbucks); both are types of competitive advantages.

Translating Buffett's comment to various global environments, we immediately see complications. Competitive advantage implies a certain range of competitive behavior. But at this time, some Chinese solar panel manufacturers are selling their products at below the manufacturing cost. In fact, the competitive dynamics can go all the way from monopolies to credit-fueled hypercompetition. There is also the competitive impact of shifting state-commercial collusion. None of this actually conflicts with the previously mentioned competitive-advantage economics, but it does complicate things when looking at individual companies. A sustainable competitive advantage in the U.S. may not be sustainable in Russia or Africa.

But here I mention one main factor that needs to be considered alongside Buffett's comment on competitive advantage—defensibility. This is a basic all-inclusive term to recognize that, in some cases, competitors are not the only players on the field, and competitive forces are not the only threats to profits. Whether it's Russian seizures of foreign-invested companies or French companies being squeezed out by their Chinese JV partners, profitable investments can face many more threats than just competition, particularly if the owner is perceived as foreign.

It's easy to focus on competitive forces and give mild or cursory consideration to these other factors, considering them anomalies to be avoided (various types of long-tail risk). But they are fundamental to many different politico-economic systems and need to be structured in to the investment. For these risks, like any other, Graham's sage advice holds that the ultimate test of an investment is its ability to withstand adversity, whether it be a depression, a government action, extreme volatility, actions by nonmarket players, or something else equally dire. A sustainable competitive advantage can be seen as a strong ability to withstand competitive adversity. But in other systems it fails to incorporate other adverse conditions.

An example of a company that both has a sustainable competitive advantage and is well defended is General Biologic in Shanghai. Run by Jon Zifferblatt and Matthew Chervenak, the company provides information and advisory services for the growing pharmaceutical and biotechnology businesses of Mainland China. Its clients include both local and Western pharmaceutical companies, for which it does in-depth analysis on the increasing number of pharma and biotech companies across China. It also supports targeted acquisitions. In terms of competitive advantage, General Biologic has built local economies of scale in information, advisory, and increasingly in transactions. But it is also highly defended. In value-point-speak, its foreign capability key is its foreign customers, who are evaluating something highly technical and with significant financial and clinical risk. It would be very difficult for local Chinese companies, governments, and other entities to enter General Biologic's business in a significant way. Additionally, research and development in general, and biotech in particular, is an area government actors are attempting to bring to China in a large way. General Biologic is well defended from various government officials and other nonmarket forces. Unsurprisingly, as the biotech market is growing, General Biologic is doing very well.

Defensibility is not a bunker mentality. It means preparing for serious threats to your profits from more than just competitors. And defensibility can be achieved through foreign capability keys, reputation, trust, political access, geography, and many other approaches. It's sometimes a requirement but certainly isn't a pessimistic worldview. In the Gulf Cooperation Council (GCC), India, and Brazil, and in cross-border situations such as U.S.-India and Europe-GCC, defensibility usually is a consideration, but usually not a big one.

Finally, defensibility has a curious twist. Although competitive advantage implies that there are few threats other than competitors, it also implies that profits are the result of competing successfully. Defensible investments imply that there are more threats to a company but also that high profits do not necessarily have to come from competitive performance. In many markets, you have to be better defended, but you don't necessarily have to be very competitive to make a lot of money. Many times it's not about being smart and competitive, but being functional and defended.

All Your Eggs in One Basket Versus All Your Baskets Tied Together

Interlocking investments in unstable environments

Value investors minimize the risk of a single investment by getting the price way below the intrinsic value (a quantitative approach) and by staying in their circle of competence (a qualitative approach). But after you've made about five of these types of value investments, the question of portfolio risk arises. How much risk am I really exposed to here? What if all the investments have problems at the same time (value at risk)? Does a marginal increase or decrease occur in the portfolio risk with each additional investment?

Buffett's classic answer to the question about portfolio risk is to "Put all your eggs in one basket, and watch that basket." Natural follow-up questions are how many eggs are enough and how many are too many to watch carefully. In his book *You Can Be a Stock Market Genius: Uncover the Secret Hiding Places of Stock Market Profits*, Joel Greenblatt argues that once you have six to eight investments, you have minimized your portfolio risk, and each additional investment doesn't decrease your net risk. However, the number of investments in many good investors' portfolios does seem to vary widely.

As you construct a portfolio that includes investments in both developing and developed economies, it is unclear if the overall risk is decreasing or increasing. One can argue that having a lot of businesses concentrated in Kenya exposes you to risk if there is a political problem there. However, one could similarly argue that having extensive real estate assets in the U.S. in the last 2 years has been equally risky. I have seen some groups attempt to diversify across emerging-market geographies (Middle East, Latin America, Asia) or to focus only on companies with a global footprint, but I find both arguments unconvincing. When going global, the question of portfolio risk and how many eggs one can responsibly watch is one question I haven't found a convincing answer to. But it's an important question.

A tactic I have seen that I do believe is effective is to *interlock investments*. If investing in the U.S. is sailing on relatively calm waters (a big if), global investing can be seen as sailing on more turbulent seas. So when the seas get rough, you lash your boats together and ride it out. Or, to use Buffett's "eggs in a basket" analogy, you tie all your baskets together for greater stability.

Waleed's Riyadh skyscraper complex, named Kingdom Centre, is a good example of six interlocked investments and some particularly clever deal structuring. The development itself occupies a 1 million square feet site and is made up of a 984-foot tower (approximately the same height as the Eiffel Tower), a shopping center, and a wedding hall. Completed in 2002, it has become the city's landmark development. If you've ever seen a picture of Riyadh, you can't miss his big tower with the hole in the top.

In terms of market positioning, Waleed heavily branded the project with his name and targeted the luxury sector with its high-end hotel and Grade A office, retail, and residential space. In the shopping center, he built a large Saks Fifth Avenue store as the anchor tenant and as a separate direct investment. It was the first Saks store to open outside the U.S., a testament to Waleed's persuasive abilities and to his status as a major Saks shareholder (he purchased 10% of Saks for $100 million in 1993). Having such a highly branded anchor store makes it much easier to get Ralph Lauren, Gucci, and other luxury tenants to come to somewhere such as Riyadh.

In the 984-foot tower, United Saudi Bank purchased six floors for its new headquarters. United Saudi Bank (USB) (now Saudi American Bank [Samba]) was a Waleed holding and the direct descendant of his first Saudi bank investment in the late 1980s. Also occupying 18 floors of the tower is Saudi Arabia's first Four Seasons hotel (Waleed is one of the owners). The tower's 65th floor was taken by Rotana, the Arab media company owned by Waleed (and now also by News Corp.). And the top floor became the Kingdom Holding Company headquarters.

The net result is six interlocked investments in one project. This has the benefit of maximizing the profits captured at various levels of the project. But it also increases both control and options in the event of an adverse event. If the tower's vacancy rate increases, Waleed can see if Samba will take a few more floors. If the market collapses and the luxury stores start losing money, you can restructure the leases. This is similar to Graham's thinking that you structure your investments to be able to withstand true adversity. So if you have already maximized your margins of safety for the individual companies and you are watching the companies closely, it seems the next step you can take to reduce the risk of loss is to increase your options in difficult times. Interlocking investments increase both control and options.

A side note on Kingdom Centre in terms of its clever value-added deal-making. Kingdom Centre was launched through a $453 million private placement, in which Waleed put in previously purchased land at a $100 million valuation (twice what he paid for it in the early 1990s), $22 million in contributed assets, and $50 million in cash—capturing 65% of the project's shares. He both added and captured value at each stage of the project. Additionally, he captured the increased value of the adjacent land guaranteeing a large secondary return. The highly lucrative project was a greenfield development that closely followed the previously discussed value-add approach for his one-mile skyscraper in Jeddah (reputable capital + political access).

Kingdom Centre's success also came much to the consternation of the owners of Alfaisalia Tower, located just down the road. The Alfaisalia Tower was built first, with the goal of becoming the iconic structure of Riyadh. Like Alfaisalia, Kingdom Centre's height was limited by Riyadh regulations to 30 occupied floors. However, Waleed noticed a sort of loophole in the rules. Although a building can have only 30 occupied floors, additional unoccupied floors are permissible. So on top of the occupied floors, he added 394 feet in the form of a giant sculpture. This made his tower reach 984 feet, 184 feet taller than Alfaisalia, and gave it its distinctive hole in the top (large enough for a Boeing 727 to fly through). Also for good measure, before Waleed sold the surrounding land, he divided it into smaller pieces separated by new roads. This makes it effectively impossible to build anything very tall nearby, both protecting Kingdom Centre's place in the skyline and ensuring that no other tower can block its views.

The net result is that Kingdom Centre dominates the Riyadh skyline and has become the symbol of the city. Next time you see a photo of the Riyadh skyline, note the much shorter Alfaisalia Tower next to Kingdom Centre.

The Intelligent Global Investor

Going global is about high-speed, incremental microfundamentalism

Going global is a lot about adopting a posture that not only will be successful but that also enables you to consistently improve over time and expand into more types of opportunities. The posture is arguably as important as the strategy. I suggest that intelligent global investing has three aspects.

Remain Strictly Microfundamentalist

I am aware that this book is about global investing but strikes a
somewhat odd, almost anti-macro, anti-globalization stance. It's the
anti-globalization global worldview of a microfundamental fundamentalist (if that makes any sense).

Something about going global makes smart people become
untethered and kind of stupid. Everyone starts talking in grand theories. Indian versus Chinese growth rates. Sovereign wealth funds'
impact on global capital flows. Something about the topic makes normally fundamentals-focused analysts start talking in big theories.
Where I have spoken in generalities, I hope it has come across that
this is purely for orientation purposes (i.e., cloud-naming) and that
such comments should be discounted as much as possible. I argue for
a staunchly microfundamentalist approach, both because it works and
to serve as a counterweight to this "untethering" tendency. It's both a
logical and prejudicial approach.

First, the world does look different depending on where you are
standing. Investors in Singapore do view the world differently than
those in New York. And it really does look different from the ground,
as compared with flying over at 30,000 feet. So getting out of the
clouds (both literally and figuratively) and back on the ground is critical. If macroeconomics is high-level, much of globalization today
tends to be discussed at an order of magnitude above this (macro^2
economics). If you get the microfundamentalist approach right, the
analysis and decision-making become easier. If you start talking globalization theories, things get murky pretty quickly.

Second, I am fairly prejudiced against multivariable modeling of
complex systems. I have done quite a lot of it, and it is becoming
more commonly used with the improvements in computing power.
But even when done by the best practitioners, it has a fairly low yield
rate and the correct conclusion is almost always "inconclusive." And
even if it is accurate and yields a conclusive answer, it can almost
never (with the exception of macro trading) be translated into consistent micro actions, such as buying companies. Note that much of the
analysis in this book has been presented empirically: equations and
graphs. There are no quantitative methods. I have found that if I

force myself to do things empirically and in long-hand, it restricts my tendency to computer-crunch the models.

To be fair, those of us who focus on small micromodels can suffer from notoriously poor uncertainty analysis. You routinely find micro-analysts predicting earnings with a specificity that is analogous to pre-dicting to within 2 inches where a rubber ball will stop after being thrown off a roof. So there is plenty of criticism to go around. But rec-ommendation #1 is when going global, stay in the trenches, firmly tethered to value and microfundamentals.

Incrementally Expand Your Circle of Competence

In his book *The Age of Turbulence*, Alan Greenspan compared his career to making a quilt. He worked on one square at a time, building deep experience and expertise in an industry, such as manufacturing or retail. Then he moved on to the next square. His understanding grew like a quilt, square by square. This is analogous to Graham's cir-cle of competence, but you add cantos instead of squares as you go through your life.

My experience has been the same, but I have been adding invest-ment terrains as well as industries—private U.S. healthcare, Saudi royal-owned real estate, government-backed Chinese banks, chaotic Brazilian retail, developing Indian financial services. And I seem to be adding adjectives as well as geographies and industries.

This type of incremental approach has power over time. Although it's not as good as interest compounding, it is similarly cumulative, and each new area of expertise tends to enhance all the others. Time is the real ally of the global microfundamentalist who is building expertise (and wealth).

Increase Your Velocity

In a world full of opportunities, your ultimate limiting factor is not your capital but the number of hours in a day. There are far more opportunities, more geographies, and more industries now than time to look at them. So against this constraint, your velocity matters. The faster you move, the more you can accomplish.

Chatting with a colleague in a Macau casino one night, we got to talking about a quirky article I had read titled "V-speed." It argued that velocity has become a measure of wealth and ability in modern life. Driving a car, you can go farther in a day than when you ride a bicycle. Therefore, the faster you can move in life, the more freedom and ability you have (that is, wealth).

V-speed is a twist on this idea. You take your miles traveled per year and divide by time. Business leaders like Prince Waleed and GE's Jeff Immelt have V-speeds of over 30 mph, meaning that they are moving at that average speed every moment of their lives. My V-speed tends to be 13 to 15 mph. This is more of a quirky idea than a serious one (moving quickly in investing is not the same as traveling). But the term has an energetic quality to it that I like. In a global gold rush of opportunities, how fast you are moving does matter.

Most of the global investors I look to for insight and inspiration have this sort of posture. They are all fundamentalists focused at the micro level. They are all incrementally building their expertise over time. And they are all moving as fast as they possibly can right now. This sort of intelligent global investor posture is a good tee-up for the next chapter in which I lay out a global investment playbook.

12

A Global Investment Playbook

This book started with a central question: "How do you value-invest long-term in inherently unstable and uncertain environments?" Or alternately, given the rise of such environments and their increasing collision with the West, "What would Ben Graham do now?"

I have asserted that in practice this theoretical question usually boils down to five practical problems: limited access, increased current uncertainties, increased long-term uncertainties, weakened or impractical claims to the enterprise, and foreigner disadvantages. If you can overcome these problems, the circle of attractive value investments expands dramatically, and a host of companies jump from the "too hard" to the "good" bucket. And my best answer to these problems (not the only answer for sure, but my best one) is to combine traditional value-investing methodologies with value-added deal-making. To not just expand the margin of safety by demanding a lower price (the traditional answer to increased uncertainty), but to also expand it upward through added value and then to stabilize it into the future through structured deal-making.

However, I could have opted to start this book instead with a description of various projects. Currently I am working on about $175 million of investments and deals, including a Swiss water company with concessions in Madagascar, a Libyan construction project, a Saudi business school, several Chinese quasi-healthcare real estate projects, a Middle Eastern insurance company, and a South Carolina physician home-monitoring company. And I'm doing this while commuting between New York and Shanghai, where I live; Beijing and Cambridge, where I teach; and Hong Kong and Paris, where I normally stop over for a few days to rest and write. But I suspect that starting out with such an account would have seemed chaotic and somewhat bizarre to the reader.

Hopefully at this point such activity appears more logical. It's really just one consistently applied value strategy. The investment version of Occam's razor is that when a small group of investors is making significant money in a seemingly random way, look for the simplest strategy.

In general, I hunt for negotiated deals in underpriced and/or underperforming companies where I can surgically add value, both perceived and economic. Such deals can sometimes be enhanced with debt at entry, asset sales, or IPOs at exit, but these are bonuses and not core to a longer-term value approach.

In this chapter, I present nine value strategies as a global investment playbook. These are the strategies that I think are particularly attractive for the coming years, although many have been used by practitioners for decades. They are all variations of value investing + value point.

A Global Investment Playbook

1. Buy underpriced good-to-great stocks (ie., traditional global value investing).

2. Buy great companies on their knees.

3. Buy "potentially great" companies, and make them great.

4. Launch a "value tank" for global acquisition and development deals.

5. Build a "direct spectacular" investment.

6. Buy or build a "bird on a rhino" investment in a rising environment.

7. Buy small-medium private companies in high growth environments.

8. Buy cheap companies in environments or situations that others avoid.

9. Structure political deals with guaranteed returns, or buy companies with politically limited competition.

I present them in the order I think will seem most comfortable and familiar to Western-based readers. The first strategy is just a reiteration of traditional global value investing approaches per Graham and Buffett. The next two are value point strategies focused on the growing intersection of developed and developing markets. The next three are value point approaches for moving into a truly global posture. The final three go fairly deep into the developing-market weeds. Their order can been viewed as a "going global" step-wise progression, a pathway for transitioning from Western to global value investing. The progression can also be seen as an incremental expanding of the sphere of companies that can be captured with a long-term value approach.

Strategy #1: Buy Underpriced Good-to-Great Stocks

In addition to being the most familiar to investors in developed economies, this traditional long-term value approach is also the most efficient for global investing. Buying the public shares of a great company at a cheap price enables the investor to stay liquid and make their returns at the time of investment. It is still the most surgical and elegant of approaches.

Much of the strategy in this book addresses the fact that this approach is too limited in most rising markets, and their increasing collision with the West. Buying Chinese stocks on the Hong Kong exchange or buying European stocks with emerging market exposure is just too limited. Most of the mispriced companies in developing markets are private. And, most importantly, within this approach you have very limited tools for dealing with the five going global problems. Trying to compensate for the increased uncertainties that are fundamental to many of today's investment terrains with an increased margin of safety leads to an impractical posture of extreme precaution. It's not that the method isn't great; it's that we don't get to use it that often. We only have one tool to deal with most problems: wait for an even lower price and thereby capture an even larger margin of

safety. We get stuck between choices of shrinking our pool of potential investments, staying in Western markets, going short-term, or
doing some other type of contorted posturing. I am arguing that a
better solution is to build additional tools to directly address the
increased uncertainties and other going global problems: searching
for value + adding value + structured deal-making.

However, it's still difficult (and a bit more work) to beat the traditional value approach of buying the public shares of a great company
at a cheap price. If you can find such opportunities on the exchanges
of Hong Kong, Dubai, New York, or other places, this remains the
best approach. It is listed here as Strategy #1 to reiterate it as the
starting point and the most efficient approach for capturing mispriced value globally. Within global investing, value point picks up
where this primary strategy leaves off.

Strategy #2: Buy Great Companies on Their Knees

Earlier, I discussed some of the definitions of "great" companies.
There is general agreement about what constitutes a great company's
financials for a longer-term approach: stable and protected profits
with minimal capital required to run and grow the business. Different
investors look for different types of companies that can generate such
a financial picture. Many look for a large and stable market share or a
sustainable competitive advantage that commands a share of the consumer mind. Some look for global presence and good brands. Some
pursue one-of-a-kind, nonreproducible assets. And in many markets,
government-limited competition remains one of the biggest factors in
creating such great companies.

The objective of this second strategy, like the first strategy, is to
buy *already-great companies for a cheap price*. However, we are
expanding to private transactions, which means that we usually are
looking for companies struggling with a real problem—real enough
that they will agree to a private transaction at a low price. So most
often we are looking for temporary business or financial problems.

Such situations can include cyclical industry events, economic down-turns, management problems, financial problems, and protracted underperformance. But the situation is such that we believe the company will now recover *without significant intervention on our part outside of capital*. We want an already-great company, just exiting a problem situation, on the cheap.

This approach works well in both developed and developing economies and is well known by value investors. I have mentioned several examples, including Prince Waleed's purchase of stakes in Citigroup, Canary Wharf, and Euro Disney, many done as negotiated private investments in public equity (PIPEs). He is one of the most successful at this approach and has been particularly effective at going between developed and developing economies this way. Reputation, as discussed, is particularly important in this approach, and targeting underperforming companies is a way of capturing the amplified power of reputation in developing economies. Warren Buffett would be given privileged access to just about any underperforming company in India or China today. This strategy (shown in Figure 12.1) can sometimes be applied to companies that have no significant performance problem and instead are looking for growth equity or other. In all of these scenarios, access is often the primary challenge, and our response is reputable capital (and sometimes political access).

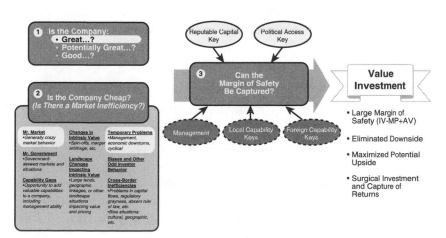

Figure 12.1   Strategy #2: Buy great companies on their knees

Recall that one of the key questions when crossing borders and going global is what is your advantage? How do you avoid being one of ten smart investors bidding for a company? How do you beat out often well funded local investors? This is a strategy in which foreigners crossing borders can have significant advantages. One advantage is greater expertise. If the company is facing issues of underperformance, you must make an important decision: Has the company been overpenalized for its problems, and has it now solved (or will it, with the injected capital)? It takes significant often technical expertise to know whether both price and performance will improve rapidly. This is an advantage that can eliminate much of the competition, particularly local.

Reputation can be a second critical advantage in such deals, because it has an outsized impact in both developing economies and in underperforming situations. When you are on your knees, whom you turn to for help has a lot to do with reputation and relationships. Third, the amount of capital required can sometimes limit competition. Both going very big and going small can eliminate many competitors.

The net result is a situation where an investor can cross borders, say from the UK into China or from the Middle East into the United States, and be in an advantaged situation relative to local investors. It is a very effective strategy for global investing, particularly in the form of PIPEs. And as previously disconnected parts of the world continue to collide, more and more variations of this strategy are becoming possible. Middle Eastern investors are buying underperforming Indonesian companies; Chinese companies rescuing discussed Africa resource companies, and so on.

A twist on this strategy is to connect large capital in one geography with struggling companies in another. Being able to come in rapidly with big capital from overseas can be a big weapon at certain points. It has more to do with size than reputation or expertise, so this is often about putting together a consortium. This technique has historically been seen as large Middle Eastern capital or emerging market sovereign wealth funds acquiring Western assets during economic downturns.

But being able to rapidly deploy large amounts of Chinese capital into Singapore or India during downturns is now becoming possible as well. If the Indian economy has a recession, investment consortiums from distant geographies can enter with this type of big capital strategy. And as developing markets are more unstable and more prone to booms and busts, this is possible on a fairly regular basis.

Strategy #3: Buy "Potentially Great" Companies, and Make Them Great

Earlier, I added a new definition of "potentially great" companies. Since we are in the business of both searching for and adding value, that means we don't have to settle for the company as it is today. We can rapidly add value and make a company better by improving or augmenting capabilities, political access, reputation, or management. And in developing markets and cross-border situations, we have far more ability to do this surgically than in the West. The other big tool we have with this approach is orchestrating mergers. I haven't discussed this strategy extensively, but it's a very effective way to build great companies.

Buying a potentially great company and making it great is analogous to buying homes and fixing them up, but with three important criteria. The first is that we look only for companies that can be made into great institutions. The second is that, per Graham's Method, we are surgical. We don't do long-term management or other, more gradual improvements. The returns are locked in at the time of the investment. The third and most important criterion is that we depend mostly on our capability keys and management. I have characterized much of the interaction of the developed and developing worlds as consisting of capability migration and consolidation. This investment strategy rides that wave and relies on bringing in management and capabilities at various points in time.

This strategy is shown in Figure 12.2. Note that it is all about getting a low price and ending up with a great company. It also re-raises an important Graham question—whether it is better to target an attractive company at an unattractive price or an unattractive company at an attractive price. This approach basically splits the difference.

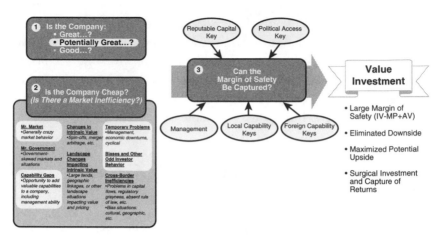

Figure 12.2   Strategy #3: Buy potentially great companies, and make them great

Strategy #1 was a quantum jump in the number of "cheap companies" we can target with a long-term value approach. Strategy #2 was about expanding from underpriced to underperforming great companies. This strategy is about expanding from great companies to potentially great ones. And when looking at most developing economies today, the number of "potentially great" companies is dramatically larger than the "great" ones. Also, the more value keys you have, the more companies of this type you can look at. In many ways, this strategy also just makes a lot more intuitive sense in developing economies—a developing companies value approach for developing economies.

I have mentioned several Waleed investments of this type. The George V, now Europe's top hotel, required a $125 million refurbishment by renowned architect Pierre Yves Rochon and then a rebranding and repositioning through a management contract with the Four Seasons. The Savoy in London is currently undergoing a similar renovation. The Fairmont required a series of mergers and acquisitions to turn it into the world's largest luxury hotel chain. More recently, Waleed's 2007 purchase of distressed NAS airline is a "potentially great" play. NAS is one of the two private airline licensees in Saudi Arabia. It is well positioned to become a great company with some targeted political and operational help.

This is a pure value point strategy, as shown in Figure 12.3. We can target a truly large array of companies this way, and not only does it have a strong answer to the "What is my advantage?" question, it also handily takes care of most of the five going global problems.

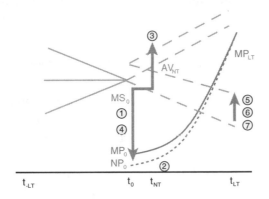

Figure 12.3   Impact on potentially great companies

Recall also the section "B2B: Back to the Balance Sheet" in Chapter 3, "Value Point." Potentially great companies expand us from Earnings Power Value (EPV) > Asset Value (AV) cases to those we assess to have EPV = AV and even those with EPV < AV, depending on the management and capability keys we can deploy. A politically connected company in a management-weak environment might well have EPV < AV and be a prime "potentially great" target company.

These previous two strategies are about hunting for deals at the intersection of developing and developed economies, at the points where the markets collide. They are also an expansion of the tools used—from capital and reputation in Strategy #2 to capabilities and political access in Strategy #3—and an expansion of traditional value investing to value point. The next three strategies are about moving from here into a committed global posture.

Strategy #4: Launch a Value Tank for Global Acquisition and Development Deals

Value tanks (focused value-adding vehicles) are stand-alone entities created to house specific value keys. The objective is a focused vehicle that, by virtue of its ability to add tremendous value, is able to roll comfortably across borders and geographies. The preceding chapters described examples of value tanks, such as Kingdom Zephyr in Africa and Kingdom Hotels in emerging markets. Note that although they are all value tanks, the translations can vary from public share purchases to illiquid private asset development to traditional private equity.

Private equity groups housed within investment banks, a fairly common situation in many developing economies, could also be considered an example. By buying shares in private companies in, say, China or India two to three years before they go public, these PE groups effectively warehouse the company within the investment bank for a later IPO. However, the important point is to note how the approach succeeds when traditional PE would not. Traditional PE looks for majority shares, an ability to use debt, and/or an ability to add management value. But these "pre-IPO value tanks" have a built-in value key—their investment banking businesses. Many rising companies would like to be taken public by Morgan Stanley or Goldman Sachs and see value in having an investor with such ties. The PE firms basically use a capability key (investment banking) to secure access to the deal and eliminate the risks of being in a minority position.

Another example is GE Money, which uses long-term added value to buy into public banks, retailers, and other companies across the world. Their preferred approach is to buy 10% to 20% of a public bank (typically $200–500 million) in a developing economy, such as Turkey, Eastern Europe, the Middle East, or India. At the same time, they do a development deal to plug their consumer finance products and capabilities into the bank's platform. And as the bank shares are publicly traded, they rapidly increase in value with the new consumer finance products, as well as with the GE name. The GE Money approach is that of a particularly powerful value tank primarily using capability and reputable capital value keys.

In terms of the presented frameworks, value tanks can target good, potentially great, and great companies and any of the discussed market inefficiencies (cross-border inefficiencies, capability gaps, and so on). We're both buying and building good to great companies, and the more value we can add when closing the deal, the greater our advantage, the more likely we are to get a cheap price, and the more attractive the investment economics. Again, we are dramatically expanding the circle of companies we can target with a long-term value approach.

This strategy is probably the most effective and accessible for Western-based investors, PE funds, value investors, and business development executives. It is a fairly easy step that leverages their current capabilities into direct global investments, while at the same time building up the political and other softer value keys along the way. Generally speaking, the stronger the capability keys built into the focused vehicle, the more easily the vehicle can roll across borders. It solves many of the going-global problems and tends to naturally make the investor into a "value-added partner of choice."

Strategy #5: Build a "Direct Spectacular" Investment

This is the other "five value keys" approach I discussed in Chapter 10, "Global Tycoons, Value Tanks, and Other 'Go for the Jugular' Strategies." We build as much value as possible into a single direct and spectacular investment, either locally or in an overseas location. These investments can result in large, rapid returns and the creation of a truly great company. These are the cruise missile analogs of value tanks. We are building one great company in one big move.

I have seen this strategy only in developing markets. However, it does often rely on bringing in developed-economy partners and capabilities, so it can have a cross-border component. You could characterize Middle Eastern mega real estate, Macau gaming, Chinese operating giants, and many of the other fairly eye-catching emerging-market phenomena as versions of "direct spectacular" investments.

Strategy #6: Buy or Build a "Bird on a Rhino" Investment in a High Growth Environment

In Chapter 10, I argued that sometimes it is mostly about the environment, that certain environments are more responsible for the attractive company financials than the company itself. I described Macau and Liujiazui as two examples.

A subset of such attractive environments is when separate economies become linked and experience rapid economic booms. The most spectacular "link surges" have been the explosive growth of Dubai and Macau. These small, shallow economies surged on the back of massive inflows of international customers and capital. The recent flood of mainland Chinese capital into Hong Kong real estate is another link-surge example. Saudi Arabia's 2005–2006 real estate and stock market booms were the result of its link with the Western economies and oil reaching $100 per barrel. Certainly such rapid-growth situations create the opportunities for trading stocks, real estate, and other assets. But such attractive environments can also be approached with a longer-term value mindset that benefits from growth but does not depend on it.

The best approach I know for such environments is the "bird on a rhino" strategy described in Chapter 5, "How Political Access Adds Value." Such situations almost always go hand in hand with the actions of the large corporate and government rhinos, particularly in shallow economies. Dubai's boom was mostly created by the large state-backed companies. So we take advantage of the opportunity by buying or building smaller, highly scalable investments that directly benefit from the actions of these large companies (a bird on a rhino). The most direct method is to buy a smaller company and then sign revenue contracts with several rhinos. And although these booms can end quickly, and badly, if we focus on highly scalable businesses and come in at the right price, we can do very well in the long term.

This strategy is shown in Figure 12.4, but it can involve any combination of value keys.

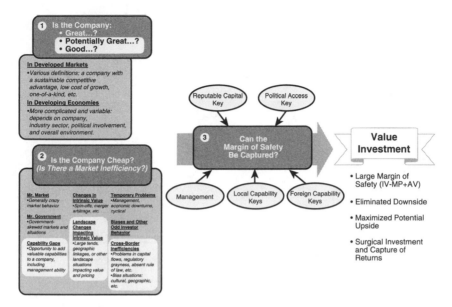

Figure 12.4   Strategy #6: Buy or build a bird on a rhino in a high-growth environment

China's outbound M&A activity over the past 2 years is a compelling example of a link surge. These cross-border deals have been primarily focused on acquiring natural resources in Africa, Australia, and Latin America; technology in Europe; and technology and distribution in the U.S. (more attempted than realized). If you have a company that benefits long-term from the trend shown in Figure 12.5, it is virtually impossible not to make money.

In practice, such investments can be traditional value investing, value point, or PE. You can build, buy and hold, buy to sell, and so on. Within the next 5 years, we can anticipate many more of these link-surge opportunities, as they seem to be a natural occurrence in a colliding world. Figure 12.6 lays out the areas I am following at the current time, but it's more for illustrative purposes than a detailed accounting.

Thus far, I have presented three strategies focused on the intersection of developed and developing markets and three focused on switching to a global posture. And with each one, the number and types of companies targetable with a long-term value approach have incrementally increased. The final three strategies are focused on direct hands-on investing deep within developing markets.

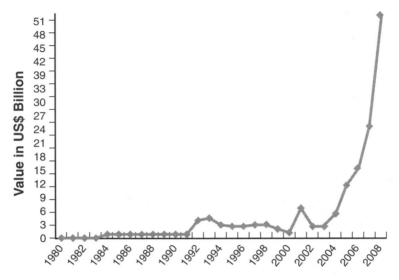

Sources: ODCE, MOFCOM, China Statistics Bureau re SinoLatin Capital

Figure 12.5   China's outbound foreign direct investment (FDI)

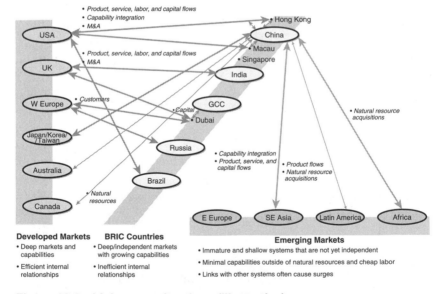

Figure 12.6   Link-surge situations (illustrative)

Strategy #7: Buy Small-Medium Private Companies in a Rising Environment

Several billion people are furnishing their first homes, taking their first cars to the garage, and discovering everything from over-priced lattes to luxury handbags. And similar to the West, most of this daily activity, by both consumers and companies, happens at small and medium-sized businesses.

In rising markets, rising small and medium companies offering local, regional, and national services and products are attractive investment targets. It turns out that the West's most successful export has been entrepreneurial capitalism. You can basically pick any first- or second-tier city in any BRIC country and start discovering good businesses benefiting from attentive owner-managers, local economic development, and market growth. It is worth noting that in the first 6 months of 2010, while the West was still firmly in recession, more than 100 companies went public on Shenzhen's new small-medium-sized company exchange.

Most of these small-medium companies are run by owner-managers and operate effectively as family-owned companies. They are hands-on, and they appreciate reputable investors who can help them move their business to the next level. In many cases, they are looking for longer-term smart capital as opposed to the relatively abundant local "hot" capital. In terms of deals, these are opportunities typically in the $10–40 million investment range, almost always for a minority equity stake. So it's about creating a value-added partnership over time.

This is the value point equivalent of small cap stock picking, of scouring the world's antique shops for mispriced situations. You are as likely to find such companies in Wuhan and Bangalore as in Shanghai and Mumbai. So this strategy is often about going well off the beaten path. Generally, you are looking for good, not necessarily great, companies that are significantly mispriced primarily because there are so many of them. Occasionally you'll find a really good small franchise, but the strategy is mostly about *getting a great price on a good company in an attractive environment*. And these situations benefit from all sorts of investor biases and inattention. They are small companies.

They are in developing markets. They are illiquid. They are minority shares. They are out of the way. However, as the population of companies of this size is quite large, you do have to dig a lot to find the gems.

The challenge with this approach is basically every problem listed at the start of the book: how to deal with the risks of a small, illiquid minority investment and how to proceed with a long-term value approach in an unstable, uncertain environment. But the main approach, adding value, can also be much more powerful in these smaller companies. It takes a particularly powerful approach to add significant economic value to a $150 million enterprise. But the $50 million range offers lots of options, particularly when capability keys can be deployed. So it's mostly about becoming a valuable partner, particularly relative to often cash-rich, better-connected local investors.

This approach also works well with softer types of value-add, such as reputation, expertise, and capital. In this, it is similar to the competition you see between foreign and local PE firms in many emerging markets. How can a foreign PE firm like Kohlberg Kravis & Roberts (KKR) compete with a local PE firm like Industrial Credit and Investment Corporation of India (ICICI) Ventures in India? ICICI Ventures, which grew out of a large domestic bank with branches and corporate customers across the country, is able to position itself as a national provider of capital and a source of financing options. KKR smartly focuses more on building value-added relationships with entrepreneurs who are looking for more than just money. This approach becomes easier in more technical fields such as healthcare, technology, media, and oil and gas. A foreign investor with deep expertise in these fields can become a far more valuable partner than a local investor.

Another good example of an investor pursuing a hunt for mostly unrecognized value in unusual geographies is Tom Barrack, founder of Colony Capital. Barrack is also illustrative of someone going global successfully without a strong value-add (it's tough to have a big non-political value-add in real estate). Colony Capital's emerging market investments are much closer to standard value investing tageting undermined areas.

Barrack has been called the world's greatest real estate investor. And as one of the West's PE/real estate giants, he is well on his way to global tycoon status, having invested over $45 billion in 12,000 assets worldwide. He originally focused on U.S. real estate with a strategy he described as "cautious contrarianism" and the "exploitation of inefficiencies." Eschewing "chasing the yield," he generally focuses on identifying value that others do not see. And this approach, unsurprisingly, has led him to look at far-flung locations. He purchased 55% of Mars Entertainment, Turkey's leading movie theater chain. He purchased 10% of Megaworld Corporation, a Manila development company. He has purchased private hospitals in Switzerland and pubs in the UK. And he famously purchased Japan's Fukuoka Dome based on the value of the titanium in the roof. I also suspect that his global approach has something to do with the fact that he started his investment career working for Middle Eastern investors. I'm guessing this gave him a level of comfort in unusual locations early on.

Real estate is both the easiest and most difficult industry to go global in. It's easy in that real estate globally is similar to real estate in the West. A building in Japan or Turkey is pretty similar to a building in Australia or Spain. And fixed assets tend to avoid many of the longer-term problems of operating assets in state capitalist or godfather systems. As mentioned, it's easy to lose customers, products, or managers, but it's hard to lose a building. If you can get the real estate deal done, you are 80% of the way home in terms of returns.

However, real estate is also the hardest industry for foreigners to add value or have an advantage. It's just not that difficult to replicate the expertise. In countries such as China and Russia, local companies have built real estate expertise and possess better networks and deeper pockets. It's hard for foreigners to have a substantial advantage that will overcome their disadvantages. In godfather economies such as Singapore and Qatar, real estate tends to be tightly held by the ruling family, and getting deals is difficult without political access. So Colony Capital's going global is similar to the targeting of smaller private companies. You are hunting further afield where you either have an advantage or where you are looking at something others have not seen. In practice, it's most often value investing with a little value point. So the best approach is to target regions that have little capital (real estate in the Philippines) or just a rising sea of undermined companies (small-medium private companies in the BRIC and GCC).

Strategy #8: Buy Cheap Companies in Environments or Situations That Others Avoid

At a low-enough price, everything is a good investment. Wherever I go, I always find it worthwhile to occasionally put aside my investment strategy and just take a look at the cheapest things I can find. Or if there is no clear price, I look for the asset that all the other investors avoid. A little hubris can sometimes go a long way.

An investment strategy based on avoided companies is well known and not discussed here. Hunting among small companies, bad industries, bankruptcies, and others is in many ways value investing at its purest.

Looking at the global landscape in this way today, three opportunities jump out. The first is *distressed companies in weak management environments*. I have argued that the most important capability migrating from developed to developing economies is management ability. And I have written a lot about dealing with hypercompetition and the often-intense competitive threats that can result from rapidly increasing management ability globally. However, the inverse of this situation is environments that have very little management ability. Central Asia, Western China, the Middle East-North Africa (MENA), and Africa have some very weak management regions. Weak is a somewhat harsh term to use, but the management ability of these regions is definitely several levels below that of advanced economies. And there can be a widespread lack of specialized skills, such as asset management, software development, or insurance underwriting.

A company organization chart in such a region usually shows a few very senior manager-owners and possibly one or two technically proficient advisors and then a large gap as it drops to lower-level administrative or clerical staff. Middle management and other skilled professionals (engineers, designers, underwriters, etc.) are few.

Meeting with potential partners in the Kingdom Holding office, my standard tactic was to give them a tour of the office (people always seem to want to know about Waleed's Airbus 380). At the boardroom window, I would ask the potential partner to look down the 984 feet to the borders of the Kingdom property. You can see the manicured gardens, clean sidewalks, and well-designed layout. But looking across the street in any direction you see garbage, cracked sidewalks, ugly buildings, and fairly terrible businesses. My point being that even in the prime central business district, Kingdom Holding is literally an island of quality management.

In weak management environments, investors usually prefer fixed assets (mines, infrastructure, real estate) or fairly simple operational entities (retail stores, operations and maintenance companies, factories). A cement factory can sell in a few days in the Middle East. You can sell luxury apartments almost anywhere. But investors will stay far away from more technical operating companies, and they strenuously avoid distressed and operationally intensive turnaround situations. A historically leveraged buyout-focused company like KKR will have a hard time getting these deals in many developing economies. But a distressed-focused company like Cerberus will find itself the only bidder in deal after deal in many of these regions.

Distressed turnarounds in management-weak countries are situations where you can get a ridiculously low entry price. And you can find those attractive situations where AV is above EPV. So if you can impact management rapidly, not only do you get a quick jump in EPV relative to AV, but you can sometimes create a surprisingly sustainable competitive advantage in the market (ie., management). Much of the competitive theory assumes the presence of effective management in the market. I am continually surprised at how, in many markets, effective management is a really strong and durable competitive advantage in itself. And even in developing economies that have some management ability, there is still a strong preference by investors for development, not turnarounds. In high-growth markets, investors always seem to want to stay at the front of the development curve. It's just more exciting, and there is much less interest in fixing broken businesses.

Turnarounds have an additional political and reputational dimension that can further limit competing bids. Distressed situations in godfather economies (Singapore, Hong Kong, Saudi Arabia) are often kept quiet and handled discreetly. They are discussed between families and are not floated for open bid. When I first met Prince Waleed, I recommended that he close his private hospital because it was taking operational losses and would be a very difficult turnaround given the immaturity of the country's private healthcare system. He made it clear that because the hospital bore his name, there was no way he would ever close or sell it. Turnarounds can be those rare situations when even fairly powerful local investors can find themselves in weak positions. And to Waleed's credit, he turned around the hospital. Kingdom Hospital Consulting Clinics is now arguably the highest-quality private medical group in the country.

Such distressed situations also seem endemic to developing economies. Things are being built very fast, and fairly regular market swings occur. Development can easily get ahead of actual demand. And although well-managed companies might survive the periodic market busts, the poorly managed ones collapse quickly. Weak management, rapid development, and highly volatile markets create a steady stream of distressed assets. If the U.S. stock market is a deep pool that continually presents mispriced companies, developing economies are advancing markets that continually leave behind distressed assets.

The "go after what others avoid" strategy in this context is to acquire the companies and improve the management in a surgical fashion. It's buy and surgically fix. This typically means a rapid turnaround effort and/or a merger. One common approach is to put in a technical or management agreement with a Western company. If this can be done, it looks like a very low-priced value point investment. If it requires a longer-term turn-around effort, it starts to move outside the strategy.

A similar opportunity today is the *avoided and ignored geographies of Africa and Central Asia (and several other places)*. Everyone is looking at Grade-A real estate in Shenzhen, but few investors are looking at Grade-B real estate in Mongolia. Tertiary hospitals in Bangalore and Mumbai are now overbuilt, but the second- and third-tier cities are underserved. There are lots of industries and geographies where you can be the only investor and can get a very low price—if you are willing to go to places others avoid.

A third very low-price opportunity today is *avoided cross-border deals*. If Africa is actively avoided by most investors, cross-border deals between places such as Africa and Russia are even more so. Most Russia investors think about Russia. Most Africa investors think about Africa. Obscure cross-border deals tend to be orphans.

I like to start business school courses with a game called Global Jeopardy in which I present the students with various leading global companies and investors and see if they can identify them. (Answer: Carlos Slim. Question: Who is the world's richest person?) And because the class locations can vary between New York, London, Dubai, and Beijing, the contrasts between the students' answers are interesting. European and Chinese students do OK. They can usually identify about half my list of leading companies and investors. Southeast Asian and Middle Eastern students are particularly good at this. American students do the worst. Their knowledge generally is limited to things that are American or maybe European. I find that the degree of someone's international knowledge corresponds pretty closely to how many opportunities there are in one's home market. It also tracks with how "foreign" an area is perceived to be. Whether it's from lack of interest or comfort, there are quite a few places in the world today that nobody really knows much about or is paying much attention to.

Obscure cross-border situations offer these types of avoided and ignored opportunities, where you can be the only bidder and enter with a very low price. American investors are becoming increasingly comfortable doing deals with Chinese and Indian companies. But Russian and Brazilian companies are still very uncomfortable dealing with each other. My approach is to target inefficiencies that are both large dollars and very awkward and/or ignored (U.S.–Russia, India–Africa, Middle East–Southeast Asia). It also helps if there is already significant trade or other business occurring between the targeted regions.

An example of a company doing well with this approach is SinoLatin Capital, a Shanghai-based investment and advisory group, that was one of the first companies to target Latin American–Chinese resource deals. The consumption of Chinese natural resources is surging, and this is driving resource acquisitions in Latin America, among other places. This is the type of very big and very awkward cross-border deal situation we look for. How often do you see a trend like Figure 12.7 within a developed economy?

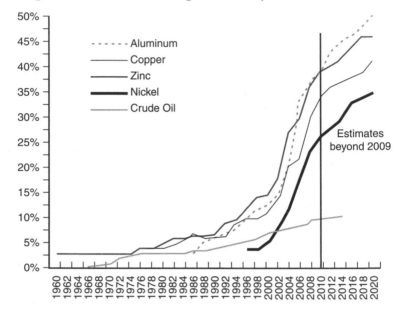

Sources: UN Comtrade, SinoLatin Capital

Figure 12.7   China's percentage share of world commodity usage

Cross-border activity between China and Latin America, both M&A and direct investments, is as awkward and uncomfortable as you can imagine. Virtually no Chinese managers and professionals have experience in Latin America (or speak Spanish), and vice versa. There is a knowledge gap, a cultural gap, a language gap, a politico-economic gap, and a comfort gap. It's the kind of situation that gets the value crowd excited.

SinoLatin's approach is to capture the difference between the intrinsic value of mines and other Latin American resource assets, and their value to knowledgeable Chinese buyers (an emerging markets' version of Mario Gabbelli). Deal structures are based on providing reputable capital (to overcome the lack of comfort and knowledge) and surgical management. As a trusted third party with respected management, they can purchase such assets, restructure them, and then sell them to Chinese state-owned enterprises (SOEs). With the right price, it is really pretty difficult to lose money in this sort of situation.

One cautionary note regarding avoided deals, cross-border orphans or others, is that the business strategy has to be compelling enough to overcome the difficulty in getting the deals done. The awkwardness is an opportunity to get a good price, but it also means that the parties are not terribly comfortable doing deals together. Is the business strategy and the investor's reputation strong enough to get such people to actually sign? Or will they just meet and drink tea for 6 months? The reason awkward China–Africa deals now get done is because of China's growing need for natural resources. Western development deals into China and India get done because of the multinationals' need for high-growth markets. If your target is the avoided deals between the Middle East and Russia today, it will likely be difficult to find a compelling-enough business strategy (maybe oil and gas?) for large dollars to actually start moving. There can be lots of first-mover disadvantages with this approach.

In practice, avoided cross-border deals are mixed value investing-value point investments. They use the reputable capital and some political access value keys against very large inefficiencies. And they can easily be done by value investors, PE firms, entrepreneurs, and other groups.

Looking forward, I think the most attractive of these cross-border orphans will still be between the developed economies and the BRIC + GCC countries. Second to this, the interactions between the BRIC countries and other smaller emerging markets (Vietnam, Africa, Mexico) are becoming more interesting, particularly as BRIC companies start to go international. Figure 12.8 shows the trends and interactions I am keeping an eye on at the moment. Again, this chart is mostly illustrative.

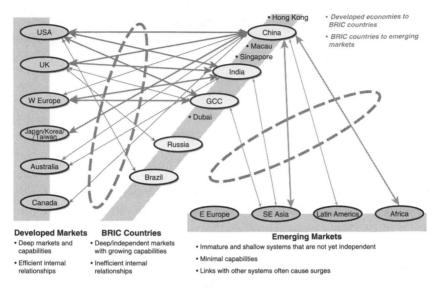

Developed Markets
- Deep markets and capabilities
- Efficient internal relationships

BRIC Countries
- Deep/independent markets with growing capabilities
- Inefficient internal relationships

Emerging Markets
- Immature and shallow systems that are not yet independent
- Minimal capabilities
- Links with other systems often cause surges

Figure 12.8   Cross-border situations

Strategy #9: Structure Political Deals with Guaranteed Returns, or Buy Companies with Politically Limited Competition

Political access can effectively break the relationship between market forces and profits. Instead of profits and value following from a company's performance within the competitive dynamics of a market, profits follow mostly from the actions of state actors.

As mentioned, government involvement distorts markets, both positively and negatively, for investors. It can create everything from politically mandated monopolies to hypercompetition, from frozen to excessive credit, and from a stable and predictable to a constantly shifting investment landscape. However, direct government involvement in specific projects and companies goes far beyond skewing the landscape and can directly, and overwhelmingly, impact profits (and intrinsic value).

In this sense, we can characterize an entire class of "political deals." The traditional value investing form of this strategy is to simply buy companies that have politically limited competition. However, as one moves to hands-on, valued-added deal-making in such environments, this becomes a much larger class of deals. This can include securing contracts for the construction, maintenance, or management of government-run development projects, which can be very large in cash-rich developing countries. This can include building and maintaining airports or renovating schools and hospitals. It can be securing a bank or financial service license. It can be acquiring supplier contracts to large SOEs or cheap loans from state-owned banks.

This is usually the point where Western-based investors start to get uncomfortable. I don't expect most readers to pursue this type of strategy, but I do want to highlight it as it is so common. If you ask an MBA in the U.S. how to become rich, he or she will probably tell you to become an entrepreneur or investor. Ask any Chinese MBA, and he or she will likely say, "Rise up in the government." It is simply understood that the government and its state-owned vehicles are the largest players in the economy, so they are partners or players in just about every type of transaction. If you want to do telecommunications deals in China, these will absolutely depend on your relationships with the state-backed mobile companies and the government ministry.

In 2008, I attended a Middle East–China conference in Riyadh, where I was scheduled to speak near the end of the day (never a great time slot). Per protocol, a representative of the Royal Court was seated in a special front row and had been sitting there silently for the entire conference. By the time I spoke, various Asian and Middle Eastern industrial companies and professional services firms had given presentations, one after the next, about the historic silk road between the Middle East and Asia and the growing oil and gas trade.

Because I believe it is the duty of the afternoon speakers to wake people up a bit, I opened my talk by telling the crowd that I planned to spend my time giving a counterargument to almost everything previously said during the conference. I laid out the data to show why few MENA–China deals were happening and why Middle Eastern oil and gas and construction projects would not be going to Chinese firms any time soon.

I argued that the key to creating a real relationship between the regions and opening the door to investments was to focus not on construction or oil and gas, but on education, healthcare, power and water, and agriculture. I went on to detail how to incorporate Chinese nurses into Saudi hospitals, how to launch joint ventures in African farming and natural resources, and how to create cultural and educational projects between the regions. The key was to turn the unique Chinese capabilities and scale in these sectors into game-changers for long-standing Middle Eastern problems. At the end, the Royal Court representative stood and spoke for the first time during the conference, saying he had finally heard what he thought the way forward was.

This was a bit of a setup on my part. If you're unfamiliar with Middle Eastern governments, you need to appreciate how many times each week for the past 30 years they have heard pitches from foreign companies wanting oil and gas allocations and parts of large development projects. The representative had probably heard those same speeches hundreds, if not thousands, of times. The truth is that Middle Eastern governments are good at oil and gas and development and have no real problems in those areas. You cannot add value there. Rather, their problems are in diversifying the private sector, improving healthcare, controlling food price inflation, and educating their workforce. If your objective is to add value, you speak to these issues. Then the deals and investments follow naturally. Value investing has traditionally been about understanding competitive dynamics. Value point in many places is about understanding political dynamics, as shown in Figure 12.9.

Previous chapters discussed some of Waleed's early years (1978–1985), when he was primarily using political relationships at a point in time when the Saudi economy was almost entirely political. The combination of a highly political economy and the first Saudi oil boom created a situation where structuring value-added deals with the government enabled arguably the greatest moment of wealth creation in human history.

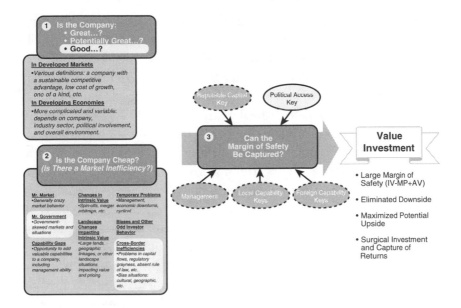

Figure 12.9   Strategy #9: Political deals

In the late 1970s and early 1980s, Saudi Arabia had only 9 million people and was experiencing an influx of approximately $130 billion in oil revenue each year. Given the government's direct involvement in most industries, political access was the key skill for doing deals. Additionally, the country was relatively closed off, creating large cross-border inefficiencies. Structuring government contracts on one side, you could then contract or subcontract with operating firms internationally, capturing returns on both sides of the deal (in the range of 30%). Waleed's first major contract was a construction project for a military academy, which he did as a joint venture with an ailing South Korean contractor. This was followed by a contract for a $70 million airport project. By 1981, his revenues had reached $1.5 billion, mostly from these types of deals. Over time, he expanded into operations and maintenance (someone has to maintain all those new government facilities) and real estate. The political and economic aspects of the environment have since cooled, and the country has opened up, but one can argue that Middle Eastern governments today have even larger problems. They are struggling with young populations and a need to diversify their economies; value-added investments and deals can speak to these issues and do very well.

Note: If you think political deals are purely a state capitalist or godfather capitalist phenomenon, you would be well advised to look at a few of the more reliably profitable American enterprises. Moody's, S&P, and Fitch for years had been the only U.S. ratings agencies designated by the Securities and Exchange Commission as Nationally Recognized Statistical Ratings Organizations. Or investigate the executive salaries and accumulated real estate holdings at some of the larger nonprofits receiving various types of government support. Note that the SAT is administered exclusively by the College Board, a nonprofit with awesome cash flow. Or read David Einhorn's book *Fooling Some of the People All of the Time*, a fascinating look at some of the interactions between government providers of credit, such as the Small Business Administration, and public companies, such as Allied Capital. How much government is involved in the economy in practice is a sliding scale, and staying in the purely private market areas is not necessarily the best strategy. Mr. Market and Mr. Government can equally create opportunities for value investors.

A final note regarding companies that have politically limited competition: Being one of two mobile service providers in Sichuan or the only outdoor signage company in Qatar can be very lucrative. Monopolies, oligopolies, and other limited-competition situations most often result from government actions (limiting the number of licenses, awarding exclusive contracts). For example, China has intentionally created limited-competition markets in automotive, telecommunications, and several other sectors. However, sometimes limited-competition situations are just the natural result of emerging markets. In many landscapes, both the markets and the competitors are still developing, and one or two companies just sort of end up in a strong position. If you get to Hainan first, you can buy a lot of the beachfront property. If you get to Bangalore first, you can own a lot of the outdoor advertising spaces. And these situations can often be found on a smaller scale and in places where few people are looking. Nobody really knows what's going on in many parts of these chaotic, rapidly changing markets, and no one has any real control. Both too little and too much politics can create such situations.

In practice, these are mostly value point investments. Getting access is very, very difficult (people with monopolies usually don't need cash or want to share). If these are government-created situations, they are, of course, fairly political: getting prime land, securing one of two licenses. If they are purely private, you need a large value-add to buy in. The dominant retailer in Western China won't sell unless you bring significant value to the enterprise. And if they are simply unnoticed situations in emerging markets, you need to do development work to create a business that captures the oligopoly position. But the primary challenge is almost always getting access, and that means value point. Defensibility is also a big issue.

A final note on political deals. A politically focused strategy reflects the fact that government players are often dominant in an economy. However, this in no way implies or condones the fairly wide range of inappropriate and disreputable behavior that can occur at the intersection of government and commercial interests. Back to my earlier point, reputation is an investor's most valuable asset. Regardless of the environment, I hold strictly to a strategy of creating value for my partners (government and commercial) and projects. I have found that this keeps one on an honorable path, even in murky environments. Any deal with significant political components should be able to be published in great detail on the front page of any newspaper without anyone having concerns.

A Multiprong Approach to Global Investing

Combining the nine strategies creates a robust going global approach

The presented global playbook constitutes a multiprong approach to global investing, as shown in Figure 12.10. And the nine strategies all support each other in practice. If you do traditional global value investing, value point makes this easier and vice versa. For example, value tanks create a very effective market entry approach, but also enable the building of direct spectacular investments. And both approaches can position the investor for traditional value investments or acquisitions of underperforming companies. All the strategies help each other, and the end result, which you can see in many of the world's global tycoons today, is the ability to do direct long-term value investments almost anywhere in the world.

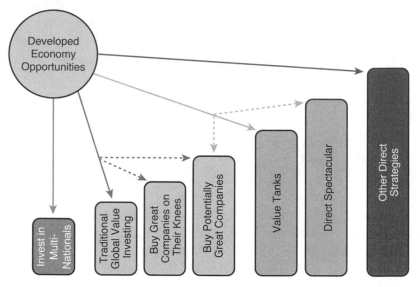

Figure 12.10   Developing economy opportunities

13

After Markets Collide: The Next Twenty Years

The start of a new age can be confusing, and it's often heralded not by grand pronouncements but by peculiar headlines. I challenge you to look at the *Wall Street Journal* on any given day and not notice a story or deal that strikes you as odd. Something you just wouldn't have seen 10 years ago. A Chinese state-owned company is trying to buy Unocal? Indian Reliance is buying U.S. shale assets? Tom Barrack is buying the largest movie theater chain in Turkey? In ways large and small, a new investment landscape has arrived. And this is posing serious questions for value investors.

I never had the opportunity to meet Ben Graham, and I have taken quite a few liberties in using his work as a framework for addressing these questions. This is presumptuous, and I hope my method of looking at various environments through his frameworks is not taken as anything but the highest respect. My best guess is that Graham would have found global investing as thrilling and fascinating as most of us do. It's profitable, and there's plenty of room for ambition. It's also an opportunity to understand many new things about investing, business, and life. The satisfaction is equally in the money and the adventure. Global investing is ultimately about bending your brain against a fundamentally changing reality—and particularly its sea of new uncertainties. Paraphrasing Frank Herbert, knowledge is the adventure that lives at the edge of uncertainty.

My objective has been to gently push you a little out of your comfort zone. If you are a traditional value investor, whether operating globally or not, I am arguing that you need to start thinking more in terms of negotiated deals. If you are in private equity, I am arguing that you need to start doing a bit of business development. If you are a business development executive, you need to start thinking like a surgical value investor. In all cases, I am not suggesting that you change your profession, but that you extend your methodology by about 20%.

If you do, I think you will discover that your opportunities expand exponentially. Suddenly attractive and capturable investments are everywhere, and you can walk comfortably and confidently across most parts of the world. We are the first generation of investors to really have the entire world as our playing field—and it is shame not to be out playing on it.

For global investors, the 2009 financial crisis was the official firing of the starter's pistol. Pre-crisis, there were certainly lots of good global deals, but they were overwhelmingly the result of inbound development into the still relatively small BRIC countries and some turbulent interactions in the global financial system. Post-crisis, we have finally arrived in a multipolar economy—defined by multiple full-fledged economies with differing politico-economic systems and constantly shifting interactions. It is noteworthy that China was the first economy to recover from the financial crisis. And most importantly, we now have a critical mass of companies and professionals in every geography. Investors and deal-makers from all over the world are now meeting and exploring the deals and investments now possible. The result is a global investing gold rush.

This last chapter is about the next 20 years—what to do post-collision. I detail what various professionals are doing, and what I humbly suggest what many could be doing. If you have aspirations of going global, these are my recommendations for your next steps.

The New Wall Street

Investors and deal-makers from around the world are starting to meet

In 2009, I found myself sitting at a conference speakers' dinner in Cambridge. The conversation on my right was about the likelihood of Dubai's defaulting on its debt (one of my better predictions). The conversation on my left was about how Moscow lawyers had extracted what can only be described as government-supported hit men from a Qatar jail. From there the conversation swung wildly between surging Chinese acquisitions in Hong Kong, falling UK real estate prices (now being targeted by Middle Eastern groups), New York bank acquisitions, and Eastern European consumer finance opportunities.

It was the second annual Cross-Border M&A and Investment conference. As I looked around the room, the assortment of speakers was unusual by any measure. There were Western investment, banking, and legal leaders such as Peter Clarke (group executive, Man Group in UK), Richard Gnodde (co-CEO, Goldman Sachs International), and Martin Lipton (partner, Wachtell, Lipton, Rosen, & Katz). There were prominent Asian leaders such as Jiang Jianqing (chairman, Industrial Commercial Bank of China) and Richard Li (chairman, PCCW in Hong Kong). There were Western trade ministers, Russian lawyers, Japanese development bank officials, Beijing government M&A officials, Indian PE professionals, and pharmaceutical and industrial acquisition specialists. It was one of those odd experiences that gets flagged in the brain as being symbolic of something.

I decided that a significant point had been reached and that we are really at the beginning of something new. The world's markets have collided, and now a critical mass of professionals, companies, and opportunities exists in virtually every geography. And we were all just starting to meet and explore the new possibilities.

It seems reminiscent of the first meetings on Wall Street in the 1790s. Traders and investors would come to Wall Street and, having nowhere to meet, would talk under a buttonwood tree. They didn't have fixed investment structures and didn't quite know how things would play out, but they were starting to meet and talk. This eventually resulted in the Buttonwood agreement, signed at 68 Wall Street on May 17, 1792, which gave rise to the New York Stock Exchange.

A similar event seems to be happening today. A new global Wall Street is being assembled. We don't know each other that well yet. We don't exactly know where all this is going. But we are all meeting (we prefer bars to buttonwood trees) and putting together deals. I fully suspect the next decade will go down as a golden age of global investing.

How to Become a Global Tycoon

Value investment giants, private equity kings, industry moguls, and other lords of finance are evolving into global tycoons

There is something truly spectacular about Waleed's hotel investments, and it is worth standing in awe of it for a moment. His hotel footprint now covers virtually every major city in the world. Through direct and indirect ownership, he has stakes in over 200 hotels and resorts. And he built it all from scratch in less than 20 years.

Waleed almost always has a hotel transaction going on somewhere in the world. In the Middle East, it might be building a Four Seasons Hotel in Riyadh or designing Four Seasons branded service apartments into luxury real estate developments. It might be a greenfield development, such as the Movenpick in Beirut. In Kenya, it might be buying or building additional Fairmont hotels. The hotel investment strategy itself is actually fairly flexible. It can be standard acquisitions. It can be greenfield developments. It can be an acquisition with extensive renovation. And deals can also be occurring at the management company level, purchasing hotel companies and orchestrating mergers, such as the Fairmont-Raffles merger in 2006.

Waleed and his hotels are something new in the world. Proof that one person in one lifetime can create a personal empire that circles the globe. That a single investor, like the British Empire of old, can create an empire on which the sun never sets. This is particularly exciting for investors and financiers, who, already soaked in ambition, can now raise their sights and become even more ambitious. Why be just a lord of finance when you can be a global tycoon? You can now have assets and investments on every continent and can spend your days traveling within your own personal global empire. Waleed is probably the first pure investor to reach global tycoon status, traveling the world and staying in his own luxury hotels everywhere he goes.

Waleed's investments have been described at length. And his insane V-speed is usually detailed in every article written about him. I have yet to meet anyone who can match his pace for more than a week or two. Figures 13.1, 13.2, and 13.3 are my summary of the evolution of his investment strategies over his 30-year career. He might not agree with it, so this should only be considered a possible "how-to guide" for becoming a global tycoon.

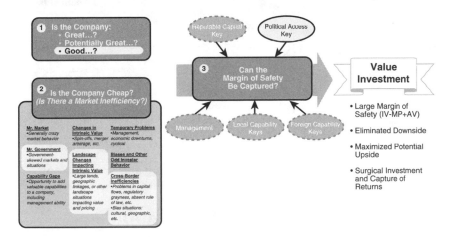

Figure 13.1   Stage 1: Political deals in high-growth, government-infused markets

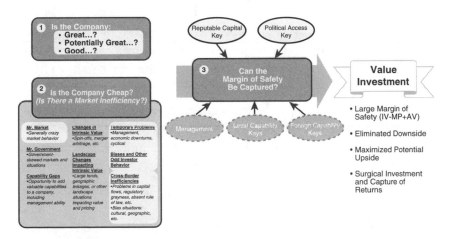

Figure 13.2   Stage 2: Domestic and cross-border acquisitions of under-priced and underperforming assets

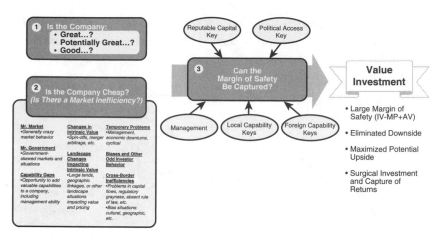

Figure 13.3   Stage 3: Global value-added investing and deal-making

Value Investors Should Go Global

Traditional value investors can easily and comfortably expand into multiple, complementary, global strategies

A colliding world is primarily a value opportunity. While the growth rates are impressive, the mispricings are even more so. Therefore, the primary approach of this book and the primary recommendation to investors is to expand traditional value approaches into a broader effort to target the inefficiencies inherent in a colliding age.

In terms of next steps, the investment strategies presented in the previous chapter are a logical step-wise progression to expand into global opportunities. The end result is the multiprong approach shown in Figure 12.10 in the previous chapter.

Buffett's first major China investment was in the public shares of PetroChina in 2002–2003 (Strategy #1). His second major China investment was through a negotiated purchase of 10% of BYD (Strategy #2). Any Western-based value investor could easily go global by simply expanding within these first two strategies. And from there, a natural and comfortable next step would be to target potentially great companies and leverage in Western assets (expand to Strategy #3) or to launch a focused vehicle with a surgical value-add approach (expand to Strategy #4)—and so on down the list—the end result being a full multiprong global investment approach. And this could all be done comfortably and confidently from a single office anywhere in the world with only a handful of people. The strategy is global, but the method remains focused and surgical.

Business Development Executives Are the Uncrowned Princes of Global Investing

Corporate executives are well positioned to expand their capabilities into global investing

Business development for Western companies has traditionally meant capturing new products and services, acquiring capabilities, or finding ways to expand markets. Genentech acquires biotech start-ups to expand its product pipeline. American Express might acquire an Internet company to expand its online and e-business capabilities, a very lucrative consulting sector in the late 1990s. Kaiser does hospital deals to expand geographically from California to Washington, DC. And In-N-Out Burger, America's much-loved corporate recluse, has finally, after 60 years, expanded from Southern California to Arizona and Nevada (coming in 2050 to a town near you).

But such business development activities have overwhelmingly occurred within developed geographies and economies, particularly for medium-sized and small companies. And deals are almost always driven by strategic and competitive considerations, not strict investment returns. A technology is needed. A market entry approach is needed. It's part of a vertical or horizontal consolidation strategy.

However, more and more corporate executives are finding themselves in strong investment positions globally. As the great migration of capabilities continues, executives have found themselves holding valuable capabilities (value keys). Much of value point is about a mild blurring of lines between business development and investment strategy. Investors are starting to think beyond price and valuation, and more in terms of business strategy and adding capabilities ("buy and sell" plus "build and fix"). And business development and other corporate executives are starting to think more like investors. If my technology will increase the value of this private Indian company, and the company is eager to have me as a partner, shouldn't I buy in?

Recall the previous discussion of GE Money as a value tank. They are one of the most effective groups at combining business development with direct investing around the world. They also have the advantage of sitting on an already global corporate platform and of having technology capabilities that are particularly valuable and transportable.

Consumer finance is also one of the more attractive industries in terms of emerging market economics, and GE Money has three powerful capability keys to use in constructing investments in this space. The first is sales and marketing/customer service expertise related to credit cards, mortgages, car loans, and other consumer finance products. They have hundreds of staff globally who are experts at increasing sales force effectiveness, determining pricing, building Internet capabilities, and mining customer relationship management (CRM) data. If a local Turkish bank can supply the customer list, GE Money can process and manage the rollout of consumer finance products to this group.

Their second capability key is risk management, which is obviously critical for offering consumer finance products in unusual locations. GE Money's more than 15,000 risk and collections professionals can analyze the risk of consumer finance products at any local bank. In practice, this is a combination of data analysis, portfolio modeling, portfolio monitoring, and setting policies and terms.

Their third capability key is technology and systems, always GE's biggest strength. This includes everything from software applications and databases to cellular banking platforms. By linking a local banking or retail operation with their global IT team, GE can offer a level of technical expertise effectively unmatched in any developing economy. This also creates a strong foreign value key, because such deep technical infrastructure cannot be easily replicated or localized.

These valuable, and nicely scalable and transportable, capabilities can be leveraged into direct investments. Note the power of this approach when compared to standard PE or value investing. In deals, they can add large value and can be comfortable taking only a 10% to 20% minority share of companies. It is also telling that in 2008, GE Money, much to the consternation of several U.S. Congressmen, moved their headquarters from Connecticut to London, which is a much more convenient location from which to do global deals.

In terms of the presented playbook, business development executives are very well positioned to go global by Strategy #3 (Buy a Potentially Great Company and Make It Great), Strategy #4 (Launch a Value Tank), or Strategy #5 (Build a Direct Spectacular Investment). All three of these strategies leverage in the capabilities these executives have access to. Of the three, launching a value tank (#4) is likely the most comfortable first step as it creates a full structure for developing investments.

Luxury brands and retail operations are another interesting "business development into direct investing" opportunity. It can be a very attractive strategy within this industry, if you can get it right. Unfortunately, Marks & Spencer's flagship Shanghai store has, whether fairly or unfairly, become the symbol for getting it wrong. Launched on Nanjing Xi Lu, down the street from my home, the Shanghai store at opening was as bad as the press gleefully proclaimed it was. It was ugly. The products seemed geared toward foreigners in terms of prices, tastes, and sizes. And it was just a really unpleasant store to be in. Additionally, my favorite Starbucks was demolished during construction, so I feel some personal resentment there. But apart from the operational problems, which are quickly being addressed, and my own pettiness, it was also a very difficult strategy and a problematic structure for a direct investment.

A Western retailer going direct by launching a flagship store in Shanghai today has a somewhat low chance of success from an investment perspective. Retail in China is ruthlessly competitive, and the key step is getting land and/or retail locations—and foreign groups typically are at a disadvantage in this. Going direct into one location in Shanghai today means a lot of challenges and no clear, overwhelming advantage.

The key is to have the right "business development into direct investment" approach. Marks and Spencer, and most other large retailers and luxury companies, are actually in a fairly strong position to do such cross-border investments today. A value-added approach would be to enter by building strategic partnerships around the operating capabilities and thereby compensate for a weak ability to acquire sites. You want to think like an investor and both build a strong deal advantage and capture the economic value of the enterprise (and if possible the ancillary real estate). Basically, you want to play to your strengths and extend your operating and brand advantages to compensate for your weaknesses.

For retailers such as Marks & Spencer and luxury brands such as Polo Ralph Lauren, the most effective approach I have seen is to do Strategy #4 (Launch a Value Tank) and use a hybrid structure. The foreign company creates a wholly owned vehicle, which maintains ownership of the key capabilities (luxury capabilities can be fairly intangible). Then the company does joint ventures for the fixed assets such as the stores and real estate. The wholly owned company oversees marketing, merchandising, supply chain, and, most importantly, customer care. But the joint ventures give you local strategic partners, strengthen your political access, and let you capture the real estate investment returns.

For example, a top branded retailer such as Saks Fifth Avenue with an interest in China can create a wholly owned vehicle in Hong Kong that houses all the critical operating functions. This is traditional business development going into a new market. The retailer then creates a series of real estate joint ventures in second-tier cities, such as Hangzhou, Chongqing, and Dalian. Saks owns the operating company and directly invests in the real estate assets, which are contracted with the wholly owned vehicle. According to the value approach, this sort of hybrid structure has six main benefits:

- You maintain your key advantages (brand, customer base, sourcing) in your own vehicle thereby addressing the long-term downside uncertainties.

- You maintain ownership of the higher ROE vehicle, which is where much of the economic value per share will be created.

- The local joint ventures overcome the problems of acquiring locations and getting political access.

- You can raise local funding for the local assets, which have lower ROEs and are more exposed to market downturns, but which are also at less risk from a weakened claim to the enterprise-perspective.

- You can launch multiple stores immediately in multiple cities without financial risk.
- You can often capture the increased value of the ancillary real estate, which provides larger near-term returns.

In practice, it looks a lot like the Coca-Cola case. Once you begin mixing business development with direct investing, you have a lot of room for such creativity. You have more lines of attack than simply expanding the margin of safety with a low price. Structures and terms can be put together to solve the problems with access, uncertainty, claim to the asset, and foreigner disadvantages.

Private Equity as the Value-Added Partner of Choice

Global private equity can amplify structured transactions with deeper partnerships

If business development executives are thinking more like investors, PE firms are thinking more like business development executives. As detailed previously, the approach of looking for leveraged buyouts globally hasn't been that successful. There aren't that many suitable candidates, debt options are limited, and you rarely have the governance structure you need. It also misses the bigger story of the developing economies, which is development.

Pure growth equity similarly has its own challenges—the biggest being that lots of local capital is already hunting for and usually overpaying for growth. Arguing that you are "higher quality capital" is possible but difficult. This leaves globally ambitious PE firms with the conundrum of how to access attractive deals without their debt tools and with some natural disadvantages relative to overpaying local capital. As local PE firms increasingly focus on doing larger and larger fast transactions, most foreign PE firms are increasingly thinking about how they can add value to an enterprise. How can I help an entrepreneur in Mumbai? Or a family office in Qatar? How can I help a Chinese firm trying to enter the United States? If value investors such as Warren Buffett strive to be seen as the "buyer of choice," PE firms going global are more and more striving to be seen as a "value-added partner of choice."

This value-added partner of choice approach works quite well when going global and has multiple variations. It can be adding very tangible capabilities, similar to GE Money. Or it can be providing intangible value such as expertise and connections. But you'll know it when you achieve it, because the doors to private deals will open in your field. In terms of the playbook, PE firms do well going global with Strategy #2 (Buy a Great Company on its Knees), Strategy #3 (Buy a "Potentially Great" Company and Make it Great), Strategy #6 (Bird-on-a-Rhino), and Strategy #7 (Buy Small-Medium Private Companies in Attractive Environments). For larger firms, Strategies #2 and #3 work well. For smaller firms, Strategies #6 and #7 are often more appropriate.

In Chapter 12, I described the competition between KKR and ICICI Ventures in India. ICICI Ventures generally positions itself as a provider of private capital and financial products to a wide national network. They focus on securing majority positions, LBOs (you can't do an LBO in India, but you can do equity and then a loan later), and large effectively controlling minority positions. They mostly stay at the Board level and watch the financials while avoiding active involvement in management. The strategy is to stay transactional and deploy as much capital as possible, operating like a big CFO. Since the launch of their first PE fund in 2003, ICICI has expanded quickly to real estate and now infrastructure. We see similar local PE approaches across the developing economies.

KKR's position as a value-added partner of choice for entrepreneurs and owner-managers is a natural contrast to this. They do deals that are far closer to foreign direct investment (FDI) than LBO. The key question with this approach is how much value to add, and how tangible will it be. Additionally, it helps to focus on industry sectors with greater technical or cross-border components, where expertise will be seen as more valuable.

A PE firm that has always been global and uses this approach effectively is Investcorp. Founded in 1982 to facilitate the flow of Gulf capital into Western PE investments, Investcorp's strategy stands out as a contrast to the standard PE strategies within the U.S.

Instead of having a geographically focused strategy, Investcorp has opened offices in Bahrain, London, and New York. Instead of having an industry strategy such as Welsh Carson in healthcare, Investcorp works across all industries. Instead of focusing on LBOs or growth equity, it does PE, real estate, hedge funds, venture capital, and GCC development.

Investcorp succeeds in this because it has created a bridge between GCC capital and Western investments, a long-standing cross-border inefficiency. Although one could say that Investcorp is not as competitive at the deal level (a U.S. healthcare growth equity deal will likely go to Welsh Carson over Investcorp), they are very competitive at fund-raising in the GCC and have captured a very secure long-term capital position. Sometimes being a value-added partner means adding value on the capital side.

Accelerating Out of the Downturn

Everyone else should reposition and hit the gas

A final group to consider is the catchall category of developed- and developing-economy family offices and smaller investment firms. Many of these groups are now considering global investing for the first time. And as the great credit crisis recedes, my recommendation to most is to reposition and accelerate.

I find that smaller investment firms in the Middle East and Singapore are good models for family offices and small firms thinking of going global. They have been crossing borders the longest, having always had more cash than local opportunities. They usually don't have the extensive assets and long reach of large investment houses, multinationals, or PE firms. And they are geographically agnostic, usually equally willing to consider the U.S., Europe, and Asia. For family offices and smaller investment firms in the West, they are a very instructive group to watch.

For most Middle Eastern firms, the recent financial crisis hit like a shock wave from the West. The first wave produced large losses in their Western portfolios, against which many had borrowed locally. The second wave decreased demand for local products and services. It was this second wave that collapsed Dubai. The rapid disappearance of

Western and Russian tourists and homebuyers shrank its income statement at the same time its debt ratio was soaring on its balance sheet.

Now post-crisis and looking at a changing world with wiser eyes, Middle Eastern investors are rapidly repositioning, some out of desperation. With large losses in the West and the dreams of Dubai shattered, most have gone back to basics and refocused on where the best opportunities are in the world today. They are now beginning to rapidly accelerate out of the downturn. In terms of the playbook, most are focusing on Strategy #6 (Bird-on-a-Rhino) and Strategy #7 (Small-Medium Private Companies in Attractive Environments).

Keep in mind, the prototypical Middle Eastern or Singaporean family office has traditionally relied on a few cash-producing domestic businesses (construction, logistics, ports, retail, cement, etc.) and has fairly limited management and capabilities. They are now refocusing on these core competencies and businesses and actively pruning their international ventures. For Saudi family offices, projects started in secondary geographies such as Egypt or Jordan are being dropped. Previous visions of regional dominance are no longer compelling. Back to basics is about going back to situations where strong advantages for deals exist. But it's also about speeding up. At the same time they are withdrawing from Jordan, they are expanding to Singapore and other parts of Southeast Asia.

This family offices going back-to-basics phenomenon has some important lessons for Western family offices and smaller investors going global. It's a reminder that most of the cash-producing businesses in developing economies are concentrated in a few core industries. In the GCC, it is businesses that track government spending and oil wealth (banking, real estate, petrochemicals). In Asia, it is businesses that track growth (construction, logistics, infrastructure, banking) and manufacturing. And this is a clear rebuttal of the approach of grouping several developing economies under a regional strategy. It's a reminder to go focused and surgical in a big world— and to increasingly specialize, particularly in technical fields where large advantages and value-adds can be deployed.

Dedicated to the Skeptical Optimists

Summing up, what a global investment world really needs is more of Graham's disciples

At the start of this book, I postulated that Graham's work is so widespread because it has a deeper impact on readers than just showing a consistently profitable investment strategy. It speaks powerfully to the other seemingly inherent characteristics of a value personality. The value crowd is highly rational. They are logical. They have a deep respect for the inherent uncertainties of a complex reality. And many of us are perpetually restless and endlessly curious. Graham's work fits our worldview, but it also fits our personality.

Within the value temperament, there is an almost visceral gut reaction to hyped trends, stories of easy riches, rosy future predictions, and other oversimplifications of complex systems. If we have a deep respect for the inherent complexity of the world on one hand, we have a healthy disdain for the tendency of the human brain to seek simplistic patterns and causal relationships within it on the other.

Skepticism runs deep within Graham's fans. We are usually polite but merciless when presented with faulty logic, weak data, optimistic business plans, and overly predictive models. The truth of things is very rare to find, and killing off the weak ideas and the bad investments is the only way to get there. Our fairly deeply entrenched skepticism follows from a belief that most things are complicated and we, as pattern-seeking mammals, are particularly susceptible to pretty PowerPoints.

You'll note that much of this book has focused on describing the most difficult situations and investigating low probability events. Yes, many foreign strategic investors will lose control of their businesses in Russia and China (this is not the same thing as losing money). Managers will abruptly quit. Governments will change their policies. Emerging markets won't emerge—at least, not fast enough for your financing plan. You will discover corruption and theft hidden in your company. Credit will get pulled. And government officials will threaten to revoke your license if you don't agree to refurnish their homes (true story). I realize this can all read pessimistic.

But such skepticism is not pessimism. After you discover all the problems, strip out the inaccuracies and uncertainties, and mercilessly shoot down the weak ideas, you ultimately are left with the truth—and the really good investments. You can then confidently make money and achieve a real bottom-up understanding of the world as it is. There is something both optimistic and inspiring about this process. About the power of a few stubborn people to slowly and doggedly get to the truth of things. I have found that the skepticism and the optimism go hand in hand.

My hope is that this book will convey an optimism about investing and life at a time of historic change. Previous generations of investors never got to have this much fun. And as the investors and dealmakers on the ground and in the trenches, we are getting front-row seats to possibly the most transformative decade in human history. This is a truly great time for Graham's disciples.

So this book is dedicated to the brutally skeptical but deeply optimistic value crowd—the ornery shorts, the combative analysts, the infuriatingly difficult researchers who just won't take your word for it, and all the other curious characters whose craft is skeptical inquiry. What the global investment landscape really needs today is more of you.

Notes

Chapter 1

The Intelligent Investor, Benjamin Graham, Collins Business, 2003 (revised edition)

Security Analysis, Benjamin Graham and David Dodd, McGraw-Hill, 2008 (6th edition)

"The World's Most Influential Arabs," *Arabian Business*, 2007

"The World's 50 Richest Arabs," *Arabian Business*, August 21–27, 2005

Chapter 2

"Carlos Slim, the richest man in the world," Stephanie Mehta, *Fortune*, August 20, 2007

When Markets Collide, Mohamed El-Erian, McGraw-Hill, 2008

Globalization: The Irrational Fear That Someone from China Will Take Your Job, Bruce Greenwald and Judd Kahn, John Wiley and Sons, 2009

"Buffett-Backed BYD Goes Electric," Forbes.com, December 2008

"Buffett Continues to Shave Stake in PetroChina," Shu Ching and Jean Chen, Forbes.com, 2007

The Age of Turbulence: Adventures in a New World, Alan Greenspan, Penguin, 2008

The Alchemy of Finance, George Soros, Wiley Investment Classics, 1987

Chapter 3

Value Investing: From Graham to Buffett and Beyond, Bruce Greenwald, Judd Kahn, Paul Sonkin, and Michael van Biema, Wiley Finance, 2001

"The Prince of Bargain-Hunters," *The Financial Mail*, July 31, 1998

"The Ultimate Investment Club," *Money*, October 1998

Alwaleed: Businessman, Billionaire, Prince, Riz Khan, William Morrow, 2005

Chapter 4

"Little-Known Carlyle Scores Big. Advisors Landed Citicorp's Prince," Kenneth Gilpin, *New York Times*, 1991

"Saudi Prince Tells Fed He Plans to Limit His Holding in Citicorp to Less Than 10%," Fred Bleakley, *Wall Street Journal Europe*, 1991

"Saudi Prince to Become Top Citicorp Shareholder Investor by $590 Million," Michael Quint, *New York Times*, 1991

Liar's Poker, Michael Lewis, W.W. Norton & Company, 2010 (reprint)

Competitive Advantage of Nations, Michael Porter, Free Press, 1998

Asian Godfathers. Money and Power in Hong Kong and Southeast Asia, Joe Studwell, Grove Press, 2007

"Kuwait must change to fulfil potential—Blair," Andy Sambridge, Arabian Business, March 2010

"UAE Investment firm Mubadala, GE launch $8 bln JV," Reuters, July 22, 2008

"GE to sell plastics unit to Sabic for $11.6 billion," Laura Mandaro and Padraic Cassidy, Marketwatch, May 21, 2007

"ExxonMobil, Aramco, Sinopec announce $5 billion venture," *USA Today*, March 30, 2007

"Contrarian Investor Sees Economic Crash in China," David Barboza, *New York Times*, January 7, 2010

The Black Swan: The Impact of the Highly Improbable, Nassim Taleb, Random House, 2010 (2nd edition)

Pity the Nation: The Abduction of Lebanon, Robert Fisk, Nation Books, 2002 (4th edition)

"Visa, China UnionPay in Dispute on International Transactions," *Bloomberg Businessweek*, June 4, 2010

Chapter 5

"Vincent Lo's Stunning Reversal," Russell Flannery, *Forbes Asia*, February 8, 2010

Sale of the Century: The Inside Story of the Second Russian Revolution, Chrystia Freeland, Abacus, 2005

"The Casino Billionaires," Andrew Farrell, Forbes.com, April 17, 2008

"Google vs. China," *Red Herring*, July 14, 2010

"After Yahoo Talks, Alibaba Says Its Buyback Bid Is Over," Bloomberg News, September 20, 2010

"Dubailand Set to Launch Developments Worth DH30b," Zawya, February 10, 2006

"Shanghai Disneyland a step closer to reality," David Pierson, *Los Angeles Times*, November 6, 2010

Chapter 6

"Alwaleed to Bid for Second Mobile License—Saudi Arabia," MENAFN, February 29, 2004

"Saudi prince to bid for Canary Wharf," Simon London, *Financial Times*

"Waleed buys stake in Fairmont Hotels," Javid Hassan, *Arab News*, 1994

"Saudi Arabia to build world's tallest building," *The Telegraph*, October 13, 2008

Chapter 7

"Morgan Stanley's China property head resigns," George Chen, Reuters, December 31, 2008

"The Carlyle Group establishes Middle East investment operation," AMEinfo, November 27, 2006

"Kingdom Zephyr raises USD492m for Africa Fund," Private Equity Wire, December 1, 2010

"Harvest starts 2010 with $800m double fund launch," LexisNexis, January 5, 2010

"Asia Alternatives Closes $950 Mn Fund of Funds," VCCircle, November 4, 2008

"China's Anti-Goldman Sachs Book," Gady Epstein, *Forbes*, September 9, 2010

"Danone Exits China Venture After Years of Legal Dispute," David Barboza, *New York Times*, September 30, 2009

"Coca Cola to make China its largest market," *China Daily* (Xinhua), September 16, 2007

Mr. China: A Memoir, Tim Clissold, Harper Paperbacks, 2006

Financial Shenanigans: How to Detect Accounting Gimmicks and Fraud in Financial Reports, Howard Schilit, McGraw-Hill, 2002 (2nd edition)

Chapter 8

"Geely's Volvo Plans Take Shape," Norihiko Shirouzu, *Wall Street Journal*, August 27, 2010

"Huawei's Middle East sales revenue hits US$3 bln in 2009," Alibaba.com, March 11, 2010

"Marina Bay Sands in Singapore to Open Its Doors on April 27, 2010," BNET, February 2010

Chapter 9

"I'm not finished yet," William Barrett, *Forbes*, August 8, 1988

"A Bull Roams Arabian Desert," *USA Today*, May 17, 2000

Kingdom Holding Company initial public offering prospectus, 2007

"Buffett of Arabia? Well, maybe," Douglas Jehl, *New York Times*, March 28, 1999

"Kingdom Holding Sells Stake in Raffles," New York Times Dealbook, April 5, 2010

"Murdoch finalizes stake. News Corp. buys into Middle East's Rotana," Ali Jaafar, *Variety*, December 1, 2009

"GM, SAIC Reshape Partnership," Norihiko Shirouzu and Patricia Jiayi Ho, *Wall Street Journal*, December 5, 2009

"SAIC Takes Controlling Interest of GM Joint Venture. Automotive balance of power and jobs shift toward Chinese," Ken Zino, The Detroit Bureau, December 5, 2009

"China's SAIC Expresses Interest in Buying GM Stake," Sharon Terlep, *Wall Street Journal*, September 21, 2010

"Fiat Focuses on China. After two failures in China, the Italian automaker has struck a deal with Guangzhou Auto to make cars for the Chinese market," Ian Rowley, Bloomberg, July 7, 2009

"Fiat rethinks Nanjing Auto joint venture," John Reed in London and Geoff Dyer in Shanghai, *Financial Times*, May 23, 2007

"Fiat quits money-losing Nanjing car JV in China," Gilles Castonguay and Jason Subler, Reuters, December 26, 2007

"Bosch and its partners celebrate the 10th anniversary of United Automotive Electronic Systems (UAES)," Bosch press release, September 8, 2005

Rupert Murdoch's China Adventures: How the World's Most Powerful Media Mogul Lost a Fortune and Found a Wife, Bruce Dover, Tuttle Publishing, 2008

"How Baidu Won China. Robin Li beat Google and made his search engine No. 1 in China," Brad Stone and Bruce Einhorn, *Bloomberg BusinessWeek*, November 11, 2010

"Japan's Softbank boasts of a rare China success story," CNET Asia, May 31, 2010

"Tech Innovator in Japan Sets Its Sights on China," Hiroko Tabuchi, *New York Times*, May 30, 2010

"Softbank Invests in China's Alibaba as 'Next Yahoo!,'" Hans Lombardo, Internet News, January 18, 2000

"Battle looms as Alibaba strains at Yahoo leash," Kathrin Hille in Beijing and Joseph Menn in San Francisco, FT.com, September 22, 2010

Chapter 10

The Little Book That Beats the Market, Joel Greenblatt, Wiley, 2006

"United Saudi Commercial Bank stages a comeback," *Middle East Economic Digest*, March 3, 1989

"A small bank with a difference," *Middle East Economic Digest*, May 14, 1993

"SCB, USCB merger plans to go ahead," Ibrahim Alfakeeh, *Arab News*, December 27, 1996

"Saudi Cairo Bank cleans out balance sheet," *Middle East Economic Digest*, February 28, 1997

"Saudi American, United Saudi agree to US$1.35 bn merger," *Business Times*, May 26, 1999

"Waleed and three groups acquire 50% of NIC," *Arab News*

"Prince Al-Walid buys 50.1% stake in Panda," *Arab News*

"Saudi prince buys IEC stake," *Financial Times*, April 25, 1998

Kingdom Hotel Investments annual report, 2008

"Hotel George V Closes for Update," *Herald Tribune*, 1997

"Kingdom Hotel Investments sells stake in Four Seasons Cairo," Gulfnews.com, September 2, 2010

Kingdom Zephyr Africa Management Company—Funds Description and Investment Strategy presentation

"Prince Alwaleed leads $2bn Saudi bid for Bank of China stake," *The Telegraph*, May 24, 2006

"Beijing's 'Marshall Plan,'" Ben Simpfendorfer, *New York Times*, November 3, 2009

Chapter 11

"Soros Injects Another US $25M into Hainan Airlines," Zeng Qingkai, *China Daily*, October 17, 2005

"Betting on the Bad Guys," Scott Adams, *Wall Street Journal*, June 5, 2010

You Can Be a Stock Market Genius, Joel Greenblatt, Fireside, 1997

"Desert Diaries. Inside the Private World of HRH Prince Alwaleed," *Arabian Business*, May 13–19, 2007

"A Day in the Life of Prince Alwaleed bin talal Al Saud," *Arabian Business*, December 2002

Kingdom Centre Private Placement memorandum, November 21, 1998

"Not Since Babel Has a Tower So Tall Risen from the Sands," Mitchell Pacelle, *Wall Street Journal*, December 18, 1997

Chapter 12

"Kingdom Consolidates. Why Alwaleed is shaking up his Saudi interest," *Middle East Business Weekly*, June 18, 1999

"USCB Buys Stake in Saks Fifth Avenue," S. Sidahmed, *Arab News*

"Saudi prince saves fashion diva in distress," *The Guardian*, September 30, 1997

"Saudi Prince Acquires 5% in Apple," *Herald Tribune*

"Prince buys more than 5% of Apple Computer," Paul Taylor, *Financial Times*

"Saudi Prince's investment in Apple doubles in value," Bloomberg News, July 17, 1998

"Prince Waleed Invests $850 Million in News Corp., Netscape, Motorola," Robert Frank, *Wall Street Journal*

"Prince Al Waleed buys stakes in News Corp and Netscape," William Lewis, *Financial Times*

"Saudi Prince Buys Stake in News Corp.," Robert Frank, *Wall Street Journal Europe*

"Prince Al-Walid plans bid for Canary," *Arab News*

"Will the Saudi stock market boom continue?," AMEinfo.com, February 18, 2006

"As Hong Kong Property Prices Soar, Analysts Grow Worried," V. Phanl Kumar, Marketwatch, September 18, 2009

"Shenzhen Takes Over as China's Listing Hub," Robert Cookson, FT.com, October 18, 2010

"I'm Tom Barrack and I'm Getting Out," Shawn Tully, *Fortune*, October 31, 2005

"Prince Alwaleed Orders Flying Palace," K.T. Abdurabb, *Arab News*, November 13, 2007

"Sino Latin Capital to Manage RMB Private Equity Funds," Private Equity Wire, November 10, 2010

"SinoLatin launches firm focused on China-Latin America transactions," Global Fund Wire, July 2009

Fooling Some of the People All of the Time: A Long Short Story, David Einhorn, Wiley, 2010

Chapter 13

"Prince Waleed signs resort pact," *Riyadh Daily*, July 2, 1997

"Saudi Prince to Pay $122.4 Million to Acquire 25% Stake in Four Seasons Hotels Group," Peter Truell, *Wall Street Journal*, 1994

"Trump Is Selling Plaza Hotel to Saudi and Asian Investors," David Stout with Kenneth Gilpin, *New York Times*, 1995

"Prince Al-Waleed Buys Copley Hotel," Javid Hassan, *Arab News*, 1996

"Saudi Prince Scoops Up the George V," *Herald Tribune*, 1996

"Prince Alwaleed buys 30% shares in Movenpick Hotels," *Riyadh Daily*, 1997

"GE Money to Acquire Platform in Romania," GE Money press release, May 2006

"Marks and Spencer Admits Mistakes in China," ChinaRetailNews.com, February 16, 2009

INDEX

FT Press

FINANCIAL TIMES

In an increasingly competitive world, it is quality
of thinking that gives an edge—an idea that opens new
doors, a technique that solves a problem, or an insight
that simply helps make sense of it all.

We work with leading authors in the various arenas
of business and finance to bring cutting-edge thinking
and best-learning practices to a global market.

It is our goal to create world-class print publications
and electronic products that give readers
knowledge and understanding that can then be
applied, whether studying or at work.

To find out more about our business
products, you can visit us at www.ftpress.com.